War Economies and Post-war Crime

I0882222

Even when armed conflicts formally end, the transition to peace is not clear-cut. This comprehensive volume explores the mounting evidence which suggests that it is rather 'unlikely to see a clean break from violence to consent, from theft to production, from repression to democracy, or from impunity to accountability'. The authors analyse the complex endeavour of transitioning out of war, studying how it is often interrelated with other transformations such as changes in the political regime (democratisation) and in the economy (opening of markets to globalisation). They explore how, in the same way as wars and conflicts reflect the societies they befall, post-war orders may replicate and perpetuate some of the drivers of war-related violence, such as high levels of instability, institutional fragility, corruption, and inequality. This book thus suggests that, even in the absence of a formal relapse into war and the re-mobilisation of former insurgents, many transitional contexts are marked by the steady and ongoing reconfiguration of criminal and illegal groups and practices.

This book will be of great interest to students and researchers of political science and peace studies. It was originally published as an online special issue of *Third World Thematics.*

Sabine Kurtenbach is a political scientist, Acting Director of the GIGA Institute of Latin American Studies, and Honorary Professor at the University of Marburg, Germany. Her research focuses on peace processes, post-war societies, youth, and institutions, with a specific regional focus on Latin America but also beyond.

Angelika Rettberg is Professor in the Political Science Department at Universidad de los Andes, in Bogotá, Colombia, and a Global Fellow at the Peace Research Institute of Oslo (PRIO), Norway. Her research focuses on the political economy of armed conflict and peacebuilding.

ThirdWorlds

Edited by Shahid Qadir, *University of London, UK*

ThirdWorlds will focus on the political economy, development and cultures of those parts of the world that have experienced the most political, social, and economic upheaval, and which have faced the greatest challenges of the postcolonial world under globalisation: poverty, displacement and diaspora, environmental degradation, human and civil rights abuses, war, hunger, and disease.

ThirdWorlds serves as a signifier of oppositional emerging economies and cultures ranging from Africa, Asia, Latin America, Middle East, and even those 'Souths' within a larger perceived North, such as the U.S. South and Mediterranean Europe. The study of these otherwise disparate and discontinuous areas, known collectively as the Global South, demonstrates that as globalisation pervades the planet, the south, as a synonym for subalterity, also transcends geographical and ideological frontier.

The most recent titles include:

Class Dynamics of Development
Edited by Jonathan Pattenden, Liam Campling, Satoshi Miyamura and Benjamin Selwyn

Third World Approaches to International Law
Edited by Amar Bhatia, Usha Natarajan, John Reynolds and Sujith Xavier

Fragility, Aid, and State-building
Understanding Diverse Trajectories
Edited by Rachel M. Gisselquist

Rural Transformations and Agro-Food Systems
The BRICS and Agrarian Change in the Global South
Edited by Ben M. McKay, Ruth Hall and Juan Liu

Sustainable Development in Africa-EU relations
Edited by Mark Langan and Sophia Price

New Mechanisms of Participation in Extractive Governance
Between Technologies of Governance and Resistance Work
Edited by Esben Leifsen, Maria-Therese Gustafsson, María Antonieta Guzmán-Gallegos and Almut Schilling-Vacaflor

The Development Dictionary @25
Post-Development and its Consequences
Edited by Aram Ziai

Power and Illicit Drugs in the Global South
Edited by Maziyar Ghiabi

Hybridity in Peacebuilding and Development
A critical and reflexive approach
Edited by Lia Kent, Miranda Forsyth, Sinclair Dinnen, Joanne Wallis and Srinjoy Bose

The Agency of the Governed in the Global South
Normative and Institutional Change
Edited by Anke Draude

Innovations in 'Sport for Development and Peace' Research
Edited by Megan Chawansky, Lyndsay M. C. Hayhurst, Mary G. McDonald and Cathy van Ingen

Global Debt Dynamics
Crises, Lessons, Governance
Edited by Andreas Antoniades and Ugo Panizza

Developmental States beyond East Asia
Edited by Jewellord T. Nem Singh and Jesse Salah Ovadia

Gendering Security and Insecurity
Post/Neocolonial Security Logics and Feminist Interventions
Edited by Navtej Purewal and Sophia Dingli

Property Rights and Governance in Artisanal and Small-Scale Mining
Critical Approaches
Edited by Chris Huggins

War Economies and Post-war Crime
Edited by Sabine Kurtenbach and Angelika Rettberg

Post-conflict Reconstruction and Local Government
Edited by Paul Jackson and Gareth J. Wall

For more information about this series, please visit:
https://www.routledge.com/series/TWQ

War Economies and Post-war Crime

Edited by
Sabine Kurtenbach and Angelika Rettberg

Routledge
Taylor & Francis Group
LONDON AND NEW YORK

First published 2020
by Routledge
2 Park Square, Milton Park, Abingdon, Oxon, OX14 4RN

and by Routledge
52 Vanderbilt Avenue, New York, NY 10017

Routledge is an imprint of the Taylor & Francis Group, an informa business

First issued in paperback 2021

British Library Cataloguing in Publication Data
A catalogue record for this book is available from the British Library

ISBN 13: 978-0-367-20335-1 (hbk)
ISBN 13: 978-1-03-208957-7 (pbk)

Typeset in Myriad Pro
by RefineCatch Limited, Bungay, Suffolk

Publisher's Note
The publisher accepts responsibility for any inconsistencies that may have arisen during the conversion of this book from journal articles to book chapters, namely the inclusion of journal terminology.

Contents

Citation Information

The chapters in this book were originally published in *Third World Thematics*, volume 3, issue 1 (February 2018). When citing this material, please use the original page numbering for each article, as follows:

Chapter 1
Understanding the relation between war economies and post-war crime
Sabine Kurtenbach and Angelika Rettberg
Third World Thematics, volume 3, issue 1 (February 2018), pp. 1–8

Chapter 2
Can organised crime shape post-war transitions? Evidence from Sicily
James Cockayne
Third World Thematics, volume 3, issue 1 (February 2018), pp. 9–27

Chapter 3
What drives post-war crime? Evidence from illicit economies in Liberia and Sierra Leone
Judith Vorrath
Third World Thematics, volume 3, issue 1 (February 2018), pp. 28–45

Chapter 4
Commanding abuse or abusing command? Ex-command structures and drugs in Liberia
Anders Themnér
Third World Thematics, volume 3, issue 1 (February 2018), pp. 46–62

Chapter 5
Lost in transition: linking war, war economy and post-war crime in Sri Lanka
Shyamika Jayasundara-Smits
Third World Thematics, volume 3, issue 1 (February 2018), pp. 63–79

Chapter 6
Peacebuilding and white-collar crime in post-war natural resource sectors
Philippe Le Billon
Third World Thematics, volume 3, issue 1 (February 2018), pp. 80–97

Chapter 7
Large-scale land acquisitions and violence in post-war societies
Annegret Kuhn
Third World Thematics, volume 3, issue 1 (February 2018), pp. 98–115

Chapter 8
Gold mining in Colombia, post-war crime and the peace agreement with the FARC
Frédéric Massé and Philippe Le Billon
Third World Thematics, volume 3, issue 1 (February 2018), pp. 116–134

Chapter 9
Ex-combatants and violence in Colombia: are yesterday's villains today's principal threat?
Enzo Nussio
Third World Thematics, volume 3, issue 1 (February 2018), pp. 135–152

Notes on Contributors

James Cockayne is Director of the Centre for Policy Research and represents the United Nations University at the UN in New York, USA, and in the UN's High-Level Committee on Programmes and the Frontier Issues Reference Group.

Shyamika Jayasundara-Smits is Assistant Professor in Conflict and Peace Studies with the International Institute of Social Studies (ISS) of Erasmus University Rotterdam, the Netherlands. Her research focuses on security sector reform, civil-military relations, and European Union common security and defence policy.

Annegret Kuhn is a Research Fellow at Kiel University, Germany. Her research interests are peace and conflict studies, the political-economy of natural resources, international institutions, and indigenous rights.

Sabine Kurtenbach is a political scientist, Acting Director of the GIGA Institute of Latin American Studies, and Honorary Professor at the University of Marburg, Germany. Her research focuses on peace processes, post-war societies, youth, and institutions, with a specific regional focus on Latin America but also beyond.

Philippe Le Billon is Professor in the Department of Geography and the Liu Institute for Global Issues at the University of British Columbia, Canada. He works on the political economy of war, resource governance, and illicit financial flows.

Frédéric Massé is Director of the Research Center and Special Projects (CIPE) at the University Externado de Colombia. He works on conflict resolution, peace processes, and illegal/criminal armed groups in Colombia and Latin America.

Enzo Nussio is a Senior Researcher at the Center for Security Studies at ETH Zurich, Switzerland. His research is on the causes, consequences, and reduction of violence, mostly focusing on Latin America.

Angelika Rettberg is Professor in the Political Science Department at Universidad de los Andes, in Bogotá, Colombia, and a Global Fellow at the Peace Research Institute of Oslo (PRIO), Norway. Her research focuses on the political economy of armed conflict and peacebuilding.

Anders Themnér is a Senior Researcher at the Nordic Africa Institute and an Associate Professor in the Department of Peace and Conflict Research at Uppsala University, Sweden. His research focus is on post-civil war democratisation; disarmament, demobilisation, and reintegration of ex-combatants (DDR); and informal military networks in post-civil war societies.

Judith Vorrath is a Researcher in the International Security Division of the German Institute for International and Security Affairs (SWP). In recent years, she has conducted different research projects dealing with illicit economies and organised crime in fragile and conflict-affected states, particularly in West Africa.

INTRODUCTION

OPEN ACCESS

Understanding the relation between war economies and post-war crime

Sabine Kurtenbach and Angelika Rettberg

ABSTRACT

Even when armed conflicts formally end, the transition to peace is not clear-cut. Mounting evidence suggests that it is rather 'unlikely to see a clean break from violence to consent, from theft to production, from repression to democracy, or from impunity to accountability'. The transition out of war is a complex endeavour, interrelated in many cases with other transformations such as changes in the political regime (democratisation) and in the economy (opening of markets to globalisation). In addition, in the same way as wars and conflicts reflect the societies they befall, post-war orders may replicate and perpetuate some of the drivers of war-related violence, such as high levels of instability, institutional fragility, corruption, and inequality. Thus, even in the absence of a formal relapse into war and the re-mobilisation of former insurgents, many transitional contexts are marked by the steady and ongoing reconfiguration of criminal and illegal groups and practices.

Even when armed conflicts formally end, the transition to peace is not clear-cut. Mounting evidence suggests that it is rather 'unlikely to see a clean break from violence to consent, from theft to production, from repression to democracy, or from impunity to accountability'.[1] The transition out of war is a complex endeavour, interrelated in many cases with other transformations such as changes in the political regime (democratisation) and in the economy (opening of markets to globalisation). In addition, in the same way as wars and conflicts reflect the societies they befall, post-war orders may replicate and perpetuate some of the drivers of war-related violence, such as high levels of instability, institutional fragility, corruption, and inequality.[2] Thus, even in the absence of a formal relapse into war and the re-mobilisation of former insurgents, many transitional contexts are marked by the steady and ongoing reconfiguration of criminal and illegal groups and practices.

At the same time, there is variation in post-war crime and violence. In some countries, violence effectively decreases, in others it increases, in yet others it remains constant. Even within these large categories, violence and crime may assume new forms and combinations, for example, a decline in conflict-related homicides, massacres, and kidnappings, but a rise in street crime and thefts, illicit markets, corruption, sexual, and domestic violence, or environmental crime.[3]

This collection explores the links between different manifestations of violence during and following war, as well as variation in form and intensity. Also referred to as the 'crime-conflict nexus'[4] – understood as the extent to which armed conflict patterns and mechanisms shape post-war crime.[5] The implications for international peace, cooperation, and development are significant as post-war crime, violence, and corruption produce insecurity. They endanger or undermine trust in fragile and incipient reform processes or they divert funds necessary for reconstruction and development either to private pockets or to different priorities such as to enforce security. The direct or indirect links and interactions between wartime and post-war violence are rarely visible and obvious. The same holds true for the relations between armed actors, criminal actors, and the state.[6] This calls for a connected understanding of conflict and post-war periods as well as for the design of policies and monitoring mechanisms bridging both.

Post-war crime and war economies

This collection focuses on an understudied factor in shaping post-war crime: war economies. This encompasses the organisation and development of a society's legal and illegal resource flows in support or as a result of conflict and violence. In recent decades there has been a vibrant debate on war economies as a major explanatory factor for the onset, continuation, and transformation of dynamics of violence.[7] The link between war economies and post-war crime has been analysed mostly in relation to three aspects: (1) persistently low levels of state capacities regarding the regulation of violence and the provision of public goods; (2) the ongoing control of licit and illicit flows of resources and weapons by non-state armed actors; and (3) changing patterns of violence.[8] Of course, these three elements are connected, suggesting a relationship of mutual reinforcement.

Institutional weakness

Regarding institutional weakness, it has been widely documented that both the formation of grievances and of illegal organisations is strongly related to the opportunity provided by domestic and international institutions incapable of, or unwilling to, respond to structural inequality and illicit markets. At the same time, it has been shown that conflict and crime further weaken existing state and development institutions.[9] This is reflected in the growth of military budgets to the detriment of investments in health, education, and infrastructure, as well as inertia in policy approaches or in practices developed during and in function of war. These practices are difficult to modify and adapt to changing circumstances. Not surprisingly, the literature on building sustainable peace tends to put state-building front and centre.[10]

Several articles in this collection illustrate the legacies of war-related institutional adaptations and particularities for post-war crime. Jayasundara-Smits,[11] for example, illustrates the links between war economies and current crime in Sri Lanka. Similarly, Themnér[12] focuses on former command structures and their relation to the ongoing post-war drug trade in Liberia. Nussio[13] addresses ongoing institutional incapacity as a source of recruitment for members of new criminal groups in Colombia. Finally, Cockayne[14] provides a historical perspective to demonstrate that post-cold war conflicts have brought little that is new despite some of the claims made in the 'new war' debate.[15] A look at the evolution of the Sicilian mafia illustrates how weak institutions and illicit markets remain mutually dependent for generations.

Flow of licit and illicit resources

Weak resource governance not only accounts for the onset of violence, but also for the resilience of crime after war's end.[16] Illicit markets thrive in and fuel conflict contexts, but also remain a challenge once formal fighting has ceased. They are difficult to dismantle, enduringly lucrative, and at the disposal of new actors once the previous controllers have demobilised. In addition, most illicit markets escape the control of and weaken domestic institutions, due to their shifting patterns as well as to international networks of weapons, drugs, and other resources. Demand arises mainly from beyond national borders. It has been shown that different forms of domestic crime and war-related violence depend on and are shaped by participation in international networks, as globalisation blurs the lines between the domestic and the international.[17] However, attention to the role of international markets, governments, and networks is often only explored during war, and ceases at war's end. Yet, integration into international networks may intensify the impact of illicit resources on domestic stability, especially in the volatile contexts of transitional countries. [18]

In this collection, Vorrath's[19] text on illicit economies and post-war crime in Liberia and Sierra Leone illustrates illicit markets' resilience and capacity to adapt, causing new sources of instability and unrest. Nussio[20] points to the ongoing drug trade as a critical point of vulnerability for the recently demobilised members of the Colombian FARC guerrilla. Massé and Le Billon [21] complement the look at the drug trade with a focus on illegal gold mining, also in Colombia. Kuhn[22] tackles the seemingly intractable issue of land, and asks whether large-scale land acquisitions stimulate or dampen prospects of peace in post-war contexts.

Of course, the question of resources cannot be limited to tradeables alone and crime is not necessarily violent.[23] Corruption, or the use of public resources for private good, has also been analysed under the lens of war economies contributing to post-war crime. In any context, corruption erodes confidence, deviates resources, and affects institutional strengthening.[24] In the aftermath of war, these effects are a result of the windows of opportunity provided by the authority gap between the retreat of illegal groups and the slow and uncertain presence of state authorities, as well as by the inflow of domestic and international resources in institutionally weak contexts. This compromises the stability and progress of post-war societies. Le Billon[25] has pointed to the importance of paying attention to conflict-related institutional deficits taking more subtle forms than physical violence. At the same time, some authors have shown that certain forms and levels of corruption may preserve needed structures of authority and promote bargaining and power-sharing conducive to the kind of stability required for implementing peacebuilding related policy.[26] In this collection, Le Billon[27] illustrates how post-war corruption reflects practices developed under the auspices of war-related institutions and further feeds the perpetuation and adjustments of post-war crime. Cockayne[28] contributes a historical perspective on the role of Sicilian mafias in providing government services.

Changing patterns of violence

When conflicts end, war-related practices such as forced displacement, massacres, and kidnappings give way to petty crime, domestic violence, and gangs.[29] In part, this may be a question of perception: during war, domestic and international authorities and citizens privilege attention to the more heinous crimes and, once war subsides, other practices gain increased public consideration. From this perspective, petty crime awareness is a post-war 'privilege' as other forms of collective organised violence decrease. However, as documented in many transitional countries, the void produced by demobilising armed structures in addition to the ongoing weakness of state institutions is, in fact, filled by new organisations and members, including drug-related gangs, which thrive in the unstable political and social contexts that mark the aftermath of war. Vorrath's text[30] on the role of the drug trade in transforming post-war crime in Sierra Leone and Liberia, as well as Themnér's[31] contribution on Liberia, illustrate the vagaries of this process.

Conclusion

None of these realities is specific either to the post-cold war setting or to particular regions in the world, so the articles included in this collection apply a comparative and historically grounded perspective in addressing these three aspects and in identifying the mechanisms linking periods, actors, practices, states, and society. Such an approach suggests the overarching reality of path dependence, as the legacies of war and violence dynamics interact with other political, economic, and social dynamics well beyond the formal end of war. Hence, a focus on war economies and their transformation or the lack there-off is essential to tackle the related social, political, and economic problems. Otherwise this is reflected in persistent institutional weakness and the influence of, and co-optation by, illicit actors, in state responses to violence and non-state armed actors; in the ongoing interaction with international markets for crime; in the reality of organisational learning and adaptation; and in the cultural propensity and historical embeddedness of practices related to violence before, during, and after war.

The message of the documents contained in this special issue that war economies do not disappear after the end of war but rather adapt and change to survive could be interpreted as fatalistic premonitions of inescapable disaster. Nothing further from our intentions. Rather, we seek to acknowledge the sizable difficulties involved in transitions and the many legacies wars have on societies for years after formally ending. As has also been proposed by Bosetti, Cockayne, and de Boer,[32] our purpose is to point at the risks involved in what we perceive as a futile compartmentalisation of duties and responsibilities among institutions involved in facilitating transitions between war and post-war periods, as well as a division of labour within academia between scholars studying conflict and those studying crime. The contributions to this collection make a powerful statement in favour of identifying practical and conceptual links between war and post-war contexts, as well as mechanisms that should be understood in greater detail and integrated more effectively into peacebuilding and development practice. Indeed, the emerging academic and policy related debate on the links between war and post-war developments points towards a promising future research agenda. This agenda on the transformation out of war needs to address the dismantlement of war economies in a systematic manner.

Acknowledgements

We wish to acknowledge the enthusiastic participation of all the authors involved in this collection, who attended preliminary workshops and have remained involved in discussions throughout the duration of this project. Special thanks to Désirée Reder, who provided valuable and thorough editorial assistance. Finally, thanks to all the peer reviewers, whose sharp and insightful comments doubtlessly contributed to strengthening all the articles included in this collection.

Disclosure statement

No potential conflict of interest was reported by the authors.

Funding

This work was supported by a Research Linkage Grant of the Alexander von Humboldt Foundation no. 3.3-IP-DEU/1159566. The research linkage grant builds on Angelika Rettberg's previous affiliation with the GIGA German Institute of Global and Area Studies as an Alexander von Humboldt Foundation Georg Forster Fellow.

Notes

1. Keen, "War and Peace", 10.
2. Licklider, "Obstacles to Peace Settlements"
3. See Darby, *Violence and Reconstruction*; Autesserre, "Peacetime Violence"; and Krause, "Hybrid Violence"
4. de Boer and Bosetti, "The Crime-conflict 'Nexus'"

5. Cockayne, "Chasing Shadows"; Gutiérrez Sanín, "Criminal Rebels?"; Jesperson, "Development Engagement with Organised Crime"; and Kalyvas, "How Civil Wars Help Explain"
6. Kurtenbach, "The 'Happy Outcomes' May Not Come at All"
7. Ballentine and Nitzschke, *Profiting from Peace*; Le Billon, "The Political Ecology of War"; Liebenberg, Haines, and Harris, "A Theory of War Economies"; Pugh and Cooper, *War Economies in a Regional Context*; and Ross, "What do we know about Natural Resources"
8. Andreas and Wallman, "Illicit Markets and Violence"; Newman and Richmond, "Peace Building and Spoilers"; Pugh, *Regeneration of War-torn Societies*; Stedman, "Spoiler Problems in Peace Processes";and Suhrke and Berdal, *The Peace In Between*.
9. Gates et al., "Institutional Inconsistency and Political Instability"; and Rodrik, Subramanian, and Trebbi, "Institutions Rule, The Primacy"
10. Paris and Sisk, *The Dilemmas of Statebuilding*.
11. Jayasundara-Smits, "Lost in Transition"
12. Themnér, "Commanding Abuse or Abusing Command"
13. Nussio, "Ex-combatants and Violence in Colombia".
14. Cockayne, "Can Organised Crime Shape"
15. Kaldor, *New & Old Wars*; and Kaldor, "In Defence of New Wars"
16. Le Billon, *Fuelling War*; and Ross, "What have we Learned"
17. Cockayne, *Hidden Power*.
18. UNODC, *Transnational Organized Crime*; and UNODC, "Transnational Organlzed Crlme in West Africa"
19. Vorrath, "What Drives Post-war Crime"
20. See note 13 above.
21. Massé and Le Billon, "Gold Mining in Colombia"
22. Kuhn, "Large-scale Land Acquisitions"
23. Andreas and Wallman, "Illicit Markets and Violence"
24. Cheng and Zaum, *Corruption and Post-conflict?*
25. Le Billon, "Buying Peace or Fuelling War"; Le Billon, "Corrupting Peace? Peacebuilding"
26. Belloni and Strazzari, "Corruption in Post-conflict Bosnia-Herzegovina and Kosovo"; Goodhand, "Corrupting or Consolidating the Peace?"; and Zabyelina and Arsovska, "Rediscovering Corruption's Other Side"
27. Le Billon, "Peacebuilding and White-collar Crime"
28. See note 14 above.
29. Experiences in post-war Central American and West-Africa provide evidence for these developments; see Cruz, "Criminal Violence and Democratisation"; Neumann, "(Un)Exceptional Violence(s) in Latin America"; Liberia Armed Violence Assessment, *Reading between the Lines*; and Themnér, "Former Military Networks and the Micro-Politics"
30. See note 19 above.
31. Themnér, "Commanding Abuse or Abusing Command"
32. Bosetti, Cockayne, and de Boer, "Crime-Proofing Conflict Prevention, Management"

Bibliography

Andreas, Peter, and Joel Wallman. "Illicit Markets and Violence: What is the Relationship?" *Crime, Law and Social Change* 52, no. 3 (1 September 2009): 225–229. doi: 10.1007/s10611-009-9200-6.

Autesserre, Severine. "Peacetime Violence: Post-Conflict Violence and Peacebuilding Strategies." *Columbia University Academic Commons,* Http://Hdl.Handle.Net/10022/AC:P:11208, 2010. https://academiccommons.columbia.edu/download/fedora_content/download/ac:138942/CONTENT/autesserre_bunche.pdf.

Ballentine, Karen, and Heiko Nitzschke, eds. *Profiting from Peace. Managing the Resource Dimension of Civil War. a Project of the International Peace Academy*. Boulder: Lynne Rienner, 2005.

Belloni, Roberto, and Francesco Strazzari. "Corruption in Post-Conflict Bosnia-Herzegovina and Kosovo: A Deal among Friends." *Third World Quarterly* 35, no. 5 (28 May 2014): 855–871. doi:10.1080/01436597.2014.921434.

de Boer, John, and Louise Bosetti. "The Crime-conflict "Nexus": State of the Evidence." *Occasional Paper*, 2015. http://collections.unu.edu/eserv/UNU:3134/unu_cpr_crime_conflict_nexus.pdf

Bosetti, Louise, James Cockayne, and John de Boer. "Crime-proofing Conflict Prevention, Management, and Peacebuilding: A Review of Emerging Good Practice." Occasional Paper. New York: United Nations University Centre for Policy Research, 2016.

Cheng, Christine, and Dominik Zaum (eds.). *Corruption and Post-conflict Peacebuilding Selling the Peace?*. London: Routledge, 2012.

Cockayne, James. "Can Organised Crime Shape Post-war Transitions? Evidence from Sicily." *Third World Thematics*, 2017. doi: 10.1080/23802014.2018.1413952.

Cockayne, James. "Chasing Shadows: Strategic Responses to Organised Crime in Conflict-affected Situations." *The RUSI Journal* 158, no. 2 (April 2013): 10–24. https://doi.org/10.1080/03071847.2013.787729.

Cockayne, James. *Hidden Power: The Strategic Logic of Organized Crime*. Oxford University Press, 2016. http://kclpure.kcl.ac.uk/portal/files/44634722/2015_Cockayne_James_1018212_ethesis.pdf.

Cruz, José Miguel. "Criminal Violence and Democratization in Central America: The Survival of the Violent State." *Latin American Politics and Society* 53, no. 4 (2011): 1–33.

Darby, John, ed. *Violence and Reconstruction*. Notre Dame, IN: University of Notre Dame Press, 2006.

Gates, Scott, Håvard Hegre, Mark P. Jones, and Håvard Strand. "Institutional Inconsistency and Political Instability: Polity Duration, 1800–2000." *American Journal of Political Science* 50, no. 4 (2006): 893–908.

Goodhand, Jonathan. "Corrupting or Consolidating the Peace? The Drugs Economy and Post-conflict Peacebuilding in Afghanistan." *International Peacekeeping* 15, no. 3 (June 2008): 405–423. doi: 10.1080/13533310802058984.

Gutiérrez Sanín, and Francisco Gutiérrez. "Criminal Rebels? A Discussion of Civil War and Criminality from the Colombian Experience." *Politics & Society* 32, no. 2 (1 June 2004): 257–285. doi:10.1177/0032329204263074.

Jayasundara-Smits, Shyamika. "Lost in Transition: Linking War, War Economy and Post-war Crime in Sri Lanka." *Third World Thematics*, 2018. doi: 10.1080/23802014.2018.1473046.

Jesperson, Sasha. "Development Engagement with Organised Crime: A Necessary Shift or Further Securitisation?" *Conflict, Security & Development* 15, no. 1 (January 2015): 23–50. doi:10.1080/14678802.2014.978182.

Kaldor, Mary. "In Defence of New Wars." *Stability: International Journal of Security and Development* 2, no. 1 (7 March 2013). doi:10.5334/sta.at.

Kaldor, Mary. *New & Old Wars. Organized Violence in a Global Era*. 2. aktual. Auflage. Oxford, 2001.

Kalyvas, S. N. "How Civil Wars Help Explain Organized Crime–And How They do Not." *Journal of Conflict Resolution* 59, no. 8 (2015): 1517–1540. doi:10.1177/0022002715587101.

Keen, David. "War and Peace: What's the Difference?" *International Peacekeeping* 7, no. 4 (December 2000): 1–22. doi:10.1080/13533310008413860.

Krause, K. "Hybrid Violence: Locating the Use of Force in Postconflict Settings." *Global Governance* 18, no. 1 (2012): 39–56.

Kuhn, Annegret. "Large-scale Land Acquisitions and Violence in Post-war Societies." *Third World Thematics*, forthcoming.

Kurtenbach, Sabine. "The 'Happy Outcomes' May Not Come at All – Postwar Violence in Central America." *Civil Wars* 15, no. sup1 (4 November 2013): 105–122. doi:10.1080/13698249.2013.850884.

Le Billon, Philippe. "Buying Peace or Fuelling War: The Role of Corruption in Armed Conflicts." *Journal of International Development* 15, no. 4 (May 2003): 413–426. doi:10.1002/jid.993.

Le Billon, Philippe. "Corrupting Peace? Peacebuilding and Post-conflict Corruption." *International Peacekeeping* 15, no. 3 (2008): 344–361.

Le Billon, Philippe. *Fuelling War: Natural Resources and Armed Conflicts*. London: Routledge, 2013.

Le Billon, Philippe. "Peacebuilding and White-collar Crime in Post-war Natural Resource Sectors." *Third World Thematics*, 2017: 1–18. doi:10.1080/23802014.2017.1365626.

Le Billon, Philippe. "The Political Ecology of War: Natural Resources and Armed Conflicts." *Political Geography* 20, no. 5 (2001): 561–584.

Liberia Armed Violence Assessment. *Reading between the Lines. Crime and Victimization in Liberia*. Small Arms Survey Issue Brief 2. Geneva: Liberia Armed Violence Assessment, 2011.

Licklider, Roy. "Obstacles to Peace Settlements." In *Turbulent Peace. The Challenges of Managing International Conflict.*, edited by Chester A. Crocker, Fen Osler Hampson, and Pamela Aall, 2nd., 697–718. Washington, DC: USIP, 2001.

Liebenberg, Sybert, Richard Haines, and Geoff Harris. "A Theory of War Economies: Formation, Maintenance and Dismantling." *African Security Review* 24, no. 3 (3 July 2015): 307–323. doi:10.1080/10246029.2015.1075412.

Massé, Frédéric, and Philippe Le Billon. "Gold Mining in Colombia, Post-war Crime and the Peace Agreement with the FARC." *Third World Thematics*, 2017. doi: 10.1080/23802014.2017.1362322.

Neumann, Pamela J. "(Un)Exceptional Violence(S) in Latin America." *Latin American Politics and Society* 55, no. 1 (March 2013): 168–175. doi:10.1111/j.1548-2456.2013.00188.x

Newman, Edward, and Oliver Richmond. "Peace Building and Spoilers." *Conflict, Security & Development* 6, No. 1 (April 2006): 101–110. doi:10.1080/14678800600590728.

Nussio, Enzo. "Ex-combatants and Violence in Colombia: Are Yesterday's Villains Today's Principal Threat?" *Third World Thematics*, 2017: 1–18. doi: 10.1080/23802014.2018.1396911.

Paris, Roland, and Timothy D. Sisk (eds.). *The Dilemmas of Statebuilding: Confronting the Contradictions of Postwar Peace Operations*. 1st ed. London: Routledge, 2009.

Pugh, Michael (ed.). *Regeneration of War-torn Societies*. New York: St. Martin's, 2000.

Pugh, Michael, and Neil Cooper. *War Economies in a Regional Context. Challenges for Transformation*. Boulder: Lynne Rienner, 2004.

Rodrik, Dani, Arvind Subramanian, and Francesco Trebbi. "Institutions Rule: The Primacy of Institutions over Geography and Integration in Economic Development." *Journal of Economic Growth* 9, no. 2 (2004): 131–165.

Ross, Michael L. "What do we know about Natural Resources and Civil War?" *Journal of Peace Research* 41, no. 3 (May 2004): 337–356. doi:10.1177/0022343304043773.

Ross, Michael L. "What have we Learned about the Resource Curse?" *Annual Review of Political Science* 18, no. 1 (11 May 2015): 239–259. doi:10.1146/annurev-polisci-052213-040359.

Stedman, Stephen John. "Spoiler Problems in Peace Processes." *International Security* 22, no. 2 (1997): 5–53. doi:10.2307/2539366.

Suhrke, Astri, and Mats Berdal (eds.). *The Peace in between: Post-war Violence and Peacebuilding*. London: Routledge, 2012.

Themnér, Anders. "Commanding Abuse or Abusing Command? Ex-command Structures and Drugs in Liberia." *Third World Thematics*, 2018. doi: 10.1080/23802014.2018.1429227.

Themnér, Anders. "Former Military Networks and the Micro-politics of Violence and Statebuilding in Liberia." *Comparative Politics* 47, no. 3 (2015): 334–353.

UNODC. *Transnational Organized Crime in Central America and the Caribbean. a Threat Assesssment.* United Nations Office on Drugs and Crime. Wien, 2012. http://www.unodc.org/documents/data-and-analysis/Studies/TOC_Central_America_and_the_Caribbean_english.pdf.

UNODC. A. Threat 'Transnational Organlzed Crlme in West Africa.' 2013. https://www.unodc.org/documents/data-and-analysis/tocta/West_Africa_TOCTA_2013_EN.pdf.

Vorrath, Judith. "What Drives Post-war Crime? Evidence from Illicit Economies in Liberia and Sierra Leone." *Third World Thematics*, 2017. doi:10.1080/23802014.2018.1408426.

Zabyelina, Yuliya, and Jana Arsovska. "Rediscovering Corruption's Other Side: Bribing for Peace in Post-conflict Kosovo and Chechnya." *Crime, Law and Social Change* 60, no. 1 (August 2013): 1–24. doi:10.1007/s10611-013-9446-x.

Can organised crime shape post-war transitions? Evidence from Sicily

James Cockayne

ABSTRACT

Many developing states that have undergone post-war transitions have emerged with significant organised crime presences and systematic corruption. Why? Is the criminalisation of post-war transitions inevitable? Is there something about them that is inherently criminogenic? Are criminal groups mere by-products of, and passive bystanders to, these transition processes, or do they actively shape them? This article seeks to shed light on these questions by examining three Sicilian post-war transitions following Italian unification, the First World War and the Second World War. Using archival research and mafia memoirs, the article argues that post-war transitions generated and facilitated mafia competition and collusion with political actors in a single market for governmental power, including setting norms, resolving disputes, and allocating resources. Mafias shaped the political system in ways that maximised their own governmental – and economic – power. This included collaboration with the Italian state and foreign occupying powers, and, on occasion, military and strategic competition with the state. The article explores how these mafia strategies shaped the transitions, and concludes with reflections on how we should understand – and respond to – the strategic agency of organised criminal groups in post-war transitions.

Introduction

A quick scan of today's post-war states – from Afghanistan to the Balkans, from Colombia to Libya – suggests they have at least one thing in common: relatively high rates of systemic corruption and criminality.[1] Why is that? Is the criminalisation of post-war transitions inevitable? Is there something about the experience and economies of war, or of post-war transition, that is inherently criminogenic? And are criminal groups mere by-products of, passive bystanders to, these transition processes – or do they actively shape them?

Traditional explanations of organised crime have not focused significantly on these questions. Instead, they have explored how illegality in otherwise peaceful contexts shapes the economic and socio-legal conditions within which criminal groups operate.[2] It is only more recently that a coherent strand of scholarship has begun to emerge that considers not only the role of armed groups in criminal activities during war,[3] but also how post-war transitions resemble and intersect with criminal markets, with weak state-backed lawful orders and continued criminal spoiling behaviour.[4] This scholarship has been motivated in part by growing recognition amongst practitioners that the tools and approaches used to manage conflict and post-war transitions have not adequately accounted for the enormous power that criminal groups seem frequently to wield.[5]

There is a simple explanation for this gap. Criminologists have largely focused on economic and sociological explanations of organised crime, and its relationship to state-building.[6] Fabio Armao, for example, explains mafia systems in terms of mafias serving as brokers who help political patrons manage the costs of securing 'ownership' of office, through sub-contracting coercion.[7] Scholars have had less to say about how organised crime impacts post-war political and economic transitions – the specific focus of this article.[8] Conversely, political scientists and scholars of security studies, who do more frequently focus on those transitions, have largely ignored organised criminal groups, arguing that their profit motives and apparent disinterest in formal political authority exclude them from political scientific inquiry.[9] Thus, violent competition between criminal groups 'is not war', argues the strategic theorist Colin Gray, because criminal groups pursue economic, not political, goals.[10] As a result, the governmental power of organised crime – and the ways that war facilitates the emergence of such power – has been under-appreciated by those dealing with post-war transitions.

In this article, I show how an appreciation of the potential governmental role, power, and strategies of organised criminal groups can improve our understanding of post-war transitions and their tendency towards criminalisation. I do this by examining the post-war transition experiences of the Sicilian mafia – perhaps the paradigmatic case of organised crime. Traditional explanations of the Sicilian mafia's emergence and power have focused on the role of mafiosi as commercial providers of private protection, in the absence of effective public protection providers,[11] and how this was parlayed into political power in Italy.[12] But there has been little exploration of how the mafia was shaped by the experience of war and post-war transitions – or, conversely, the mafia's role in shaping those transitions.

To understand how criminal groups navigate and exploit transitional dynamics, this article considers the relationship between the Sicilian *mafia* and politics during three episodes of post-war transition in Sicily's (relatively) recent history: in the 1860s (after Italian unification), the 1920s (after the First World War), and 1940s and 1950s (after the Second World War). These cases are chosen for several reasons. First, while the Sicilian mafia has been deeply and widely studied, its role in post-war transitions and how those transitions have shaped its role in the 'peacetime' Italian political economy and Sicily's transition into a developed economy, have not. Second, the Sicilian mafia is frequently held up as a kind of archetype of 'organized crime' so understanding its approach to post-war transition may be instructive for understanding the behaviours of other organised criminal groups. Third, the unusual longevity of the Sicilian mafia allows examination across three separate post-war transitions, in effect holding the 'actor' as a constant variable and allowing for a rudimentary longitudinal analysis.

'Mafias' are, of course, just one type of organised criminal group. There is no single, agreed definition of 'organized crime' or 'mafia'. One line of argument, for example, suggests that there are two types of criminal actors: the 'entrepreneurs', or those who supply and move illicit goods in criminal markets, and the 'protectors' or 'violent entrepreneurs', who supply protection in these markets.[13] Mafias are often said to fall into the latter group – those who attempt to 'control the supply of protection' in a given domain.[14] Yet frequently, these two categories of actors represent ideal types, and in reality, different (or even the same) members of the same criminal enterprise often play both functions. Instead, the distinction is often between criminal actors who participate in a criminal market governed by others and those who seek to *govern* that market, setting and enforcing norms, allocating resources, and resolving disputes.[15] Here, I focus on the governmental aspect of the Sicilian mafia. I return in the conclusion to questions of whether this may limit the general applicability of the findings.

Drawing on a range of primary and secondary sources, including insider accounts such as mafia memoirs and recorded interviews, official government proceedings, and declassified intelligence analysis and diplomatic correspondence, we see the same Sicilian mafia groups adopting distinct strategies to develop governmental power in different transition periods. The article begins with an explanation of the 'governmental' role played by organised crime in war and post-war transitions. Next, it considers the way that the mafia exploited the politics and institutions of the Italian state, as well as the transition of Italy's post-war economy during each episode of post-war transition, to maximise its control of contentious resources and its extraction of criminal rents. The article then considers what we can learn from these cases about the agency of these and other criminal groups during post-war transitions, and what this may mean for contemporary policies and programming in post-war transitions.

The invisible hand of organised crime

A central thesis underlying the argument presented in this paper is that criminal groups do not operate, as conventional wisdom sometimes holds, in entirely 'ungoverned' areas or markets. Instead, if the state is not governing neighbourhoods, newly emergent markets or even industries, criminal groups may emerge that play these governing functions – setting norms, allocating resources, and resolving disputes (to follow the approach to understanding governance functions during war developed by Mary Kaldor, David Keen, and Mark Duffield).[16]

This potential governmental role of organised crime has been recognised for some time in both the theoretical and empirical literature, with some authors even referring to organised crime in terms of a theoretical 'state-making' function.[17] Yet, despite these references to organised crime as playing state-like functions, the empirical study of criminal groups' roles in post-war transitions is a very new enterprise. In particular, there has been little attention to the way that criminal groups, having developed governmental power within illicit markets and during wartime, parlay that power into political influence during post-war transitions.

During these transitions, there are arguably not two separate 'worlds' – upperworld and underworld – but rather one common but heterogeneous strategic space in which states, organised criminal groups and other actors are competing for governmental power.[18] This article shows how this common strategic space emerged in Sicily during post-war transitions following unification, the First World War and the Second World War, and looks at how the mafia navigated these spaces. I describe this space as a 'market', because different actors seem to compete to provide to individuals and communities not just 'protection', but specific forms of 'governmentality' – what Michel Foucault described as the normative systems by which subjects regulate themselves or 'conduct their own conduct'.[19] They compete for legitimacy and for loyalty. Drawing on the understanding of the role of governance in war developed by Kaldor, Keen, Duffield, and others (touched upon earlier), we can say that 'governmental power' is the ability to shape and deliver a specific system of governmentality, setting the norms by which actors participate in dispute resolution and resource allocation. A system of 'governmentality' is distinct from the governmental apparatus of the state; it implies a normative system and praxis for structuring 'the possible field of action of others'.[20] The market for government involves competition for legitimacy – that is, for the allegiance of individuals to different normative systems.[21]

For the state, the system of governmentality is the lawful order, and allegiance is a public act of citizenship. For a criminal group, this normative system is clandestine and involves active avoidance of taking a *formal* role in government, because a criminal group's profits, power, and even prestige depend on its access to criminal rents. Allegiance to criminal governmentality is often entirely hidden, frequently hidden *behind* allegiance to the state. Criminal power is thus a hidden form of governmental power and the system of governmentality may in fact be geared to ensure that hidden nature – as the Sicilian mafia's code of silence, often known as *omertà*, is.

The ways in which war creates space in this market are not hard to discern. It loosens some of the ties that bind the state to the people. It further degrades the weak institutional capacity that may have helped to give rise to war. It weakens justice systems and the rule of law, normalises the use of violence to resolve disputes, and reduces livelihood prospects, making criminal livelihoods more attractive. Post-war states lack the institutional capacity to regulate the production and extraction of resources, leading to political competition between different armed and non-armed actors to control the extraction of rents. And, amid this degradation of institutional capacity, war often lowers the cost of doing criminal business – reducing corruption prices, the price of arms, and promoting smuggling activity.[22]

Yet the empirical understanding of just how criminal groups have navigated *post*-war settings is not well developed. Are they, in fact, norm-makers or norm-takers in these environments? Do criminal groups shape events or let their options be dictated by the flow of history? What approach do they take to shaping the political economies of post-war states?

To answer this question, I look below at three episodes of post-war transition in Sicily's last 150 years.

The Sicilian mafia in post-war transitions

In the transitions following the war of Italian unification, the First World War, and the Second World War, the Sicilian mafia exploited conflict dynamics and their legacies, adopting specific – and distinct – strategies that shaped the political system to maximise its own governmental and economic power. This section examines the role of the Sicilian mafia in Sicilian and Italian government during three distinct transition episodes: first, the mafia's emergence following the war of Italian unification; second, its role in managing economic transition after the First World War, and resulting competition with the Fascist regime in the following years; and third, its relationship to the Allied Military Government – the government organised by the occupying powers, the US and UK – in the tail end of the Second World War.

Italian unification and the origins of the Sicilian mafia

The unification of Italy in the mid-nineteenth century represented a profound and abrupt transformation for the peninsula's political economy. Nowhere was this felt more strongly than in the poor, agrarian south, where wealth and power remained tied to the large rural, feudal-relic landholdings known as *latifundias*. The Sicilian *mafia* emerged through the violent entrepreneurialism of a small number of rural strongmen, many of whom had formed clandestine networks during the wars of unification. They became key brokers managing and regulating the transition of the Sicilian economy into the capital circuits and political system controlled by the north.

Sicily's political economy was at the time still largely structured on post-feudal lines, with absentee aristocratic landlords relying on local 'rent-payers' – *gabellotti* – to manage their estates, protect their holdings from violence, and control the economic flow between the Sicilian agricultural hinterland and the coastal ports.[23] This system allowed these local strongmen, as essential gatekeepers, to run protection rackets directed at both local populations and the landowners. *Gabellotti* also became increasingly important as northern capital began to refashion Sicily's supply chains, connecting rural production more tightly to littoral ports, and developing new hinterland industries, such as the mining of sulphur, a key resource for the boom in rubber galvanisation. *Gabellotti* controlled transport corridors and rural workforces and could use their muscle to push into, and through, these developing supply chains. Equally, they could use their muscle and local authority to protect commodities from theft during transit. Soon, through family networks and commercial supply chains, these rural men of influence were tied into the networks of urban traders, bankers, and lawyers.[24]

Amongst these influential *gabellotti*, those who had served with Garibaldi's revolutionaries stood out. One of the first recorded uses of the term 'mafiosi' relates to squads of brave men – *Squadri di Mafia* – that joined Garibaldi when he landed in Sicily in 1860. This revolutionary service not only provided these *mafiosi* post-war authority and legitimacy, but also gave them powerful contacts in Rome, and, in some cases, appears to have exposed them to the techniques of clandestine organisation. It was from amongst the ranks of these war-time *mafiosi* that the clandestine social networks and culture of the *mafia* as we now know it emerged.[25]

Rome's economic reform efforts struggled, however, because it did not have a significant presence on the ground. To this day a Sicilian motto runs '*La presenza è potenza*': Presence is power.[26] The *mafiosi* were present, so they became the key interlocutors for northern actors seeking to navigate Sicilian community politics and economics. And the Sicilian political economy of the time was frequently violent. Alongside the formal democratisation of politics had come a democratisation of security and policing, as the formal potentates of the Kingdom of the Two Sicilies were replaced by far-away Italian officials. As the state became even more distant, a veritable 'industry of violence' emerged, with providers of various shapes and sizes, levels of formalisation and shadiness.[27] The mafiosi emerged as central governors of this industry, just as the Russian *maffiya* would 130 years later following that country's major constitutional transition.[28] Writing in the late nineteenth Century, one keen observer noted that the mafioso

> acts as capitalist, impresario and manager. He unifies the management of the crimes committed … he regulates the division of functions and labour, and he controls discipline amongst the workers …. To him falls the judgement from circumstances as to whether violence should be suspended for a while, or multiplied and made more ferocious. He has to adjust to market conditions to choose which operations to carry out, which people to exploit, which form of violence to use best to achieve the desired objective.[29]

Mafiosi were, in other words, strategic organisers of crime who built governmental power out of crime. They developed internal norms – 'controlling discipline' and 'regulating the division of functions and labour'; they resolved disputes; and they allocated resources – choosing 'which operations to carry out, which people to exploit, which form of violence to use'.

Also as in Russia, this ability to control violence gave *mafiosi* the ability to organise corrupt exchanges with politicians and officials. The *mafiosi* who enjoyed personal relationships with post-unification politicians, developed through shared service during the wars of unification, were in a unique position to do this. Mafiosi began to use their brokering role in Sicilian communities to control local electoral politics and voting and their growing wealth to finance campaigns. In return, they received immunity and favours,[30] indulging in extortion, cartelisation, and making their middle and upper class 'friends' complicit in criminal activities.[31] Over time, these *mafiosi* developed a shared operational culture and organisational techniques, coalescing into the Sicilian *mafia* system we know today.

As the British historian Eric Hobsbawm has explained, the mafia emerged out of a 'modus vivendi with northern capitalism'[32] during Sicily's transition into a modernising Italian economy dominated by northern Italian capital, in which northern political actors had to rely on local proxies for enforcement. It was, in that sense, reminiscent of many colonial, post-colonial, and post-war transitions that we see today. The mafia emerged as a key intermediary in the system and market of government.

It was not inevitable, though, that this intermediary role should take a criminal form. Legitimate political and business brokers could have assumed these roles – as they did in other parts of Italy. Instead, the shape of the Sicilian political economy appears to have been the result of choices made by specific *mafiosi* who leveraged the techniques of violence and clandestine organisation, as well as the networks of influence, gained through their service during a revolutionary war to insert themselves into an important if clandestine governmental role in Sicily.

The mafia in the post-WWI transition

Sicily saw no major military action during the First World War, but the war did have significant social effects, including the strengthening of agitation for land reform in southern Italy, particularly by returning veterans. As the post-war economic transition created tension between leftist agitators and the aristocratic landowners, the mafia, with its central role in managing rural order, emerged as a key broker in – and brake on – progressive reform efforts, often by serving as frontmen for corrupt land deals that gave the impression of reform, while protecting hidden economic interests.[33] Yet it was precisely this intermediary role, between northern capital and political power on the one hand, and Sicilian workers, veterans and peasants on the other, that drew the mafia into competition with the fascist forces that emerged later in the 1920s, in part as a result of and reaction to economic forces unleashed by WWI.

This became clear in the 1924 general election. Benito Mussolini had ridden to power on the back of a movement of *fasci di combattimento* – 'fighting leagues' – that combined war veterans with radical nationalist rhetoric, populist economic policies (such as the eight-hour work day and confiscation of war profits) and street violence. In the 1924 general election, while his Fascist Party won a landslide victory nationally, in Sicily mafia mobilisers secured victories for the opposition Popular Party and Liberal Party. Mussolini toured the island soon after, hoping to drum up support, but received a cold reception in mafia areas. In response, he appointed an iron-fisted prefect, Cesare Mori, who was authorised to undertake a major policing and military operation against the mafia, ultimately imprisoning approximately 11,000 people on suspicion of mafia ties.[34]

Both Mussolini and Mori recognised that the mafia was not just a criminal organisation, but a competitor for normative authority and legitimacy in Sicily. Unlike most political actors, Mussolini's vision of government was specifically totalitarian. It imagined the Fascist party having the total loyalty of the people – a total monopoly in the market for government. In a telegraph to Mori as he arrived in Palermo, Mussolini ordered that '[t]he authority of the State must be absolutely, repeat absolutely, re-established in Sicily'.[35] Mori himself characterised the campaign as not simply 'a police campaign on a more or less grand scale, but instead an insurrection of the conscience, a revolt of the spirit, the action of a people'.[36] The Fascists sought to win this confrontation by representing themselves as more effective protectors than the mafia, including through the use of overwhelming force, such as sieges of entire towns known to be connected to key mafia figures.[37] As Sicilian mafia historian Salvatore Lupo has explained, 'In order to win on the terrain of folk values, the state had to gain itself a degree of "respect" by behaving in a more *mafioso* fashion than the *mafiosi* themselves'.[38]

Concurrently, Mori also attacked the bottlenecks in the Sicilian economy that provided the rents that underpinned mafia power. He tightened cattle registration systems to undermine cattle-rustling and improved state measurement of agricultural yields, to prevent mafia chicanery. And coastal elites were pressured to distance themselves from their rural mafia partners.[39] As the mafia's local power was steadily corroded, the state assumed an increased role in the economy, and coastal elites joined the Fascist Party.[40]

The Fascists appeared to have won the confrontation with the mafia, denying them the intermediary role in Sicily's political economy that the mafia at first appeared to have retained – and perhaps even enlarged – during the period of popular agitation for land reform following the First World War. The mafia's initial success at inserting itself as a buffer between leftist agitators and aristocratic reactionaries demonstrated the mafia's ability to adapt to changing politico-economic circumstances, maintaining an important dispute resolution role. But the mafia's apparent conquest by the Fascist Party, as it remade Sicily's political economy in a more unitary form, eschewing the role for *any* social intermediaries (other than itself), showed that the mafia's governmental power was not invincible.

Some younger mafia figures began to flee, several of them to New York. There, inter-factional mafia rivalries from Sicily spilled over into a war for control of the rents from Prohibition, known today as the Castellammarese War, after a faction from the small town of Castellammarese del Golfo, west of Palermo.[41] But in truth, while the upper-level mafia networks of Sicily were co-opted and bullied into supporting the Fascists, and mafia influence was driven out of the norm-setting and dispute resolution role in Sicily's supply chains and markets, mafia networks and loyalties were not dismantled altogether. Particularly in the hard-to-reach mountainous hinterlands above Palermo and further east, the clandestine governmentality of the *mafia* – its hidden, social norm-setting role – ran deep. The 'lower-level' mafia networks were not so easily displaced. Perhaps all they might require take to flicker back into life was the removal of the Fascists from power and the creation of space in the market for government in which they could once again compete.[42] Soon enough, war offered that opening.

The mafia's resurgence after the Second World War

The decline of the Fascists, it turned out, was not so long in coming. By the summer of 1942, when the Allies invaded and occupied Sicily and the Italian *mezzogiorno* (the southern regions of Italy plus Sardinia), southern Italy was essentially a failing state, with many of the characteristics endemic to today's post-war societies. Infrastructure was crumbling, most large towns faced severe food shortages, large numbers of dead were unburied, and arms and unexploded ordnance were ubiquitous.[43] The US Army observed that food shortages were leading to general unrest and were being exploited by 'criminal factions',[44] with a vibrant black market for food, weapons, and other goods and services emerging, including corrupt diversion of up to one third of Allied supplies.[45] Normative barriers to participation in criminal activity were destroyed, with up to two-thirds of household incomes derived from black market activity, and large numbers of young people joining local criminal groups.[46]

The Sicilian mafia, though weakened by Mussolini's predations prior to the war, flickered back to life, and moved quickly to position itself as the intermediary governing force positioned between the black market and the Allied Military Government (AMG). AMG efforts to dismantle the Fascist Party created the same kind of vacuum in the market for government that Coalition efforts to dismantle Saddam Hussein's Baathist Party in Iraq created sixty years later. The mafia rushed into that vacuum.[47] The AMG's own senior administrator, Major-General Francis Baron Rennell of Rodd, soon recognised that AMG personnel had fallen 'into the trap of appointing the most pushing and obvious person [as mayors], who in certain cases are now suspected as [*sic*] being the local Mafia leaders'.[48]

Although internal AMG documents show that the AMG did briefly consider options for dealing with the mafia, including confrontation and active negotiation, the policy it ultimately adopted was, essentially, one of wilful blindness to mafia resurgence.[49] This was not, however, simply a question of AMG by-standing; the governmental power of the AMG itself became a resource that the mafia penetrated and, in certain limited cases, merged with. The Sicilian mafia also capitalised on the ties forged between the US Navy intelligence and American mafiosi during the Second World War II. The New York Mob provided critical tactical and intelligence capabilities in the planning of the invasion and occupation of Sicily.[50] Once Allied forces landed in Sicily, American agents sought out mobsters who had been deported from the US to Italy to help broker access to local Sicilian mafia *capi*.[51] After the war ended, New York mobsters with close ties to the Sicilian mafia parlayed this influence into key roles in the AMG, serving as official 'interpreters' for the top US officials during the occupation and using their positions to organise the black market.[52]

The mafia became a resource for the AMG, to govern the informal and illicit markets; and the AMG became a resource for the mafia to expand their own governmental power. Its unique access to governmental power – not to mention resources, such as official ID cards, vehicles, materiel and movement licences – put the mafia in a uniquely strong position to influence the transition as the AMG began to draw down. An array of political actors was beginning to vie for power in Sicily once the war ended – including monarchists, republicans, Communists, separatists, and Unitarians. As Michele Pantaleone, a respected Sicilian journalist of the time noted, the mafia would ally itself with whichever party was 'as 'governmental' as possible' – or whichever power offered it the greatest prospect of exercising governmental power in Sicily.[53]

The mafia's first move was to maximise its power over the transition itself. '[I]nstead of inserting itself into an existing power structure' as it had traditionally, it became 'bent on contributing directly to a political hypothesis' – formal Sicilian exit from the Italian state to create a separate, sovereign political entity.[54] As the US military intelligence apparatus concluded at the time, 'the Mafia members want an autonomous Sicily because in order to accomplish their criminal aims, they can easier intimidate the Civil public servants, then [*sic*] they could those residing in far-away Rome'.[55]

By 1944, a separatist political movement backed by mafia figures had reached out directly to senior leaders in the United States and Great Britain, seeking great power protection for an independent Sicily. [56] When this support was not forthcoming, the mafia moved onto a more offensive footing, encouraging the separatist political forces that it was underwriting to develop the capacity for violence. Soon, an insurgent force was being assembled.[57] This *Esercito Volontario per l'Indipendenza Siciliana* (EVIS) managed to build a network of informants and develop a staff structure and detailed military planning, but struggled to recruit,[58] turning instead to mafia networks and the rural bandits they controlled.[59]

As the insurgency became more threatening, the mafia moved to capitalise on its increased bargaining power. It reached out to and negotiated with a series of different political parties – including the monarchists, the Communists, and the Christian Democrats – indicating its willingness to give up its support for the insurgency and separatism altogether, in return for those parties' support for a hidden governmental role in the post-war political economy.[60] The best offer, ultimately, came from the Christian Democrats. They recognised that the mafia was not, in fact, wedded to the notion of exit from Italy and the creation of a separate political system, as this might actually *reduce* mafia wealth. Instead, the mafia could be induced to support something short of exit – Sicilian *autonomy*, within which the traditional governmental role of the mafia would be accommodated.[61] After a series of secret negotiations,[62] the Christian Democrats told the Allies point-blank that a political settlement was possible, if 'the system formerly employed by the old and respected Maffia [*sic*] should return',[63] through the creation of Sicilian autonomy within the Italian constitutional system.

On 21 November 1945, mafia leaders from Palermo, Trapani, and Agrigento met to chart a new way forward. The mafia abandoned its strategy of constitutional separatism, and returned to its traditional intermediary strategy, interposing itself between the state and the local population. The decision was ratified a week later by a larger group of 47 mafia leaders from across the island. The American consul, informed of these developments, suggested this new mafia group with its ties to the Christian Democrats might provide 'the foundation of the strongest political force which has yet existed in Sicily'.[64]

Mafia leaders told the authorities that they were abandoning EVIS, and would 'work and cooperate with the authorities to maintain tranquillity throughout the island'.[65] Soon the police began to find bandit leaders dead, cause unknown; and tip-offs from the population increased dramatically.[66] In late December 1945, EVIS' leader was captured. The separatist experiment had been snuffed out; but the mafia's role in post-war government was secured.

In the years that followed, the bargain with the Christian Democrats paid off handsomely – for both sides. Mafia support transformed the northern-dominated party's electoral fortunes on the island, leapfrogging them from trailing the Communists to dominance in mafia-controlled districts, helping to secure their electoral dominance in Rome for many decades to come.[67] In return, mafia-linked business interests dominated the economic flows that now passed through the regional assembly and other autonomous Sicilian institutions that had been created by constitutional transformation backed by the Christian Democrats. To cement this partnership further, through the course of the 1950s the mafia began what was essentially a hostile 'merger' with the party, using 'branch-stacking' techniques originally refined in Brooklyn, New York, by the American Mob, to control the Christian Democratic system in Sicily.[68]

The party structures offered the Sicilian mafia a formalised political patronage apparatus within which the mafia could hide its informal power and system of corrupt exchange – and gain a direct line to the corridors of power in Rome. As the Sicilian economy increasingly integrated into the Italian, European, and international markets, this line to the capital was even more critical to ensure the mafia could maintain its power and continue to extract its criminal rents from Sicilian value chains.[69] By the period of the dominance – and 'sack' – of Palermo by the Christian Democrat mayor Salvatore Lima, the mafia and the Christian Democrats on the island of Sicily had essentially formed a governmental joint venture, with mafia assets used to maintain political power through electoral coercion and maintenance of order, and state assets used to line mafia pockets, especially through rigged public procurement and works.[70]

The manoeuvring of the mafia during the period from the Allied occupation to the formation of this governmental joint venture shows particularly clearly how an organised criminal group can choose not simply to react to post-war political and economic changes, but to shape and drive those changes itself. Organised criminal groups can shape post-war economic transitions, as independent actors in their own right.

Rethinking the criminalisation of transitions

Through the course of three post-war transitions, the Sicilian mafia emerged as a governmental power in Sicily, and as a strategic actor able to shape the strategic environment around it. Recognising that the mafia had agency in these transition processes, and that their criminalisation and the emergence of corruption was not a purely structural or epiphenomenal process, should give us pause. It challenges some of the basic assumptions built into international response to criminality and corruption in post-war economic transitions.

First, it challenges our assumption that the management of organised crime and illicit economies during transitions is a technical, regulatory, or narrowly law enforcement exercise that can be achieved through structurally oriented interventions – i.e. interventions that fail to account for criminal groups as shapers of their own destiny, and not just epiphenomena issuing from structural drivers. Clearly, it is also a highly strategic one, requiring a careful understanding of different groups' interests, identity and strategies, and how they are likely to respond, dynamically, to changes in the strategic environment *created* by these programming interventions.

Second, it challenges us to consider that different criminal groups will position themselves within the transition process quite differently – and that the same group may choose different strategies at different times. At times, the mafia opted to play the role of intermediary between the state and local populations, cooperating with the state. Following the Second World War, it threatened to exit the Italian state all together, and set up a new independent political unit. In that same period, and earlier during the 1920s, it engaged in confrontation with the state, attacking both the state itself, and, at times during the EVIS insurgency of the 1940s, attacking civilians to force a change in state policy. And yet, by the 1950s, it found itself in a localised joint venture with the Christian Democrats, controlling Sicily's political economy from within the institutions of the state.

These different approaches suggest that it may not be safe to assume that all criminal groups will adopt the intermediary or 'brokering' role of mafias mapped out by Fabio Armao and others who have previously studied these issues.[71] Instead, post-war transitions may offer a gate through which criminal groups, all developing and exploiting hidden forms of governmentality, can seek to wield influence in the 'market for government' through a variety of different approaches. Elsewhere, I have explored at greater length what six different such strategies may look like, ranging from the adoption of an intermediary approach (the typical approach for mafias), to the development of joint ventures, exit and creation of new markets for government.[72] Table 1, below, describes three different 'positioning strategies' by which criminal groups can seek to cooperate with states, and points to the implications of these different approaches for state response. Table 2, further below, explains three different approaches criminal groups seem to take when they engage in confrontation with states – and again points to some implications for response.

Empirical testing of other contexts (countries and historical periods) will shed further light and potentially add to this initial theoretical work. Understanding different types and strategies of criminal groups in post-war transitions is a fundamental component in designing international interventions in contemporary settings. Existing approaches to transition often fail to recognise that criminal groups can make their own strategic choices – and change them, as these Sicilian cases show.

So how can we do better? First, the insights here suggest a need to formally use a political economy approach to inform our efforts to manage organised crime during transitions. We will continue to struggle to manage crime during transitions if we do not understand where criminal groups are drawing their power from, and the informal functional and normative roles they play within the local political economy. The mafia's power ultimately derived from its ability to manage illicit (and licit) value chains within the circuits of Italian and European (and later, global) capital. The same might be said of other states that continue to undergo complex political-economic transitions, as Mexico has in the last two decades.

Second, we need to think about how leverage – and thus effective responses – may need to differ, depending upon what we find out about where a group's governmental power is sourced. Groups with criminal strategies are not seeking to remove or supplant the state. In fact, they need the state to remain formally in place with political authority and responsibility, so that the activities from which the criminal group reaps criminal rents *remain* criminal (and thus lucrative). But once a criminal group begins to develop governmental power – enjoying the allegiance of individuals and communities to a distinct normative system, and using it to resolve disputes and allocate resources – then it is implicitly in competition with the state, offering another form of governmentality. The episodes studied here suggest that there is a variety of positioning options available to a criminal group at any given time, depending on which strategy it thinks may maximise its governmental power (and criminal rents) – as we see in the various approaches taken by Mexican criminal groups. Existing responses to organised crime in post-war and other complex transitions tend to discount the agency criminal groups exercise during these transitions, and the various positioning strategies criminal groups may use. They, therefore, muddle the possible responses, without a clear

Table 1. Three Criminal Positioning Strategies involving Cooperation with States – and Effective Responses to them.

	Intermediation	Autonomy	Merger
Actors associated with this positioning strategy	Mafias	Warlords and gang rule	Joint Ventures
Underlying market logic	Jurisdictional sharing	Territorial segmentation	Vertical integration
Criminal rents available exceed internal costs plus…	Cost of corrupting governmental capabilities	Cost of excluding state and developing alternative governmental capabilities	Cost of integration of capabilities
Conditions for emergence	Rapid structural or normative change creates unmet demand for government	State enforcement capabilities ineffective	Elite political or military group controls state assets with weak public oversight
	Low costs of corruption	Low cost of organising alternative governmental capabilities (e.g. fragmenting military structures; or local protection groups)	Poor rent extraction opportunities in local licit economy
Geography	Mafias locate at sites of formal legislative, spending and policing power	Communities where state capabilities are consistently weak – for warlords, peripheries; for gangs, slums	State-run security and economic operations – e.g. military airports and installations, development banks, financial regulators
Contemporary examples	Russian and Kenyan mafias	Jamaican garrisons, warlords in Afghanistan and West Africa	Guinea-Bissau, Venezuela
Governmentality	Protection of traditional community values within formal political system	Protection of local identity and interests without secession	Court politics
Effective state responses	Remove unmet demand for government through regulatory reforms of markets (e.g. ending prohibition)	Physical extension of governmental capabilities	Promotion of democratic control of state institutions (armed forces, development banks, financial regulators, campaign finance reform)
	Raise costs of corruption, Inc. through higher-level enforcement (e.g. federal)	Localisation of governance, subject to centralised corruption monitoring	Inter-state accountability

Table 2. Three criminal positing strategies involving confrontation with states – and responses to them.

	Strategic alliance	Terrorism	Blue ocean
Role of third party	Common adversary of both state and criminal group	Public – source of pressure on the state	Potential new state host
Underlying strategic approach	Balance of power	Indirect strategy	Structural transformation
Criminal vulnerability	Defection and betrayal	Alienation and popular resistance	Lack of local knowledge
Effective state responses	Defection/wedge strategies	Strategic communication to delegitimise criminal violence	Inter-state responsibility and elite accountability

understanding of the underlying positioning strategies to which each is best tailored to respond.

Third, we must recognise that the central struggle during transitions is a struggle for the loyalty of the population – not just to particular parties or groups, but to different visions of government, different governmentalities. This is particularly the case in contemporary situations where armed groups have adopted mixed criminal and jihadist strategies, for example in northern Mali and the Sahel. Contemporary interventions by the international community during these transition processes pay little attention to this battle for loyalty. Multilateral approaches to post-war recovery operate on the assumption that a well-functioning state is the desired end-state, and may downplay the risks of state predation that loom large for those who have suffered it, and suffered during war.

What response can there be? For Mussolini and Mori, who *did* understand that their battle with the mafia was a normative one, the response was to be more *mafioso* than the *mafioso*. But as we have seen, this was not a successful strategy over time. The alternative approach is to take a more sophisticated – and scientific – approach to understanding how loyalty to the state, and the lawful order it represents, can be promoted, through social, familial, and other non-state networks and affiliations, and through greater attention to the role of strategic communication during transition processes.[73]

Finally, this brief review of the Sicilian mafia's experience with transitions points to the need for international actors to focus on preventing the criminalisation of specific aspects of post-war transitions that serve as key gateways for criminal groups into positions of influence and power over political actors. This notably includes elections. While elections help to restore the political legitimacy of the state, a rush to elections may provide an opportunity for actors with hidden criminal agendas, since they possess significant economic power and the organisational and coercive capabilities needed for effective political campaigning. They operate, in other words, at a significant advantage in the market for government during transitions, and elections may simply offer them an opportunity to expand their influence in the post-war order, if not carefully policed. To date, much electoral assistance by the international community overlooks these questions, risking repetition of the wilful blindness displayed by the AMG in Sicily over sixty years ago.[74]

Conclusion

Drawing on evidence from three disparate episodes of post-war transition in Sicily over 150 years, this article has argued that even as war helps to organise crime, so organised crime can shape post-war transitions. Post-war transitions offer a highly favourable environment for the organised crime groups that are nurtured by, or otherwise survive, war to transform their informal and illicit economic and governmental power into more institutionalised – and sometimes even formalised – influence over political processes and systems. A political economy approach to post-war transitions will help us to understand how informal and illicit economies operate as a source of power that organised crime groups can and do strategically leverage into wider and longer-term influence. It may also offer the outlines of an approach that will allow a more effective response to the potential criminalisation of post-war transitions.

Acknowledgement

The author thanks Amanda Roth for support during the writing of this article.

Abbreviations

BNA British National Archives: CAB = Records of the Cabinet Office; FO = Records of the Foreign Office; WO = Records of War Office and Armed Forces; FBI – US Department of Justice, Federal Bureau of Investigations. These records are taken from 1) "The FBI Vault" in the online FBI "Reading Room." http://vault.fbi.gov; and 2) NARA Record Group 65.; NARA – US National Archives and Records Administration, College Park, MD. Listed by Record Group (RG), then entry:box:folder number – e.g. RG 226, 142:2:14. Of these, the most important are: RG 59-General Records of the Department of State; RG 226-Records of the Office of Strategic Services; RG 59-General Records of the Department of State; RG 226-Records of the Office of Strategic Services; RG 226-Records of the Office of Strategic Services

Notes

1. OECD, *States of Fragility 2016*, 91–97.
2. Smith, "Illicit Enterprise: An Organized," 121–50; Southerland and Potter, "Applying Organization Theory."
3. See for example Naylor, "The Insurgent Economy," 13–51; Williams, "Insurgencies and Organized Crime," 27–72; and Felbab-Brown, *Shooting Up*.
4. See for example Cockayne, de Boer, and Bosetti, "Going Straight"; Dziedzic, *Combatting Criminalized Power Structures*; Hellman, "Winners Take All," 203–34; and Cheng, "Private and Public Interests," 62–78.
5. Bosetti, Cockayne, and de Boer, "Crime-Proofing Conflict Prevention," 3.
6. See for example Williams and Godson, "Anticipating Organized and Transnational Crime."
7. Armao, "Why is Organized Crime so Successful?", 29.
8. There are some important exceptions, including Bayart et al., *The Criminalization of the State*; Wilson, *Government of the Shadows*; Arias, *Criminal Enterprise and Governance*.
9. See further Berdal and Serrano, "Introduction," 7.
10. Gray, "What is War?" 185.
11. See especially Gambetta, *The Sicilian Mafia*.
12. See for example Pantaleone, *The Mafia and Politics*; Dickie, *Mafia Republic*; Briquet, "Organized Crime, Politics and the Judiciary,' 188–201; Lupo, *History of the Mafia*, 18–19.

13. Varese, "What is Organized Crime?" 14–20; Shaw, "We Pay, You Pay."
14. Varese, "What is Organized Crime?" 14–20.
15. Cockayne, *Hidden Power.*
16. Kaldor, *New and Old Wars,* 90–111; Duffield, *Global Governance and the New Wars*; Keen, *The Economic Functions of Violence,* 11.
17. See for example Schelling, "Economic Analysis and Organized Crime," 114–26; Schelling, "Economics and the Criminal Enterprise," 61–78; Tilly, "War Making and State Making," 169–91; Cressey, *Theft,* 110; Bequai, *Organised Crime,* xi; Jankowski, *Islands in the Streets,* 89; Grossman, "Rival kleptocrats," 143–56.
18. The argument is explored at more length in Cockayne, *Hidden Power,* on which this article draws.
19. Foucault, "Governmentality," 87–104.
20. Ibid.
21. Compare Alex de Waal's notion of the 'political marketplace' in Africa in De Waal, "Mission Without End?" 99–113; David Kilcullen's 'theory of competitive control' in Kilcullen, *Out of the Mountains,* 116–68; and Vanda Felbab-Brown's notion of states and criminal actors as 'competitors in state-making' in Felbab-Brown, "Conceptualizing."
22. Cockayne, "Chasing Shadows," 13.
23. Raab, *Five Families,* 15–7; Dickie, *Cosa Nostra,* 37–44, 48–51; Hobsbawm, *Primitive Rebels,* 40, 41.
24. Dickie, *Cosa Nostra,* 37–51; Lupo, *History,* 8, 9, 17, 18, and Chapters 2 and 3; Hobsbawm, *Primitive Rebels,* 34, 38–40; Hobsbawm, *Bandits,* 87; Arlacchi, *Men of Dishonor,* 53–56; Pantaleone, *The Mafia and Politics,* 38–40; Catanzaro, *Men of Respect,* 15, 16.
25. Fentress, *Rebels and Mafiosi,* 147–252.
26. Dickie, *Mafia Republic,* 423.
27. Franchetti, *Condizioni Politiche,* 172, 173, author's translation. See further 223 et seq.
28. Varese, *The Russian Mafia.*
29. Franchetti, *Condizioni politiche,* 172, 173, author's translation. See further 223 et seq.
30. Pantaleone, *The Mafia and Politics,* 195.
31. Catanzaro, *Men of Respect,* 17.
32. Hobsbawm, *Primitive Rebels,* 42, 43.
33. Costanzo, *The Mafia and the Allies,* 35, 36; Pantaleone, *The Mafia and Politics,* 44, 45, 85; Lupo, *History,* 159, 167–169.
34. Costanzo, *The Mafia and the Allies,* 38; Newark, *Mafia Allies,* 45; Lupo, *History,* 174.
35. Quoted in Petacco, *L'uomo della provvidenza,* 101; author's translation.
36. Mori, *Con la mafia,* 242.
37. Spano, *Faccia a faccia,* 42; Lupo, *History,* 175.
38. Lupo, *History,* 175.
39. Newark, *Mafia Allies,* 35, 36.
40. Catanzaro, *Men of Respect,* 109–112; Pantaleone, *The Mafia and Politics,* 53.
41. Cockayne, *Hidden Power,* 114–120.
42. Lupo, *History,* 22; Stille, *Excellent Cadavers,* 17; Duggan, *Fascism and the Mafia,* 195–199.
43. Rennell, "Confidential Notes," 2, 3; Pantaleone, *The Mafia and Politics,* 65–70; Scotten, "The Problem," 4, 5; Lewis, *Naples '44,* 109.
44. Notes on meeting held in HQ Island Base Section, 3 December 1943.
45. Lewis, *Naples '44,* 109, 122, 123.
46. Ibid.; Pantaleone, *The Mafia and Politics,* 70.
47. Newark, *Mafia Allies,* 142, 143.
48. Rennell, "Confidential Notes," 2, 3.
49. Scotten, "The Problem," 4, 5.
50. Costanzo, *The Mafia and the Allies,* 6, 58–60.
51. Alfieri testimony, 19, 20; Titolo testimony, 15; Herlands Report, 86.
52. Lewis, *Naples '44,* 109–110; Duff, Chapter 2, Part III, 53; Notes, Meeting of Intelligence Officers in Palermo, 4.
53. Pantaleone, *The Mafia and Politics,* 65, 71.
54. Lupo, *History of the Mafia,* 189.

55. US Joint Intelligence Collecting Agency, "Comments on Separatist Movement in Sicily," 2. See also G-2(CI) NATO to G-2(CI); AFHQ, "Separatism and Separatists."
56. US Joint Intelligence Collecting Agency, "Comprehensive Outline," 3; US Naval Intelligence, Palermo, Report; Pantaleone, *The Mafia and Politics,* 66, 75; Finkelstein, *Separatism,* 60, 61; Newark, *Mafia Allies*, 242, 243; Manley, "Report on Sicilian Separatism," 2.
57. Finkelstein, *Separatism,* 80–7.
58. Nester to Secretary of State, "Raid on Separatist Ammunition Dump"; Finkelstein, *Separatism,* 163; Rome to Foreign Office, 10 October 1945. See also Kirk to Secretary of State, 3 October 1945.
59. Jacobs, "Present Political Situation in Sicily"; Watkins, "The Situation in Sicily," 3; US Naval Intelligence, Palermo, Report, 15 February 1946.
60. Office of Strategic Services, "Monarchy Seeks Support"; Extract from Security Intelligence Summary No. 22, October 1945, 6 November 1945, BNA, WO 204/12617; Nester to Secretary of State, 'Possible Fusion'; Finkelstein, *Separatism,* 158–60.
61. Pantaleone, *The Mafia and Politics,* 76, 77.
62. Office of Strategic Services, "Notes on Separatism"; Report, "Italy, Government, Political Parties"; Manley, "Report on Sicilian Separatism," 5; Finkelstein, *Separatism,* 49, 88, 89; Office of Strategic Services, "General Castellana Seeking Maffia Accord."
63. Nester to Secretary of State, "Statements Made." See also Nester to Secretary of State, "Excerpts from"; Nester to Secretary of State, "Leaders of the Maffia"; Nester to Secretary of State, "Meeting of Maffia Leaders"; Nester to Secretary of State, "Formation of Group"; Finkelstein, *Separatism,* 122.
64. Nester to Kirk, 23 November 1945; Nester to Kirk, 5 December 1945; Italian Parliamentary Commission of Inquiry, *Relazione sui rapporti*, 110.
65. Nester to Kirk, 12 January 1946. See also Celetta and Saverio Forte to US Army CIC Naples Detachment, "Sicilian Separatist Disturbances."
66. Dickie, *Cosa Nostra*, 211; Catanzaro, *Men of Respect,* 123; Italian Parliamentary Commission of Inquiry, *Relazione sui rapport,* 56, 57.
67. Pantaleone, *The Mafia and Politics,* 198.
68. Ibid., 195–7; Catanzaro, *Men of Respect,* 180.
69. Dickie, *Cosa Nostra*, 204.
70. Cockayne, *Hidden Power*, 199–201.
71. See for example Armao, "Why is organized crime so successful?"
72. Cockayne, *Hidden Power*.
73. Bosetti et al., "Crime-proofing Conflict Prevention," 6.
74. Ibid.

Bibliography

Primary sources

Celetta, Special Agent Gabriel B. and Special Agent Saverio Forte to US Army CIC Naples Detachment. "Sicilian Separatist Disturbances." 29 January 1946, British BNA, WO 204/12617.

Counter Intelligence Corps. Naples Detachment, Memorandum, "Sicilian Political Situation." 4 February 1945, BNA, WO 204/12619.

Duff, D. S. "Narrative for Official History of Civil Affairs in Italy (the Sicily campaign)." Undated, BNA, CAB 44/171.

Extract from Security Intelligence Summary. No. 22, October 1945, 6 November 1945, BNA, WO 204/12617.

G-2(CI) NATO to G-2(CI) Allied Forces Headquarters. "Separatism and Separatists." 11 January 1944, BNA, WO 204/12618.

Italian Parliamentary Commission of Inquiry into the Mafia phenomenon in Sicily. *Relazione sui rapporti tra mafia e banditismo in Sicilia*. Legislature V, doc. xxiii, n. 2. Rome: Senate Printing Press, 1972.

Jacobs, Lt. D. M. "Present Political Situation in Sicily." 6 February 1946, BNA, WO 204/12617.

Kirk to Secretary of State. 3 October 1945, FBI, 109-12-233-111.

Lord Rennell. "Confidential Notes in Reply to Points Made in House of Commons Debate." 3 August 1943, BNA, FO 371/37327.

Nester to Kirk. 12 January 1946, NARA, RG 59, 865.00/1-1246.

Nester to Kirk. 23 November 1945, NARA, RG 59, 865.00/11-2345.

Nester to Kirk. 5 December 1945, NARA, RG 59, 865.00/12-545.

Nester to Secretary of State. "Certain Elements Within the Separatist Party." 22 August 1944, NARA, RG 59, 865.01/8-2244.

Nester to Secretary of State. "Excerpts From a Secret Report by General Castellano to Count Sforza and Carondini." 4 November 1944, NARA, RG 59, 865.01/11-444.

Nester to Secretary of State. "Formation of Group Favoring Autonomy Under Direction of Maffia." 27 November 1944, NARA, RG 59, 865.01/11-2744.

Nester to Secretary of State. "Leaders of the Maffia Meet at a Number of Secret Meetings in Palermo." 18 November 1944, NARA, RG 59, 865.01/11-1844.

Nester to Secretary of State. "Meeting of Maffia Leaders with General Giuseppe Castellano and Formation of Group Favoring Autonomy." 21 November 1944, NARA, RG 59, 865.00/11-2144.

Nester to Secretary of State. "Possible Fusion of Maffia and Separatists Under Leadership of Vittorio Emanuele Orlando." 10 April 1945, NARA, RG 59, 865.00/4-1045.

Nester to Secretary of State. "Raid on Separatist Ammunition Dump." 13 June 1945, NARA, RG 59, 865.00/6-1345.

Nester to Secretary of State. "Separatist Movement in Sicily, Enclosure No. 2." 4 September 1944, NARA, RG 59, 865.01/9-4444.

Nester to Secretary of State. "Statements Made by General Castellano Regarding Sicilian Situation and Possible Solution Thereof." 18 January 1945, NARA, RG 59, 865.01/11-444.

Notes on meeting held in HQ Island Base Section. 3 December 1943, BNA, WO 204/827.

Notes, Meeting of Intelligence Officers in Palermo. 10 February 1944, BNA, WO 204/827.

Office of Strategic Services. "General Castellana Seeking Maffia Accord." 13 October 1944, NARA, RG 226, 226/103050.

Office of Strategic Services. "Notes on Separatism: 1. Communist Leader, 2. Aldisio's Attitude, 3. Pro-American Maffia, 4. Bagheria Meeting." 7–14 August 1944, in FBI, 65-51898-3.

Office of Strategic Services. Italian Division, "Monarchy Seeks Support of Separatist Movement." 3 May 1945, BNA, WO 204/12618.

Report. "Italy, Government, Political Parties in Sicily, Maffia and Separatist Movement." 10 December 1943, NARA, RG 38, 9632-H, C-10-f.

Rome to Foreign Office. 10 October 1945, BNA, FO 371/49767.

Mallett, Sir Victor. "Giuliano and Sicilian Banditry." Memorandum, British Embassy in Rome to Foreign Office, 7 October 1949, BNA, FO 371/79312.

Scotten, Capt W. E.. "The Problem of Mafia in Sicily." 29 October 1943, BNA, FO 371/37327.

US Joint Intelligence Collecting Agency. "Comments on Separatist Movement in Sicily." 21 January 1944, BNA, WO 204/12618.

US Joint Intelligence Collecting Agency. "Comprehensive Outline of the Sicilian Separatist Movement." 17 January 1944, BNA, WO 204/12618.

US Naval Intelligence. Palermo, Report, 15 February 1945, BNA, WO 204/12618.

US Naval Intelligence, Palermo, Report, 15 February 1946, BNA, WO 204/12618.

Vice-Consul Manley. "Report on Sicilian Separatism and the Movimento per L'Indipendenza della Sicilia." 17 April 1946, BNA, FO 371/67786.

Watkins. "The Situation in Sicily." 6 September 1945, BNA, FO 371/49767.

Secondary sources

Arias, Enrique Desmond. *Criminal Enterprise and Governance in Latin American and the Caribbean*. New York: Cambridge University Press, 2017.

Arlacchi, Pino. *Men of Dishonor: Inside the Sicilian Mafia. An Account of Antonino Calderone*. Translated by Marc Romano. New York: William Morrow, 1993.

Armao, Fabio. "Why is Organized Crime so Successful?" In *Organised Crime and the Challenge to Democracy*, edited by Felia Allum and Renate Siebert, 27–38. London: Routledge, 2003.

Bayart, Jean-François, Stephen Ellis, and Beatrice Hibou. *The Criminalization of the State in Africa*. Bloomington: Indiana University Press, 1999.

Bequai, August. *Organized Crime: The Fifth Estate*. Lexington, MD: D. C. Heat & , 1979.

Berdal, Mats, and Mónica Serrano, eds. *Transnational Organized Crime and International Security: Business as Usual?*. Boulder, CO: Lynne Rienner, 2002.

Briquet, Jean-Louis. "Organized Crime, Politics and the Judiciary in Post-war Italy." In *Organized Crime and the Challenge to Democracy*, edited by Felia Allum and Renate Siebert, 188–201. Abingdon: Routledge, 2003.

Catanzaro, Raimondo. *Men of Respect: A Social History of the Sicilian Mafia*. New York: The Free Press, 1988.

Cheng, Christine. "Private and Public Interests: Informal Actors, Informal Influence, and Economic Order After War." In *Political Economy of Statebuilding: Power After Peace*, edited by Mats Berdal and Dominik Zaum, 62–78. Abingdon: Routledge, 2013.

Costanzo, Ezio. *The Mafia and the Allies: Sicily 1943 and the Return of the Mafia*. Translated by George Lawrence. New York: Enigma, 2007.

Cressey, Donald R. "The Functions and Structure of Criminal Syndicates." In *Task Force Report: Organized Crime. Annotations and Consultants Papers*. Washington, DC: The President's Commission on Law Enforcement and Administration of Justice, 1967.

De Waal, Alex. "Mission Without End? Peacekeeping in the African Political Marketplace." *International Affairs* 85, no. 1 (2009): 99-113.

Dickie, John. *Cosa Nostra*. London: Palgrave Macmillan, 2005.

Dickie, John. *Mafia Republic*. London: Sceptre, 2013.

Duffield, Mark. *Global Governance and the New Wars: The Merging of Development and Security*. London: Zed Books, 2001.

Duffield, Mark. "Post-modern Conflict: Warlords, Post-adjustment States and Private Protection." *Civil Wars* 1, no. 1 (1998): 65–102.

Duggan, Christopher. *Fascism and the Mafia*. New Haven, CT: Yale University Press, 1989.

Dziedzic, Michael J., ed. *Combatting Criminalized Power Structures: A Toolkit*. London: Rowman & Littlefield, 2016.

Felbab-Brown, Vanda. "Conceptualizing Crime as Competition in State-Making and Designing an Effective Response." *Security and Defense Studies Review Editorial Board* Spring-Summer (2010): 155–158.

Felbab-Brown, Vanda. *Shooting Up: Counterinsurgency and the War on Drugs*. Washington, DC: Brookings Institution Press, 2009.

Fentress, James. *Rebels and Mafiosi*. Ithaca: Cornell University Press, 2000.

Finkelstein, Monte S. *Separatism, the Allies, and the Mafia: The Struggle for Sicilian Independence, 1943–1948*. Bethlehem, PA/London: Lehigh University Press/Associated University Press, 1998.

Foucault, Michel. "Governmentality." In *The Foucault Effect*, edited by Graham Burchell, Colin Gordon, and Peter Miller, 87–104. Chicago, IL: University of Chicago Press, 1991.

Franchetti, Leopoldo, and Sidney Sonnino. *La Sicilia nel 1876: Inchiesta in Sicilia, 2 volumes*. Florence: O. Barbera, 1877.

Gambetta, Diego. *The Sicilian Mafia: The Business of Private Protection*. Cambridge, MA: Harvard University Press, 1993.

Gray, Colin. "What is War? A View from Strategic Studies." In *Strategy and History: Essays on Theory and Practice*, edited by Colin Gray, 185. New York: Routledge, 2006.

Grossman, Herschel I. "Rival kleptocrats: the mafia versus the state." In *The Economics of Organized Crime*, edited by Gianluca Fiorentini and Sam Peltzman, 61–82. Cambridge: Cambridge University Press, 1995/1997.

Hellman, Joel S. "Winners Take All: The Politics of Partial Reform in Postcommunist Transitions." *World Politics* 50, no. 2 (1998): 203–234.

Hobsbawm, Eric. *Bandits*. 2nd ed. New York: Pantheon Books, 1981.

Hobsbawm, Eric. *Primitive Rebels*. Manchester, NH: The University Press, 1959.

Jankowski, M. S. *Islands in the Streets: Gangs and American Urban Society*. Berkeley: University of California Press, 1991.

Kilcullen, David. *Out of the Mountains: The Coming Age of the Urban Guerrilla*. Oxford: OUP, 2013.

Lewis, Norman. *Naples '44. A World War II Diary of Occupied Italy*. New York: Carroll & Graf, 1978/2005.
Lupo, Salvatore. *History of the Mafia*. Translated by Antony Shugaar. New York: Columbia University Press, 2009.
Mori, Cesare. *Con la mafia ai ferri corti*. Verona: Mondadori, 1932.
Naím, Moisés. "Mafia States: Organized Crime Takes Office." *Foreign Affairs*, May/June, 2012.
Naylor, R. T. "The Insurgent Economy: Black Market Operations of Guerrilla Organizations." *Crime, Law & Social Change* 20 (1993): 13–51.
Newark, Tim. *Mafia Allies: The True Story of America's Secret Alliance with the Mob in World War II*. St Paul, MN: Zenith Press, 2007.
OECD. *States of Fragility 2016: Understanding Violence*. Paris: OECD, 2016. doi:10.1787/9789264267213-en
Pantaleone, Michele. *The Mafia and Politics*. London: Chatto and Windus, 1966.
Petacco, Arrigo. *L'uomo della provvidenza: Mussolini, ascesa e caduta di un mito*. Milan: Mondadori, 2004.
Raab, Selwyn. *Five Families: The Rise, Decline, and Resurgence of America's Most Powerful Mafia Empires*. New York: St. Martin's Griffin/Thomas Dunne Books, 2005.
Schelling, Thomas. "Economic Analysis and Organized Crime." In *President's Commission on Law Enforcement and the Administration of Justice, Task Force Report: Organized Crime. Annotations and Consultants' Papers*, 114–126. Washington, DC: Government Printing Office, 1967.
Schelling, Thomas. "Economics and the Criminal Enterprise." *Public Interest* 7 (1967): 61–78.
Shaw, Mark. "'We Pay, You Pay': Protection Economies, Financial Flows, and Violence." In *Beyond Convergence: World Without Order*, edited by Hilary Matfess and Michael Miklaucic, 235–250. Washington, DC: National Defense University, 2016.
Smith Jr, D. C. "Illicit Enterprise: An Organized Crime Paradigm for the Nineties." In *Handbook of Organized Crime in the United States*, edited by R. J. Kelly, K.-L. Chin, and R. Schatzberg, 121–150. Westport, CT: Greenwood, 1994.
Southerland, M. D., and G. W. Potter. "Applying Organization Theory to Organized Crime." *Journal of Contemporary Criminal Justice* 9, no. 3 (1993): 251–267.
Spanò, Aristide. *Faccia a faccia con la mafia*. Milan: Mondadori, 1978.
Stille, Alexander. *Excellent Cadavers*. New York: Vintage Books, 1996.
Tilly, Charles. "War Making and State Making as Organized Crime." In *Bringing the State Back In*, edited by Peter Evans, 169–191. Cambridge: Cambridge University Press, 1985.
Varese, Federico. *The Russian Mafia: Private Protection in a New Market Economy*. Oxford: Oxford University Press, 2001.
Varese, Federico. "What is Organized Crime?" In *Organized Crime: Critical Concepts in Criminology*, edited by Federico Varese, 1–35. New York: Routledge, 2010.
Williams, Phil, and Roy Godson. "Anticipating Organized and Transnational Crime." *Crime, Law & Social Change* 37 (2002): 335–339.
Williams, Phil. "Insurgencies and Organized Crime." In *Drug Trafficking, Violence, and Instability*, edited by Phil Williams and Vanda Felbab-Brown, 27–72. Carlisle, PA: Strategic Studies Institute, 2012.
Wilson, Eric, ed. *Government of the Shadows: Parapolitics and Criminal Sovereignty*. London: Pluto Press, 2009.

What drives post-war crime? Evidence from illicit economies in Liberia and Sierra Leone

Judith Vorrath

ABSTRACT

Crime is a reality of life around the world, but its characteristics and impact differ tremendously across states and societies. There are different reasons to believe that crime in post-war environments has specific features. First, parts of it may be a legacy of armed conflict or more precisely of war economies. Second, post-war contexts are often seen as being particularly attractive for criminal networks, because massive violence has ended while the state's authority and capacity remain weak. Despite these alleged links relatively little is known about the manifestations of crime in post-war settings. By looking into illicit economies in Liberia and Sierra Leone this article shows that neither remnants of war economies nor the specific vulnerability of states emerging from armed conflict alone can account for the key features identified. Continuing illicit activities around natural resources and cannabis cultivation as well as the more recent transit of cocaine rather seem to be shaped by incomplete state-building. The shifting boundaries of illegality in combination with informal arrangements increase the level of uncertainty and lead to a constant negotiation of what actually constitutes a crime. The article also discusses why this has so far not involved larger scale violence in both countries.

Linking conflict and crime

Crime has increasingly been discussed as a relevant factor in conflict and a source of major violence, but few conceptual bases are offered in the academic literature for identifying and explaining post-war crime. There are two common angles of approaching the potential peculiarities of post-war crime: one stressing the features of war economies and their continuing significance after war, one focusing more on the vulnerabilities of states in post-war transitions that lack the capacities and means to counter or deter criminal activities. These are not contradictory explanations, but different views on how post-war crime can be expected to take shape.

The first view builds on the extensive literature dealing with the economic dimension of armed conflict. Naturally, those focusing on war economies and the related agendas of violent entrepreneurs primarily look into ways of resolving and preventing conflict along the lines of economic transactions. From this perspective, post-war crime could be seen as an expression of the failed transformation of war economies after a violent conflict has ended by some kind of peace settlement or military victory. [1] It has frequently been pointed out for prominent cases like Bosnia that dismantling illegal activities as well as networks between state and criminal actors from wartime during post-war transitions is very difficult.[2] Of course, the 'crime-conflict nexus' can take many different forms, but war economies are usually seen as the core of it. Whether individual profit seeking and funding opportunities are actually a cause of the outbreak of civil war ('greed') or political concerns like ethnic discrimination and inequality ('grievance') are more important has been a matter of academic controversy.[3] What is less disputed is that after the end of the Cold War and the subsequent drying-out of support by powerful states, non-state armed groups had to rely increasingly on other sources of income, including the trade with oil, minerals, timber, or drugs.[4] In doing so, armed actors have to collaborate with business- and middlemen across borders in order to get these goods on the world market. Shadow economies in conflicts also frequently involve mafia-type structures, organised crime actors or generally those who already controlled illicit economies[5] before the war.[6] When relying on the 'greed' argument, it is most relevant to focus on economic incentives and opportunities to avoid a relapse into armed conflict while supporters of the 'grievance' thesis stress the significance of group identities combined with political and economic inequalities for mobilisation. It has been shown for a sample of 13 civil wars which includes those in Liberia and Sierra Leone that armed groups had only started to loot resources after the beginning of hostilities and that in 9 cases easily extractable commodities were looted, notably gemstones, drugs, or timber.[7] So irrespective of the question what caused civil war initially, the core challenge in a post-war environment is the transformation of war economies in a way that preserves the (negotiated) peace and at the same time guarantees substantial reforms in the respective sectors to formalise and (re) distribute profits.

A second interpretation of post-war crime can be derived from the more state-focused literature stressing the general attraction of fragile and conflict-affected countries for (organised) crime. The Human Security Report 2011, for example, referred to organised crime as an external stress factor penetrating already vulnerable states and contributing to repeated cycles of violence.[8] More precisely, when formal state authority is re-established, but institutions and capacities remain weak, vulnerability of those states may be exacerbated as risks of globalisation and illicit economies tend to gravitate towards them.[9] There has been a growing debate on how fragile states are exactly linked to organised crime.[10] Naturally there is some overlap with the literature on the legacy of war economies, but two differences stand out. First, post-war crime from this perspective may be characterised by newly emerging forms of (organised) crime that take advantage of the specific incentives linked to post-war transitions. [11] While wide-spread fighting and instability during a war may encourage certain criminal activities, particularly linked to the trade of natural resources for arms, it can rather discourage others like the use of affected areas for transit of illicit goods like drugs. Thus, the end of massive, wide-spread violence can provide new opportunities. Secondly, the literature has increasingly emphasised the possible convergence of interests of transnational criminal networks and power-holders in fragile states up to the point of state capture.[12] While not unique to these contexts 'the activities of organized crime can have a disproportionate and devastating impact, particularly when a political transition to peace or democracy is underway'.[13] So while a lack of transformation of war economies is one way to look at post-war crime, an important part of the picture may be newly emerging illicit activities and political–criminal arrangements.

Another general assumption for post-war contexts is that crimes such as armed robbery, child prostitution, or homicide tend to be high due to the circulation of small arms, traumatisation, and brutalisation of parts of society or a lack of income opportunities.[14] This article will look at post-war crime from the wider angle of illicit economies, mostly referring to the illicit trade in different commodities in order to see how economic and political dynamics play out. The related activities may or may not be accompanied by violence. The category of violent crime naturally is much broader and comprises inherently violent phenomena such as rape or robbery which are not the subject of this article.[15] The focus will be on illicit economies and post-war crime in Liberia and Sierra Leone where peace processes involved efforts to (re)build states as well as to transform war economies.[16] Ultimately, the article shows that it is neither the remnants of war economies nor the weaknesses of the state alone that shape post-war crime but the framework of uncertainty generated by transitions with shifting rules and power structures.

From war to illicit economies in Liberia and Sierra Leone[17]

The armed conflicts in Liberia and Sierra Leone[18] have been strongly linked, just like the related war economies. While the competition over the control of natural resources such as diamonds, gold, and timber among armed groups and state agents was particularly prominent, the trajectory of violent conflict in the two countries shows many common features of other intra-state wars in the 1990s.[19] Despite a series of regional and international efforts to negotiate lasting agreements and the holding of elections in the mid-1990s, hostilities resumed in both contexts over an extended period of time. Finally, under increasing outside pressure and a range of targeted sanctions, fighting mostly ended and peace has been guarded by large, multidimensional UN missions.

The post-war periods in the two countries stand out with regard to the level of international engagement and related efforts in state-building, particularly considering their relatively small size. Whether it is for that reason or others, Liberia and Sierra Leone are seen as relative success cases of peacekeeping. Yet, while the countries avoided a relapse into violent conflict so far, both are still commonly ranked as fragile states.[20] This combination of a 'precarious' stability and continuing challenges including a very weak formal economy as well as their strong connectedness makes the two countries useful cases for the analysis of features of post-war crime.

The legacy of war economies

Illicit economic activities formed a core part of the war economies in Liberia's and Sierra Leone's civil wars. Clearly much of the trade in West Africa had been informal before and a political–criminal nexus had already emerged in both countries. Under the leadership of President Samuel Doe in Liberia 'a networked and decentralised system based on connections to illicit commerce'[21] started to emerge. This system comprised shadowy deals with major international criminals.[22] Similarly, the governments of Siaka Stevens and Joseph Momoh in Sierra Leone entrenched illicit networks and practices related to the mineral sector.[23]

However, when warlords such as Charles Taylor in Liberia surfaced with the outbreak of conflict, they set out 'to create a new kind of political authority based on the private control of resources'.[24] Commercial activities provided income for weapons and other materials and thus, facilitated the militarisation, but also the fragmentation of public space in Liberia and Sierra Leone into different zones of authority. The most important resources to maintain control were gold and diamonds as well as timber and rubber.[25] In the process of establishing authority, Charles Taylor and his armed group – the National Patriotic Front of Liberia (NPFL) – took over some existing commercial channels while disrupting others, for example, through attacks on minority groups and foreign traders who were replaced as intermediaries.[26] Already by late 1990, the NPFL controlled almost all of the country outside the capital, including important trade nodes. Larger mining companies such as Liberian Minerals Company with their iron ore mines in Nimba County or the rubber company Firestone now had to rely on Taylor's protection for their operations.[27]

The newcomers to the scene included Ivorian, French, and Lebanese business people based in Abidjan whom Taylor had met there before the war.[28] The logging business became a central part of the economy of 'Greater Liberia', as the NPFL-controlled territory was called. Ivorian-based logging firms were allowed to operate in Nimba County and the south-east of Liberia and to export timber, mostly to European states through Côte d'Ivoire.[29] Overall, income for the NPFL was mostly derived by taxes, fees, payments of salaries to port managers or other bodies, as well as material support in the form of fuel, oil, or vehicles.[30] Taxation systems – including for diamond and gold exports – could have brought Taylor's group about $75 million a year, according to estimates.[31]

The access to the diamond fields was also an important factor leading to Taylor's involvement in Sierra Leone. He supported the Revolutionary United Front (RUF) – a Libyan-trained group of Sierra Leoneans led by former army corporal Foday Sankoh that invaded the area from Liberian territory in 1991.[32] The diamond mining areas fell to the RUF in November 1992, changed hands several times and remained the centre of the war economy in Sierra Leone until 2002. Overall, there was a break in established patterns of commerce when the RUF attacked Lebanese diamond traders and established its own marketing links to Liberia. The neighbouring country became the official export source for diamonds from Sierra Leone as well as Guinea and even Angola, so that by 1994 Liberia was the third largest supplier of diamonds to Antwerp.[33] But despite these ruptures, Lebanese diamond traders apparently remained engaged in the business as well, operating from new bases outside of the mining areas.[34] Despite Sierra Leone's war economy being more fragmented, violence and business became deeply entrenched. Categories like 'licit' or 'illicit' rendered largely undistinguishable in both countries. Other armed groups like the 'United Liberation Movement of Liberia for Democracy' (ULIMO) partly copied the NPFL model and became 'like a marketing franchise' for smaller groups of fighters controlling territory and resources.[35]

Overall, the war economies in both countries contained the two common manifestations of the 'crime-conflict nexus': the organisational link of armed groups to criminal actors (as well as to formal enterprises) and armed groups themselves engaging in 'do it yourself' forms of organised crime.[36] The latter was most visible in the exploitation of diamonds while a prominent example for the collaboration with shady entrepreneurs abroad was the cooperation of Charles Taylor and the RUF with businesses of the network of the notorious Russian arms dealer Viktor Bout. In exchange for the supply of weapons, the latter was apparently paid by diamonds and other valuable commodities acquired illegally by Taylor's associates and RUF.[37]

The emerging 'warlord politics' relied on the domination of markets, rather than the state bureaucracy[38] before the peace settlements negotiated over the course of the 1990s led to the inclusion of various armed factions into government.[39] In 1997, Charles Taylor himself became elected president of Liberia, just as the 1999 Lomé Peace Accord in neighbouring Sierra Leone made RUF leader Sankoh Vice-President and left him in charge of the diamond mines.[40] When these arrangements largely failed to secure peace, international efforts increasingly focused on disentangling violence and business. A set of UN sanctions finally tried to deprive state and non-state actors of their income from the exploitation and export of natural resources, such as the ban of direct or indirect import of all rough diamonds from Sierra Leone through Security Council resolution 1306 (2000) and from Liberia based on resolution 1343 (2001) as well as the embargo on Liberian timber and timber products through resolution 1521 (2003). The civil wars ended relatively soon after, in 2003 and 2002, respectively.

Armed conflict tends to increase the room for 'nodes' of organised criminals connected with governance structures and formal private enterprises.[41] Thus, a core challenge of the post-war transitions was to unravel at least some of those nodes without disrupting the fragile balance of the negotiated settlement. Apart from the embargos, international measures included travel bans and asset-freezing as well as the set-up of the Special Court for Sierra Leone in 2002. Ultimately, it indicted 13 persons, including Charles Taylor, who was sentenced to 50 years of imprisonment in May 2012. Some central actors of the war economies remained under scrutiny of the UN sanctions regime for Liberia, but others, as in peace processes elsewhere, managed to 'use post-conflict privatization programmes and elections as opportunities to launder their looted assets and their coerced legitimacy'.[42] A whole set of reform programmes tried to re-establish a formal state framework after the lines of 'licit' and 'illicit' had been completely blurred during the civil wars. Efforts particularly focused on re-organising the governance of natural resource sectors as foreseen in the initial mandate of the United Nations Mission in Liberia.[43]

'Old' and 'new' components of post-war illicit economies

Naturally, illicit economies in Liberia and Sierra Leone underwent changes during the post-war transitions. The end of large-scale instability may have provided a more conducive environment for licit and illicit economic activities alike. Yet, at a global scale neither country has become an important destination market for international illicit trade. There is some demand for illegal goods produced in the region (marihuana or hunting weapons) and lower priced goods that are smuggled (rice, fuel, faked medicines), but overall both countries mainly provide natural resources for illicit markets or serve as transit zones.

More of the same? The transformation of illicit resource exploitation and trade

Looking at the evolution of the minerals sector and the logging industry in post-war Liberia and Sierra Leone shows how remnants of previous illicit activities persist while the ongoing state-building also infuses doses of change. Both Liberia and Sierra Leone have become parties to the Kimberley Process Certification Scheme in 2007 and 2003, respectively. The scheme regulates the commerce with precious stones in order to prevent 'conflict diamonds'[44] from entering the world market. Therefore, all related activities – from mining and dealing to exporting – require licences.

However, the review mission of the Kimberley Process to Liberia in March 2013 found

> evidence of routine smuggling of Sierra Leonean diamonds and their certification by Liberia, evidence of illicit diamond mining in many parts of Liberia and a high likelihood that conflict diamonds from Côte d'Ivoire, [...], were being processed through the Liberian system.[45]

Even for Sierra Leone, more recent estimates of the value of diamonds lost to smuggling are between 50% and 90% of total production.[46] As the regulatory regime for gold is weak in both countries, the assumption usually is that much of it bypasses the system.[47] In 2013, the UN Panel of Experts on Liberia noted that illicit mining and trafficking of gold in the country 'continues almost entirely unhindered'.[48] In June 2014, the Panel concluded that thousands of ex-combatants who are often still tied to their former commanders engage in illicit mining.[49] There has been small-scale violence allegedly linked to illicit gold mining in the Gola Forest region bordering Sierra Leone and Liberia where ex-combatants remain allegedly under the influence of former 'generals' who commanded armed factions during the Liberian conflict.[50] Many of these groups were engaged in illicit activities – particularly diamond mining in the Liberia–Sierra Leone border areas – during and in some cases already before the war.[51]

The minerals mined illegally are either legalised by being sold to a licenced dealer inside the country or smuggled abroad. In both practices illegal diamond dealers or brokers can be involved. For example, in Sierra Leone some markets are well-established places for the illegal trade in diamonds.[52] Lebanese traders generally remain prominent in the diamond business, but nationals from other West African countries also play an important role. Yet, all kinds of actors can be involved in smuggling, including miners, licenced and illicit dealers or middlemen who buy up gold or diamonds and bring them abroad as well as foreign investors, for example, from Europe or the Middle East.[53] Different rates of taxation and systems of certification in the region set up during the transitions provided incentives for smuggling. Sierra Leone's Mines and Minerals Act of 2009 raised the tax for precious stones to 6.5%, and to 15% for special stones above a market value of $500,000.[54] When the tax was enacted, there were no official exports whatsoever the following six months, whereas exports of Guinea and Liberia increased.[55] Similarly, there was a clear drop in exports for gold after the Act raised the tax to 5%.[56]

Beyond the illicit mining and trade in minerals, there have been rather new illegal activities in the sector, such as fraud schemes with gold and diamonds. Amongst these are scams with faked gold or diamonds making use of the Internet and upfront businesses, particularly in Sierra Leone. Usually such covers are set up to attract foreign investors who initially receive real stones or gold, which are replaced by faked ones after the investor has paid an advance fee or tax.[57] Records on the exact proceedings of such scams differ. In May 2014, the US State Department published a warning on fraud and fake Kimberley Process certificates for Sierra Leone. In this scheme, individuals were 'invited to Sierra Leone to view rough diamonds that were later evaluated as fake stones and were also provided with a fake Kimberley Process certificate [...].'[58] There are no insights on how frequent these scams are, but most likely many are not reported.[59]

The impact of changing regulation and incentives can also be seen in the logging industry. Both countries saw bans on logging after the end of armed conflict, generally rendering the trade in timber illegal. In Liberia, the international embargo remained effective until 2006.

The forest sector was reformed and new logging licences were granted, but some returning companies are said to have been operating earlier under different names.[60] Finally, seven large Forest Management Contracts and ten small Timber Sale Contracts were issued by the Liberian Government, but the process was marred by violations. More importantly, private-use permits (PUPs) emerged as a new legal loophole.[61] By 2012, there were 66 such licences designed for small-scale use, which did not require the payment of any taxes. An audit revealed that none of the PUPs had complied with national forest laws and regulations.[62] Moreover, despite a moratorium placed on PUPs (with the exception of four that were already operating), the shipment of timber apparently never really stopped.[63]

Similarly, Sierra Leone placed a ban on timber exports and suspended all concession operations by January 2008 due to allegations that foreign companies had engaged in illicit activities.[64] Again it became clear that exports continued illegally when containers destined for East Asia and labelled as scrap metals were intercepted by the Anti-Corruption Commission at the Freetown port in 2011.[65] Overall, it turned out that there were 33 containers of timber with three exporting companies from Sierra Leone and Guinea involved. Finally, out of 25 people charged in the cases, 18 were convicted.[66] A paper by the EU Commission concludes that after the ban 'illegal logging is often managed by Lebanese from Guinea Conakry and Liberia, who obtain agreements with chiefs and employ local people'.[67] It is a general assumption in Sierra Leone that paramount chiefs tend to be implicated in illegal logging as they are the first entry point for any activity in an area.[68] By law, they receive surface rents from companies operating legally on land in their chiefdom.[69]

But there are also changes in illegal logging since demand has shifted – from Europe during the time of war economies to Asia. China and India are now the largest importers of timber. At the same time, the United States, the EU, and Australia have raised barriers for the import of illegal timber and products made of illegal timber through new laws.[70] Asian, particularly Chinese, organisations are often believed to be behind logging operations, whether as financiers or with a more prominent role in shipping out the wood from Sierra Leone, Liberia, or another country in the region.[71] But larger companies also need to establish links with local transport businesses as well as secure access to ports for shipping their containers. Thus, the operations in illegal logging on the ground might have remained at the level of middlemen as during the wars.

A new threat? The drug trade

While natural resources were at the core of the war economies in Liberia and Sierra Leone, drugs were part of them as well. Initially, cannabis was introduced to West Africa in the twentieth century and spread particularly by Sierra Leonean traders along the coast in the 1920s and 1930s.[72] During wartime, it was particularly consumed by combatants in both Liberia and Sierra Leone. In the post-war period, the cannabis market has remained relevant for local consumption. Growing cannabis brings high returns in comparison to crops such as rice, and it is an important source of income in areas with few opportunities.[73]

In contrast, cocaine trafficking has been linked to South American crime groups when major cases were revealed about ten years ago. Around 2005, UNODC noticed a strong increase in the number of seizures of cocaine on route to Europe via West Africa.[74] With a rising market in Europe, a decline in demand in the United States, and a better controlled Caribbean route, South American cocaine traffickers started to make extensive use of West African countries as transit zones.[75] Both Liberia and Sierra Leone had been connected with the trafficking of cocaine and heroin before, notably in the 1980s. But in 2008 two events raised the attention for the vulnerabilities of both countries. The discovery of about 700 kg of cocaine on a Cessna plane from Venezuela that had landed at Lungi Airport in Sierra Leone's capital, Freetown, in 2008 led to the arrest of three Colombians, two Mexicans, a Venezuelan, and an American as well as of eleven Sierra Leoneans.[76] At first, no adequate legal basis existed, so a retroactive new law had to be passed in 2008. In the end, 16 of the 18 arrested were found guilty,[77] which so far represents the only convictions in a higher end cocaine case in Sierra Leone.[78] Apparently, state officials had been implicated. Amongst the convicted was Ahmed Sesay, national football team manager and the cousin of the Minister of Transport and Aviation; he was fined 300 million Leones and sentenced to five years of imprisonment. Even though evidence emerged in the trial that the minister himself had knowledge of the incoming plane and gave permission for its landing, he was appointed again to high-ranking official positions after an initial suspension by the president.[79]

Liberia was directly confronted with cocaine being trafficked through the region the same year. The French Navy caught the ship 'Blue Atlantic' 100 miles offshore loaded with 2.5 tons of cocaine in 92 barrels with a value of about $500 million. Even though the vessel was apparently not destined for Liberia, it was brought to Monrovia, where the Ghanaian crew was arrested.[80] The case revealed the shortfalls of the criminal justice system in Liberia, where possession and trafficking of drugs was tried under a public health act with insignificant fines.[81] A special drug law making drug trafficking a non-bailable offence was drafted, but it was only finally signed into law by the Liberian President in October 2014. Under the very weak legal basis, the 'Blue Atlantic' case was finally dropped.[82]

The operating networks at the time comprised people from inside and outside the region. In another prominent case, for example, the responsible operating group comprised 'a Russian pilot, a Nigerian narcotics broker, a Colombian cocaine supplier and a Ghanaian maritime expert'.[83] More recently, West African traffickers are not merely providing logistical services anymore and seem to gain more influence in the market as transactions increasingly take place in the region.[84] In Liberia and Sierra Leone, there surely are upfront businesses, people involved in logistics such as transport of drugs and also in the small retail market. But there are also higher ranking cases such as the one of Gibrilla Kamara, a Sierra Leonean drug kingpin who was arrested together with seven others in Liberia through a sting operation of the US Drug Enforcement Administration (DEA) and Liberian agents in 2010. Apparently they tried to bribe high-level officials in the Liberian Government to use the country as a transhipment point for cocaine.[85]

Yet, there is little evidence suggesting that Liberia and Sierra Leone have emerged as major hubs for criminal networks. There is a common assumption that cocaine trafficking continues through the use of containerised cargo by the ports or by vessels that tranship drugs from South America onto smaller boats off the coast before they are sent by car to Guinea or on boats to Europe.[86] Clearly, the ports at Freetown and Monrovia remain vulnerable for trafficking of all kinds.[87] Frequent seizures at Roberts International Airport in 2013 and 2014, including of heroin, indicate that it remains an important entry into Liberia as well.[88] But overall, seized quantities in the region have been going down. Moreover, the cultivation and trade in cannabis seem to remain mostly locally driven with some transnational links in the region. Occasionally, plantations are discovered and destroyed by law enforcement, for example, in lower Montserrado County in Liberia[89] or in the Kambia District north of Freetown in Sierra Leone in 2012.[90] There are frequent allegations of protection of the cultivation by politicians, chiefs, or the police.[91] In a prominent case, there has been direct involvement of a Liberian police officer who was arrested in November 2013 at Bo border crossing in a joint operation. The car carrying cannabis with a street value of more than $36,000 was marked as being part of the presidential escort, and the operation led to the arrests of a superintendent, the head of the presidential escort, and four others, including a member of the Sierra Leonean armed forces.[92]

Such cases reveal the weakness of the criminal justice systems in both countries. In Liberia, the police and the courts have been rated as the most corrupt institutions in the country, indicating the common perception 'that wealth, not guilt, determines the outcome of a case'.[93] The situation might be slightly, but not fundamentally, better in Sierra Leone, particularly for drug cases where large profits are involved.[94] But despite these weaknesses, other countries have been more prominent as transit zones for hard drugs which suggests that post-war transitions are not per se attracting crime. A closer look at the incomplete state-building and underlying structures of power are necessary in order to identify patterns that bind the 'old' and 'new' components of illicit economies together and shape post-war crime more generally.

Understanding post-war crime

State authority and a legal framework have formally been (re-)established after armed conflict in Liberia and Sierra Leone. The different features of illicit economies discussed, however, show that hybrid forms of governance persist. These may be seen as a legacy of war and the underlying economic interests penetrating the post-war system or simply as an expression of fragile statehood. But it is essential to understand how this mode of governance actually works in order to shed some light on post-war crime.

State-building and protection

After violent actors pursued or facilitated illicit business during the civil wars in Liberia and Sierra Leone, illegality in the post-war context is not systematically linked to such actors anymore. Structures of non-state armed groups have only partly persisted, for example, in illicit mining operations in some areas.[95] Whilst many in higher level positions were able to 'legalize' their profits and status, those at the lower end of the chain apparently did often not manage to do so. In combination with a lack of income opportunities for the youth in general, this situation clearly remains a potential source of insecurity.[96]

The more organised components of illicit post-war economies in Liberia and Sierra Leone tend to rely on their access to patronage networks – preferably those that are core parts of the state-building process. In fact, when asking whether crime tends to be organised, respondents in Liberia and Sierra Leone frequently refer to the involvement of politicians or security agents as indicators of the level of organisation.[97] Generally, three basic patterns exist. In the first, officials facilitate illicit activities with certificates or licences, for example, to engage in mining or the export of natural resources. Naturally, this only works for legal goods, not for drugs like cocaine.

The second option is the classic 'paying somebody off' for protection. Either criminal actors arrange a cover-up in advance or they engage in negotiations with officials when caught. These two can be combined as, for example, in the case of the deputy director of the Liberian DEA, Albert Chelley, who was dismissed in August 2013 because he had conspired with Nigerian drug traffickers and on two occasions prevented the arrest of heroin smugglers.[98] In Sierra Leone, it has been reported that there is also interference by paramount chiefs and politicians on behalf of people in cannabis cultivation.[99] Despite reforms of the legal and institutional frameworks, many transactions still depend on personal relations – for legal and illegal businesses alike. These are not easy to circumvent, as one official in a Liberian border town stressed: 'People buy their way out, it is fishy. People are reluctant to enforce the law. When you take it to the bosses, there is another bargain up there. And it is a matter of social relationship, you compromise'.[100] Ultimately, the fear of falling out with the patronage system keeps it together.

In the third scheme, officials are actually entrepreneurs of illicit activities themselves, or illicit traders gain public office. For example, it is said that government officials are behind 'cartels' in Freetown where the more expensive drugs are sold[101] or that some politicians manage illicit mining operations.[102] The majority of cases of state involvement, however, seem to be in the first two categories. It is difficult to systematically analyse whether such networks of protection – or parts of them – stem from the time of the war economies. Clearly, the phenomena described are not confined to post-war contexts as crime and state politics have been linked elsewhere. In fact, markets of protection seem to be a more adequate label than organised crime in African countries in general.[103] Similarly, the distribution of resource revenues in West Africa tends to be subject to patronage politics and political bargaining involving state and quasi-state actors.[104] This raises the question of what the specific mechanisms of the related transactions are in countries that have recently emerged from armed conflict.

The shifting boundaries of illegality

Personalised structures of authority functioning inside or alongside formal rules and institutions always involve some degree of uncertainty. But in post-war Liberia and Sierra Leone laws and regulating institutions have undergone many changes. Therefore, it has often been difficult to even formally establish what legal and illegal means, let alone what is criminal. Not surprisingly, the line is even less clear-cut for goods that can be exploited and traded legally such as gold, diamonds, and timber. However, new regulations are not at all meaningless. In fact, quite a few illegally exploited minerals are 'legalized' before being exported, even more so after some incentives for smuggling have been removed by harmonising taxes between neighbour countries in the Mano River Union. Yet, most activities in gold and diamond mining and trade continue to rely on established relationships and informal rules.[105] The formal system is still met with suspicion which has an impact, for example, with regard to containing the smuggling, as one respondent pointed out:

> Who would run after who? There is officially a reward for reporting, but people are not sure it will ever happen, and then it would just complicate their life with the other people. The core is, the system is not trusted.[106]

This lack of trust means that legality and legitimacy strongly diverge in the new framework. In fact, establishing legality is often seen as a means of personal enrichment. For example, there have been protests and riots against industrial mining companies – such as Octea and London Mining in Sierra Leone[107] and China Union in Liberia[108] – that turned violent. Moreover, while violent opposition to the state has become rare, there are parallel systems of authority and dispute settlement, especially customary and statutory legal systems. Frequent conflicts occur with regard to land rights, for example when people have traditionally used land that is then assigned to a foreign company for exploitation. In contrast, the smaller scale illicit production and trade of diamonds in Sierra Leone has a high social legitimacy while scams are usually seen as criminal behaviour.[109] Tensions linked to larger extractive industry investments, to the decentralisation of decision-making and revenue distribution as well as to negative impacts of mining at the community level are common across West African countries.[110] In post-war contexts, however, informal arrangements frequently collide with the new official system, and it can be very unpredictable what the outcome will be, for example, which rules are finally enforced. Legally, it may be easy to define a crime, but in a shifting post-war framework there is a high level of uncertainty as to what new laws and procedures actually matter when and where.

This even holds true for the more organised drug trade. Until the new laws had been passed in Liberia and Sierra Leone, it was easy to release traffickers 'on bail'. Even with the new regulation and the adaptation of law enforcement in both countries, there still is the common assumption that they can easily buy their way out. In addition, due to the social stigma linked to drug consumption, there seems to be a danger that consumers and small offenders are increasingly criminalised. Yet, Liberia and Sierra Leone have not become major hubs for cocaine trafficking like some countries in the region. In fact, weak state capacities in post-war situations are real, but they are only part of the story. Clearly, other features may rather have had a deterrent effect in Liberia and Sierra Leone, for example, a barely reconstructed infrastructure and the strong international presence with large UN missions. Most importantly, an incomplete state-building process not only increases incentives for criminal activities. In fact, these settings may be attractive for outside networks compared to rather centralised authoritarian systems since the number of officials – and thus potential entry points –increases with multiparty elections, institution-building, and decentralisation during transitions. At the same time, the predictability of those settings is usually lower and the reliability of protection can decrease. Therefore, countries with a strong political influence of the military like previously Guinea-Conakry and Guinea-Bissau may be more appealing for illicit activities like cocaine trafficking.

Conclusion

The introduction to this collection has pointed out that there are many paths and mechanisms connecting different explanatory factors of post-war crime.[111] Looking at illicit economies in Liberia and Sierra Leone the most notable aspect seems to be an incomplete state-building and the related uncertainty in the new system. The illicit economies largely centre on the exploitation and trade in natural resources, cannabis cultivation and trade as well as the transit of hard drugs. When the extent of cocaine trafficking through West Africa became visible, there was the fear that the trade could 'turn the region into an epicentre of lawlessness and instability'.[112] This level of instability has not (yet) occurred in Liberia or Sierra Leone. Naturally, post-war crime cannot only materialise in violence linked to the mentioned illicit economic activities. The rates of intentional homicide have generally dropped from 4.8 in 2008 to 3.2 in 2012 for Liberia and from 3.3. in 2008 to 1.9 in 2012 for Sierra Leone.[113] The gradual improvement in crime and security also shows in population surveys for both countries.[114] At the same time, particularly Liberia is known to have high rates of robbery, burglary, and mob violence.[115] The adequacy of crime statistics in Liberia and Sierra Leone can certainly be questioned. There is, however, little visible connection of criminal violence to illicit economies so far. Is this a lasting development or rather a snapshot at the time of persisting international attention and presence?

According to the first angle outlined in the introduction, avoiding renewed violence of a larger scale will depend on balancing the spoiler potential with the necessity for reforms while also transforming the economy for the benefit of the wider population. The other view focuses on addressing fragile statehood to prevent stressors from bringing about repeated violence. The vulnerability for crime is often seen in porous borders and a lack of regulation and effective law enforcement which are aspects that are commonly cited by agencies in Liberia and Sierra Leone as well. They often refer to weak capacities and insufficient resources as being the main challenges in fighting post-war crime. These deficiencies are real, but they mask an ultimate dilemma in tackling crime in cases such as Liberia and Sierra Leone: illicit activities are often tied to the very state that is supposed to build and defend the reformed framework of legality. The danger of seeing fragile statehood merely as a matter of low capacity or a lack of technical reforms has already been pointed out with regard to other contexts.[116]

Post-war transitions provide their own set of incentives when incomplete state-building and personalised power relationships come together in the way outlined above. This kind of precarious stability means that mostly increasing the level of state coercion and capacities is risky, because 'the retention of state structures claiming but not possessing legitimate authority provoked rebellion and insurgency'.[117] The more important aspect is increasing the trust in existing rules and institutions like programmes in community policing try to do. From a global perspective, the organisational level and profits of post-war crime in Liberia and Sierra Leone may be low. But its features can undermine and de-legitimise the state if impunity for higher level offences prevails while the lower echelons of illicit economies struggle to manoeuvre under the conditions of uncertainty.

Disclosure statement

No potential conflict of interest was reported by the author.

Funding

This work was financially supported by the German Ministry for Economic Cooperation and Development.

Acknowledgements

I would like to thank all respondents in Liberia and Sierra Leone for taking the time to talk to me and providing essential information for my research. Naturally, all possible mistakes are my responsibility. I also would like to thank the reviewers and everyone who provided feedback for this article.

Notes

1. The term 'post-war crime' is usually not used in the literature; rather terms like the 'criminalization of the economy' are common (see e.g. Ballentine, *Economic Agendas in Civil Wars*, 2.).
2. Williams and Picarelli, "Combating Organized Crime," 134.
3. See e.g. Collier and Hoeffler, *Greed and Grievance in Civil War*; and Cederman et al., *Inequality, Grievances, and Civil War*.
4. Ballentine and Nitzschke, "Introduction," 1.
5. According to Shaw and Mangan (*Illicit Trafficking*, 7) illicit economies comprise transactions and commodities that are legally prohibited in production and/or trade unless they comply with respective regulations.
6. Grävingholt et al., *Entwicklungszusammenarbeit und nichtstaatliche Gewaltakteure*, 67.
7. Ross, *Natural Resources*, 52.
8. World Bank, *Human Development Report 2011*.
9. OECD, *Think Global, Act Global*, 56.
10. See e.g. Miraglia et al., *Transnational Organised Crime*.
11. Of course, remnants of war economies and the related 'spoiler' potential can also be categorized as a stress factor in post-war transitions.
12. Miraglia et al., *Transnational Organised Crime*, 11, 12.
13. Shaw and Kemp, *Spotting the Spoilers*, 1.
14. See Enzo Nussio's article in this collection for a discussion of why ex-combatants are seen as being more likely to engage in crime. Nussio, *Ex-combatants and Violence in Colombia*.
15. Similarly, there can be different types of political violence without connections to illicit economies.
16. See e.g. Pugh and Cooper, *War Economies in a Regional Context*.
17. For a detailed discussion of this process see: Vorrath, From War to Illicit Economies
18. The research paper is based on field research in Liberia from November 10 to December 9, 2013, and in Sierra Leone from January 11 to February 9, 2014. Overall, the author conducted 48 semi-structured interviews in Liberia (in Monrovia and in/around Gbarnga/Bong County and Ganta/Nimba County) and 46 in Sierra Leone (in Freetown and in/around Koidu/Kono District) with officials at various levels (national to local), representatives of security agencies, the judiciary, local NGOs, associations and private security companies as well as business people, traditional authorities, journalists, social and community workers and people engaged in or linked to specific (illicit) economic activities. Interviews conducted during these trips are anonymized and cited by codes indicating the country (LIB = Liberia; SL = Sierra Leone), the sequence number of the interview, and the date of the interview.
19. Armed conflict in Liberia lasted from 1989 to 2003, with an interruption between 1996 and 1999 when Charles Taylor became elected president of Liberia. These two periods are often

referred to as the first and second Liberian civil wars. In Sierra Leone, armed conflict started in March 1991 and basically continued until early 2002.

20. Liberia and Sierra Leone are on the OECD's list of fragile states and economies in 2015 and have both been on every such list since 2007. According to the same report they also have about the same level of fragility, see OECD, *States of Fragility 2015*, 32, 33 and 44.
21. Andersen, "Outsiders Inside the State," 137.
22. Ellis, *Mask of Anarchy*, 154–56.
23. Reno, *Warlord Politics and African States*, 123.
24. Ibid., 91.
25. Reno, *Warlord Politics and African States*, 79.
26. Ibid., 98.
27. Ellis, *Mask of Anarchy*, 89, 90.
28. Ibid., 89, 90.
29. Waugh, *Charles Taylor and Liberia*, 165.
30. Reno, *Warlord Politics and African States*, 96.
31. William H. Twaddell, "Testimony to Africa Sub-committee of the U.S. House of Representatives," 1996, The Inquirer, Monrovia 5, no. 55 (August 13, 1996), cited in Ellis, *Mask of Anarchy*, 90, 91.
32. Byman et al., *Trends in Outside Support*, 76; and Ellis, *Mask of Anarchy*, 71.
33. Waugh, *Charles Taylor and Liberia*, 188.
34. Gberie, *War and Peace*, 18.
35. Ellis, *Mask of Anarchy*, 104.
36. Williams and Picarelli, "Combating Organized Crime," 125.
37. United States District Court, *Sealed Indictment*.
38. Reno, "Liberia: The LURDs," 71.
39. Ellis, *Mask of Anarchy*, 101, 102, and 107.
40. UN investigations showed that RUF income from diamonds at the time was between 25 million and 125 million USD annually (UNSC, *Report Panel of Experts 2000*, 17).
41. Utas, "Bigmanity and Network Governance," 5.
42. Cockayne, "Crime, Corruption and Violent Economies," 202.
43. UN Resolution 1509 (2003), 4.
44. These are 'rough diamonds used by rebel movements to finance wars against legitimate governments' according to the Kimberley Process; see: http://www.kimberleyprocess.com/ (accessed August 11, 2014).
45. Cited in UNSC, *Midterm Report Panel of Experts 2014*, 18.
46. Fanthorpe and Gabelle, *Political Economy*, 22.
47. Interviews LIB-33_28-11-13; LIB-3_13-11-2013; SL-24_28-1-14.
48. UNSC, *Final Report Panel of Experts 2013*, 33.
49. UNSC, *Midterm Report Panel of Experts 2014*, 19.
50. UNSC, *Final Report Panel of Experts 2013*, 12; and UNSC, *Midterm report Panel of Experts 2014*, 18.
51. Abdullah and Muana, "The Revolutionary United Front," 179.
52. Engwicht, *After Blood Diamonds*, 12.
53. Interviews SL-44_6-2-14; SL-24_28-1-14; SL-49_3-2-14; Interview LIB-3_13-11-2013.
54. Government Printing Department of Sierra Leone, *Mines and Minerals Act*, 116.
55. Interviews SL-30_30-1-14; SC, SL-20_27-1-14.
56. Interview SL-20_27-1-14.
57. Interview SL-1_15-1-14.
58. Department of State, *Fraud Warning*.
59. Interview SL-49_3-2-14.
60. Interview LIB-38_2-12-13.
61. Global Witness et al., *Signing Their Lives Away*, 2.
62. Hettinger and James, *African Economic Outlook*, 9.
63. Special Independent Investigating Body, *Private Use Permits*, 8.
64. Walker and Burchert, *Getting Smart and Scaling Up*, 178.
65. Mano Daily and AFP, "S. Leone Anti-graft Agency."

66. Some of these were also linked to the so called 'Timbergate' affair. This scandal was triggered by an Al-Jazeera undercover story allegedly implicating two associates of Vice-President Sam Sumana, who accepted bribes in return for the promise that the vice president would back an illegal logging project (see: Reuters, "Sierra Leone Charges Two.").
67. EC, *Cross-border Flows*, 59.
68. Interviews SL-26_29-1-14; SL-33_3-2-14.
69. Conteh, "Chiefs, NGOs and Alternative Conflict Resolution," 7.
70. Global Witness, *Logging Company*.
71. Interviews SL-27_29-1-14; SL-29_30-1-14; SL-47_8-2-14.
72. Carrier and Klantschnig, *Africa and War on Drugs*, 35.
73. Walker and Burchert, *Getting Smart and Scaling Up*, 176; Interview LIB-38_2-12-13.
74. UNODC, *Drug Trafficking*, 3.
75. Numbers have to be taken with a pinch of salt, but for 2010 UNODC estimated that 10% of European seizures – meaning 18 tons of pure cocaine worth about $1.25 billion – might have passed through West Africa, see UNODC, *Transnational Organized Crime*, 17.
76. Gberie, *State Officials*, 14.
77. Walker and Burchert, *Getting Smart and Scaling Up*, 175.
78. Status in February 2014: Interview SL-45_7-2-14.
79. Gberie, *State Officials*, 14, 15.
80. Interviews LIB-3_13-11-2013; LIB-51_5-12-13.
81. UNSC, *Midterm report Panel of Experts 2014*, 21.
82. Interview LIB-26_26-11-13.
83. Gberie, *State Officials*, 22.
84. UNODC, *Transnational Organized Crime*, 4; and Shaw, *Leadership Required*, 3.
85. United States Attorney, 'Sierra Leone Man Pleads Guilty'.
86. Interviews SL-6_17-1-14; SL-5_17-1-14; SL-13_23-1-14; SL-1_15-1-14.
87. Interviews SL-29_30-1-14; SL-15_24-1-14; SL-12_23-1-14; UNSC, Midterm report Panel of Experts 2014, 21.
88. Interview LIB-11_19-11-13.
89. Interview LIB-20_22-11-13.
90. Walker and Burchert, *Getting Smart and Scaling Up*, 176.
91. Interviews LIB-24_25-11-13; SL-47_8-2-14; SL-6_17-1-14; SL-17_24-1-14.
92. UNSC, *Midterm report Panel of Experts 2014*, 21; Interviews LIB-11_19-11-13; LIB-51_5-12-13; LIB-6_15-11-2013.
93. Human Rights Watch, *No Money, No Justice*, 21.
94. Interview SL-45_7-2-14.
95. Weapons are also still circulating in the region according to UNODC, see UNODC, *Transnational Organized Crime*, S. 33.
96. Christensen, "Big Man Business," 64, 65.
97. Interviews SL-45_7-2-14; SL-31_30-1-14; LIB-11_19-11-13; LIB-19_22-11-13.
98. Gberie, *State Officials*, 22.
99. Interview SL-1_15-1-14.
100. Interview LIB-50_5-12-13.
101. Interview SL-43_6-2-14.
102. Interview SL-45_7-2-14.
103. Ellis and Shaw, "Does Organized Crime Exist."
104. Maconachie et al., *Challenge of Fragility and Security in West Africa*, 24.
105. Interview SL-30_30-1-14; Engwicht, *After Blood Diamonds*.
106. SL-26_29-1-14.
107. Interview SL-47_8-2-14.
108. Interview LIB-37_2-12-13.
109. Engwicht, "Illegale Märkte," 163, 196.
110. Maconachie et al., *Challenge of Fragility and Security in West Africa*, 9–23.
111. See Kurtenbach and Rettberg, "War Economies and Postwar Crime."

112. Antonio Maria Costa, Executive Director, UNODC, In UNODC, *Drug Trafficking*, 1.
113. See Intentional homicide count and rate per 100,000 population, by country/territory (2000–2012), In UNODC, *Homicide Statistics 2013*.
114. UNODC, *Global Study on Homicide*, 85–87.
115. See e.g. OSAC, *Liberia 2016 Crime & Safety Report*, 2.
116. Menkhaus, "State Failure and Ungoverned Space," 173.
117. Williams and Picarelli, *Combating Organized Crime*, 124.

Bibliography

Abdullah, Ibrahim, and Patrick Muana. "The Revolutionary United Front of Sierra Leone: A Revolt of the Lumpenproletariat." In *African Guerillas*, edited by Christopher Clapham, 172–193. Oxford: James Currey, 1998.

Andersen, Louise. "Outsiders Inside the State. Post-Conflict Liberia between Trusteeship and Partnership." *Journal of Intervention and Statebuilding* 4, no. 2 (2010): 129–152.

Ballentine, Karen, *Program on Economic Agendas in Civil Wars: Principal Research Findings and Policy Recommendations*, Final Report, New York: International Peace Academy, 2004.

Ballentine, Karen, and Heiko Nitzschke. "Introduction." In *Profiting from Peace: Managing the Resource Dimensions of Civil War*, edited by Karen Ballentine and Heiko Nitzschke, 1–24. Boulder: Lynne Rienner, 2005.

Byman, Daniel, Peter Chalk, Bruce Hoffman, William Rosenau, and David Brannan. *Trends in Outside Support for Insurgent Movements*. RAND: National Security Research Division, 2001.

Carrier, Neil, and Gernot Klantschnig. *Africa and the War on Drugs*. London: Zed Books, 2012.

Cederman, Lars Erik, Kristian Skrede Gleditsch, and Halvard Buhaug. *Inequality, Grievances, and Civil War*. Cambridge: Cambridge University Press, 2013.

Christensen, Maya Mynster, "Big Man Business in the Borderland of Sierra Leone" In *African Conflicts and Informal Power: Big Men and Networks*, edited by Mats Utas, 60–77. London: Zed Books, The Nordic Africa Institute, 2012.

Cockayne, James. "Crime, Corruption and Violent Economies." In *Ending Wars, Consolidating Peace: Economic Perspectives*, edited by Mats Berdal and Achim Wennmann, 189–218. London: The International Institute for Strategic Studies, 2010.

Collier, Paul, and Anke Hoeffler. "Greed and Grievance in Civil War." *Oxford Economic Papers* 56 (2004): 563–595.

Conteh, Felix Marco. "Chiefs, NGOs and Alternative Conflict Resolution Mechanisms in Post-conflict Sierra Leone." *Review of African Political Economy (online)*, (2014): 1–14.

Department of State/Bureau of Economic and Business Affairs. *Fraud Warning and Fake Kimberley Process Certificates for Sierra Leone and Guinea*, Washington, DC, May 9, 2014. Accessed August 13, 2014. http://www.state.gov/r/pa/prs/ps/2014/05/225925.htm.

Ellis, Stephen. *The Mask of Anarchy: The Destruction of Liberia and the Religious Dimension of an African Civil War*. London: Hurst & Company, 1999.

Ellis, Stephen, and Mark Shaw. "Does Organized Crime Exist in Africa?" *African Affairs* 114 (2015): 505–528.

Engwicht, Nina. *After Blood Diamonds: The Moral Economy of Illegality in the Sierra Leonean Diamond Market*. MPIfG Discussion Paper 16/9. Cologne: Max-Planck-Institut für Gesellschaftsforschung/Max Planck Institute for the Study of Societies, August 2016.

Engwicht, Nina, *Illegale Märkte in Postkonfliktgesellschaften: Der sierra-leonische Diamantenmarkt* [Illegal Markets in Post-conflict Societies: The Sierra-leonean Diamond Market.] Frankfurt: Campus Verlag, 2016.

EC (European Commission). *Cross-border Flows of Timber and Wood Products in West Africa*. Final Report by Hugh Blackett & Dr. Eric Gardette, Contract Reference: 2007/146818, October 20, 2008.

Fanthorpe, Richard, and Christopher Gabelle. *Political Economy of Extractives Governance in Sierra Leone*. Washington, DC: World Bank, July 2013.

Gberie, Lansana. *War and Peace in Sierra Leone: Diamonds, Corruption and the Lebanese Connection*. Occasional Paper No. 6, Partnership Africa Canada, November 2002.

Gberie, Lansana. *State Officials and Their Involvement in Drug Trafficking in West Africa: Preliminary Findings*. West Africa Commission on Drugs (WACD) Background Paper No. 5, Kofi Annan Foundation, 2013.

Global Witness, *Logging Company Flouts Liberian President's Timber Export Ban and Drives Breakdown in Rule of Law*, Press Release/December 20, 2012. Accessed April 12, 2017. https://www.globalwitness.org/en/archive/logging-company-flouts-liberian-presidents-timber-export-ban-and-drives-breakdown-rule-law/.

Global Witness, Save My Future Foundation and Sustainable Development Initiative. *Signing Their Lives Away: Liberia's Private Use Permits and the Destruction of Community-owned Rainforest*. Briefing Document, September 2012. Accessed April 12, 2017. https://www.globalwitness.org/sites/default/files/signing%20their%20lives%20away%20-%20liberian%20private%20use%20permits%20-%204%20sept%202012.pdf.

Government Printing Department of Sierra Leone. *The Mines and Minerals Act 2009*, Supplement to the Sierra Leone Gazette Vol. CXLI, no. 3, January 7, 2010.

Grävingholt, Jörn, Claudia Hofmann, and Stephan Klingebiel. *Entwicklungszusammenarbeit im Umgang mit nichtstaatlichen Gewaltakteuren* [Development Cooperation Dealing with Non-state Armed Actors]. Bonn: German Development Institute/DIE, 2007.

Hettinger, Patrick, and Janice James. *African Economic Outlook, Liberia 2014*. African Development Bank, OECD Development Centre and United Nations Development Programme, 2014.

Human Rights Watch. *'No Money, No Justice': Police Corruption and Abuse in Liberia, August*, 2013.

Maconachie, Roy, Radhika Srinivasan, and Nicholas Menzies. *Responding to the Challenge of Fragility and Security in West Africa: Natural Resources, Extractive Industry Investment, and Social Conflict*. Washington, DC: Fragility Conflict, and Violence Group, World Bank, 2015.

Mano Daily and AFP. "S. Leone Anti-graft Agency Stops Illegal Timber Exports." February 10, 2011. Accessed August 22, 2014. http://www.nanodaily.com/reports/SLeone_anti-graft_agency_stops_illegal_timber_exports_999.html.

Menkhaus, Ken. "State Failure and Ungoverned Space." In *Ending Wars, Consolidating Peace: Economic Perspectives*, edited by Mats Berdal and Achim Wennmann, 171–188. London: The International Institute for Strategic Studies, 2010.

Miraglia, Paula, Rolando Ochoa and Ivan Briscoe, *Transnational organised crime and fragile states, A thematic paper supporting the OECD DAC INCAF project 'Global Factors Influencing the Risk of Conflict and Fragility'*. OECD Development Cooperation Working Papers, October 2012.

Nussio, Enzo. "Ex-combatants and Violence in Colombia: are Yesterday's Villains today's Principal Threat?" *Third World Thematics* (2017): 1–18. doi:10.1080/23802014.2018.1396911.

OECD (Organisation for Economic Co-operation and Development). *States of Fragility 2015. Meeting Post-2015 Ambitions*. Paris: OECD, 2015.

OECD (Organisation for Economic Co-operation and Development). *Think Global, Act Global: Confronting Global Factors that Influence Conflict and Fragility*. Paris: OECD, September 2012.

OSAC (Overseas Security Advisory Council). Liberia 2016 Crime & Safety Report. Accessed September 8, 2017. 2014 https://www.osac.gov/pages/ContentReportPDF.aspx?cid=19759.

Pugh, Michael and Neil Cooper with Jonathan Goodhand. *War Economies in a Regional Context: Challenges of Transformation*. Boulder: Lynne Rienner, 2004.

Reno, William, "Liberia: The LURDs of the New Church" In *African Guerrillas: Raging against the Machine*, edited by Morten Bøås and Kevin C. Dunn, 69–80. Boulder: Lynne Rienner, 2007.

Reno, William. *Warlord Politics and African States*. Boulder: Lynne Rienner, 1998.

Reuters. "Sierra Leone Charges Two in 'Timbergate' Graft Case." April 17, 2012. Accessed August 22, 2014. http://www.reuters.com/article/2012/04/17/sierraleone-corruption-idUSL6E8FHBPO20120417.

Ross, Michael, "How Do Natural Resources Influence Civil War? Evidence from Thirteen Cases", *International Organization* 58, Winter 2004, 35–67.

Shaw, Mark. *Leadership Required: Drug Trafficking and the Crisis of Statehood in West Africa*. ISS Policy Brief No. 37. Pretoria: Institute for Security Studies, October 2012.

Shaw, Mark, and Walter Kemp. *Spotting the Spoilers: Guide to Analyzing Organized Crime in Fragile States*. New York: International Peace Institute, 2012.

Shaw, Mark, and Fiona Mangan. *Illicit Trafficking and Libya's Transition: Profits and Losses*. Washington, DC: United States Institute of Peace, 2014.

Special Independent Investigating Body. *Report on the Issuance of Private Use Permits (PUPs)*. Liberia, December 19, 2012.

UNODC (United Nations Office on Drugs and Crime). *Drug Trafficking As a Security Threat in West Africa*. Vienna: UNODC, November 2008.

UNODC (United Nations Office on Drugs and Crime). *Global Study on Homicide 2013: Trends, Contexts, Data*. Vienna: UNODC, March 2014.

UNODC (United Nations Office on Drugs and Crime). *UNODC Homicide Statistics 2013*. Accessed on April 12, 2017. https://www.unodc.org/gsh/en/data.html.

UNODC (United Nations Office on Drugs and Crime). *Transnational Organized Crime in West Africa: A Threat Assessment*. Vienna: UNODC, February 2013.

United Nations Resolution 1509. Adopted by the Security Council at its 4830th meeting, on September 19, 2003, S/RES/1509.

UNSC (United Nations Security Council). *Report of the Panel of Experts Appointed Pursuant to Security Council Resolution 1306 (2000), Paragraph 19, in Relation to Sierra Leone*, December 20, 2000, S/2000/1195.

UNSC (United Nations Security Council). *Final Report of the Panel of Experts on Liberia Submitted Pursuant to Paragraph 5 (f) of Security Council Resolution 2079 (2012)*, November 25, 2013, S/2013/683.

UNSC (United Nations Security Council). *Midterm Report of the Panel of Experts on Liberia Submitted Pursuant to Paragraph 5 (b) of Security Council Resolution 2128 (2013)*, May 23, 2014, S/2014/363.

United States Attorney Southern District of New York. "Sierra Leone Man Pleads Guilty in Manhattan Federal Court to International Narcotics Distribution Conspiracy." Sierra Herald, March 1, 2011. Accessed August 22, 2014. http://www.sierraherald.com/cocaine-us-trial-sesay.htm.

United States District Court. Southern District of New York, Sealed indictment, S1 09 Cr. 1002, United States of America – v. – Viktor Bout. Accessed October 9, 2015. http://star.worldbank.org/corruption-cases/sites/corruption-cases/files/documents/arw/Taylor_Bout_SDNY_Indictment_Feb_17_2010.pdf.

Utas, Mats. "Introduction: Bigmanity and Network Governance in African Conflicts" In *African Conflicts and Informal Power: Big Men and Networks*, edited by Mats Utas, 1–31. London: Zed Books, The Nordic Africa Institute, 2012.

Vorrath, Judith. *From War to Illicit Economies: Organized Crime and State-building in Liberia and Sierra Leone*. Stiftung Wissenschaft und Politik: SWP Research Paper 2014/RP 13, November 2014.

Walker, Summer, and Elisa Burchert. *Getting Smart and Scaling Up. The Impact of Organized Crime on Governance in Developing Countries. A Desk Study of Sierra Leone*. New York: Center on International Cooperation, New York University, 2013.

Waugh, Colin M. *Charles Taylor and Liberia: Ambition and Atrocity in Africa's Lone Star State*. London: Zed Books, 2011.

Williams, Phil, and John T. Picarelli. "Combating Organized Crime in Armed Conflict." In *Profiting from Peace: Managing the Resource Dimensions of Civil War*, edited by Karen Ballentine and Heiko Nitzschke, 123–152. Boulder: Lynne Rienner, 2005.

World Bank. *Human Development Report 2011: Conflict, Security, and Development*. Washington, DC: World Bank, 2011.

Commanding abuse or abusing command? Ex-command structures and drugs in Liberia

Anders Themnér

ABSTRACT

In contemporary discourses on post-war reconstruction in West Africa, ex-command structures are often assumed to play a key role in the drug economy. Such assertions have, however, not been systematically investigated. Based on in-depth field research in Liberia, this article holds that ex-command structures have not only played a limited role in the country's drug economy, the use of and trade in drugs has had a destructive impact on ex-military networks. These findings highlight that rather than seeking to dismantle strong ex-command structures, efforts to combat the drug economy may benefit from integrating them into the statebuilding process.

Introduction

In contemporary discourses on West Africa, the drug economy is commonly identified as a key challenge to post-civil war reconstruction. The presence of criminal groupings trading drugs[1] in war-ridden countries such as Guinea-Bissau, Liberia, Mali, Nigeria (Niger Delta), Senegal (Casamance), and Sierra Leone,[2] has generated concerns over the risk of illicit networks being integrated into the state. At worst, such dynamics can lead to the criminalisation of the latter. In these depictions, ex-command structures are often assumed to play a prominent role.[3] The reason for this is twofold. First, ex-commanders are commonly well positioned to use the labour of their ex-fighters to engage in illicit activities, such as drug-trading. Despite large-scale efforts to break up the command-and-control structures of armed groups by investing in disarmament, demobilisation, and reintegration programmes (DDR), ex-commanders often continue to have influence over their ex-fighters.[4] Ex-commanders can utilise this clout to transform their former armed units into drug running outfits; not only are members of the former accustomed to obeying orders and working together, they also have a history of using violence in what are often clandestine settings.[5] Second, ex-commanders are often assumed to use drugs to ensure the continued loyalty of their former subordinates. In many armed conflicts, combatants employ drugs to cope with the pressure of battle. By continuing to feed this abuse during peacetime, drug-dealing ex-commanders cannot only ensure a pool of loyal customers, but also keep their military capacity intact.[6]

The threat of ex-military networks being employed in the trade of drugs has generated a number of assumptions concerning the relationship between ex-command structures and illegal substances in West Africa. Not only are ex-military networks often presumed to thrive in milieus where drugs are traded and used, they are also believed to play a prominent role in the drug trade in the sub-region.[7] This, in conjecture with the risk that such structures are used for other social vices – such as warfare and electoral violence – has prompted policymakers to frame lingering ex-command structures as an obstacle to post-war reconstruction. However, even if there are examples of some ex-commanders and fighters having engaged in such activities in Guinea-Bissau, Liberia, Mali, and Sierra Leone, it is not clear if this is part of a broader trend. For instance, to what extent are drug-running outfits in war-ridden countries in West Africa actually based on ex-military personnel? Furthermore, does the empirical evidence actually support the idea that efforts to combat drug trafficking benefit from the dismantlement of strong ex-command structures? The burgeoning literature on DDR has so far failed to address these questions, both from a West African and global perspective. In this exploratory study, I seek to address these questions by tracing the intricate relationship between (ex) command structures and drugs during Liberia's two civil wars, and the peace implementation process that followed them. The reason for including a historical analysis of wartime drug use, is that it allows us to assess claims about ex-commanders' ability to manipulate their ex-fighters' drug addiction[8] – developed during the hostilities – to retain influence over the latter.

The article's findings speak to a number of interrelated debates concerning post-war reconstruction and the drug economy in West Africa, and beyond.[9] First, experiences from Liberia underlines the need to reassess previous assumptions in the DDR literature that ex-command structures prosper in environments where drugs are consumed and traded. In fact, due to the social stigma attached to drug abuse – especially of heavier substances – 'clean' ex-commanders and combatants tend to avoid wartime comrades who are dealers or addicts. This means that ex-command structures composed of many of the latter often crumble. This is in sharp contrast to ex-military networks situated in more legitimate economic sectors and attached to governing elites. Ex-commanders operating in similar settings are often better positioned to offer employment opportunities to their ex-fighters. As 'job brokers', such ex-commanders are commonly more successful in ensuring the loyalty of their former subordinates. By tracing the conditions under which ex-military structures are most likely to thrive contra dissolve, the article connects to a growing literature on social cohesion in the aftermath of war.[10] Second, the article highlights that contrary to previous assumptions, ex-military networks may play a rather limited role in post-war drug economies. In fact, even if some Liberian ex-commanders and fighters were involved in the drug economy they were just one of many actors. The drug distribution infrastructure also involved actors ranging from ordinary Liberians with no connections to the war, and police officers, to security personnel and foreign citizens (especially, Nigerians).

Based on these conclusions, it is questionable whether efforts to address the distribution and consumption of drugs are furthered by the dismantlement of strong informal command structures. In fact, rather than leading to the criminalisation of the state, the integration of such structures into the statebuilding process may facilitate efforts to combat the trade in drugs. By generating employment, such an approach can create incentives for ex-fighters to shun the economic opportunities present in the drug economy. As such, the article predominantly speaks to the literature on DDR and the larger debate about the benefits of using ex-wartime structures to integrate ex-military actors into the new post-war order being built.

Drugs, wars, and command structures in West Africa

In order to understand why ex-command structures are often assumed to play a key role in the drug economy in West Africa, it is first necessary to trace how scholars have, historically, depicted the usage of and trade in drugs in internal armed conflicts in the region, as well as globally.

With the end of the cold war, the international community began giving greater attention to the resolution of civil wars. Even though there had been a steady increase in the number of internal armed conflicts since the 1970s, [11] many 'Western' observers were shocked by what some believed to be a 'new' kind of wars characterised by mass-atrocities and a desire for wanton economic profit.[12] In this context, drugs became one lens through which to interpret the dynamics of intra-state violence. For instance, accounts from Bosnia-Hercegovina and Rwanda, described how the use of illegal substances blossomed amongst fighters.[13] Wartime drug abuse was particularly identified as a problem in countries suffering from civil strife in West Africa. In Liberia and Sierra Leone, the vilest abuses were attributed to combatants doped up on amphetamines, cocaine and crack-cocaine.[14] According to Gberie, drugs and violence were employed by Revolutionary United Front (RUF) to induct children into the Sierra Leonean rebel group.[15] In addition, before battle, commanders commonly distributed drugs to combatants to give them the courage to attack the enemy. Being high also made it easier for fighters to commit atrocities against civilians by dehumanising them. In many instances, combatants appear to have taken the drugs out of free will, simply to make war bearable. However, according to other accounts commanders obliged fighters to use drugs.[16] By referring to the presence of drugs – irrespective if it was employed voluntarily or through force – the violence somehow became more understandable for many commentators; it was simply incomprehensible that sober individuals could engage in such 'barbarism'.

A second strand of literature emphasised the economic role drugs had in financing armed struggles. By applying a 'greed' perspective, scholars sought to explain why some ideological conflicts – such as in Afghanistan and Colombia – degenerated into wars of profit.[17] Once rebel and militia leaders began taxing and controlling drug routes, access to the latter became a goal in itself rather than a means to win the war. Similar dynamics were also identified in several West African countries.[18] For instance, rebels of Movement for Democratic Forces of Casamance (MFDC) have for a long time financed their armed struggle against the Senegalese regime through the cultivation and distribution of marijuana.[19] Hence, according to this logic, there was also a reverse link between drugs and command structures. Instead of drugs being employed to control fighters, military elites use the latter to control the trade in drugs.

Drugs, post-war societies, and ex-command structures in West Africa

Increasingly, drugs have also been framed as a threat to post-civil war stability.[20] Scholars and practitioners have, for instance, highlighted how weak state institutions in war-ridden countries may be penetrated by internationally sponsored drug networks and turned into transit hubs for smuggling illegal substances.[21] Such developments appear to be particularly daunting in post-civil war societies in West Africa. The reason for this is that 'smuggling is widely tolerated, law enforcement is fitful and inefficient, and politicians are easily bribed or even involved in the drug trade themselves'.[22] Drugs are, however, not only negatively affecting the sub-region by criminalising formal institutions; there is also a growing domestic consumption of drugs, which risk aggravating existing problems of social marginalisation and crime.[23]

In this processes, ex-command structures are often assumed to play a key role.[24] One reason for this is that after the arrival of peace, it can be tempting for ex-commanders and fighters to try to control drug distribution routes. Incomes generated from such activities can be superior to the benefits available through participation in DDR programmes. For instance, despite efforts to reintegrate Tuareg ex-rebels in Mali during the 1990s, members of the latter employed their ex-command structures to retain control over parts of the Sahel drug trade.[25] In some instances, ex-commanders may choose to reinvent themselves as drug barons even though they had not been engaged in the drug trade during the war. In Sierra Leone, for instance, drugs played a limited role in financing the armed factions. Despite this, evidence suggests that several ex-rebel commanders transformed themselves into local drug dealers after the war, oftentimes employing their ex-fighters as pushers or mules.[26] Having wartime experiences of collectively employing violence and operating in what are often clandestine environment, ex-commanders and fighters have a competitive advantage over other actors involved in the drug trade.[27]

Irrespective if ex-military structures' involvement in the drug trade can be traced back to the previous war or not, such criminalised networks are often found in spaces of marginality – areas largely outside the control of the state and characterised by informal economies, such as urban ghettos or border areas. The reason for this is twofold. First, it is in these environments that many customers live, making it rational for ex-commanders to focus their drug business to, for instance, ghettos. Second, the people who are willing to work for ex-commanders and go on drug 'missions' – such as ex-fighters with bleak prospects of social advancement – commonly live in marginal spaces.[28]

An additional reason for why ex-command structures are believed to play an instrumental part in the post-war drug economy, is that ex-commanders have incentives to manipulate the drug addiction of their ex-fighters. In countries such as Côte d'Ivoire, Liberia, and Sierra Leone demobilisation produced a large pool of ex-fighters that were drug addicts.[29] This created an opportunity for ex-commanders to continue to control the labour of their former undermen by feeding their abuse. In fact, a popular narrative amongst local NGO representatives in both Liberia and Sierra Leone, was that ex-commanders were able to continue to ensure the loyalty of child ex-combatants by offering them drugs.[30] From a patronage perspective, this was a rational strategy; by ensuring a continued access to ex-fighters, ex-commanders could build up a network of clients that could be used for different legal or illicit business ventures or mobilised on behalf of different elites. In addition, by nurturing their ex-fighters' drug addiction, ex-commanders could ensure a loyal pool of customers that contributed to sustaining the drug trade.[31]

A new research agenda to unpack the drug–ex-command structure nexus

Even though previous research has made a vital contribution by highlighting the role that drugs can play in transitions from war to peace, it suffers from a number of shortcomings.

First, previous studies have failed to disaggregate between different types of drugs. In fact, heavier substances that are associated with higher levels of addiction (heroin, cocaine, and crack-cocaine) are often conflated with lighter drugs (marijuana, hashish, and khat). This constitutes a problem since there is growing evidence that not all forms of drug trade are detrimental to socio-economic development. Carrier and Klantschnig have, for instance, traced how the production and sale of khat and cannabis has played a vital role in reducing poverty in Lesotho, Nigeria, and Kenya.[32] These findings speak to the possibility that the role ex-command structures play in the trade and consumption of drugs, partly depends on the kind of substances involved.

Second, depictions of the trade in and usage of drugs in war-ridden societies are commonly based on the narratives of a few key informants, rather than systematic empirical analysis. To some extent this is understandable. Not only has the drug economy seldom been the key focus of previous studies analysing post-civil war dynamics, it is also notoriously difficult to receive reliable information about illegal activities such as the drug trade. However, recent studies by Carrier and Klantschnig, Laudati, and Suckling have shown that it is possible to do rigours and systematic studies about the drug economy based on in-depth fieldwork. [33]

Third, much of the literature dealing with ex-command structures has so far focused on describing the role such ties have in marginal spaces. This inclination for studying ex-military networks in urban ghettos or border areas, gives the impression that it is above all in these milieus – dominated by illicit economic activities, such as drug trading – where ex-command structures thrive. However, the assumption that there is a correlation between drug dealing and the strength of ex-command structures needs to be empirically assessed. This requires comparisons between ex-military networks operating in various socio-economic environments, for instances, marginal spaces and areas dominated by more licit activities.

Finally, there is a lack of studies investigating claims that drug dealing ex-commanders can manipulate the wartime addiction of their ex-fighters to either control the labour of the latter, or ensure a loyal pool of customers. In order to assess claims concerning the drug–ex-command structure nexus, it is necessary to historically trace what types of drugs fighters employ during war, whether the same kind of substances are used after demobilising, and if combatants predominantly acquire these illicit substances from their former superiors or other suppliers. An additional benefit of including an historical approach is that it allows us to trace the origins of the drug economy and establish what role wartime command structures had in its development.

Hence, in order to gain a deeper understanding of the relationship between drugs and ex-command structures, it is necessary to develop a research design that: (a) compares ex-military networks in different socio-economic environments (i.e. with higher and lower levels of drug penetration); (b) is based on systematic empirical collection and analysis; (c) disaggregates between different types of drugs; and (d) traces drug use from war to peacetime. Only then is it possible to ascertain whether uprooting ex-command structures should be a corner stone of policies seeking to tackle the drug economy.

A note on methods and sources

In order to critically analyse the relationship between drugs and ex-command structures, Liberia will be employed as a case study. There are several reasons for this. First, previous studies have highlighted that drugs played a vital military and psychosocial role during Liberia's two civil wars – 1989–1996 and 1999–2003.[34] Second, there is growing evidence suggesting that drugs have continued to affect the life of many ex-fighters and commanders also after demobilising, either through continued substance abuse or efforts to engage in drug trading.[35] A third reason to employ Liberia as a case study is that it shares a number of similar characteristics with other post-civil war societies in West Africa: weak state institutions, long destructive wars, growing tendency to be integrated into the international drug economy, and high levels of corruption.[36]

The empirical material comes from a research project, co-headed by the author and implemented in Liberia, which sought to understand when and why ex-commander structures continue to thrive after demobilising.[37] This project collected data on a variety of factors ranging from ex-fighters and ex-commanders' economic livelihood and participation in DDR, to access to patronage and drugs. The reason for why the collected data are useful for the purposes of this study is that it employed a network-sensitive approach. In fact, focus was on how ex-commanders and their ex-fighters interacted with each other and which types of services and resources (such as drugs) were exchanged.

More specifically, two approaches were used to gather the necessary data. First, in-depth egocentric analyses were conducted with five ex-commanders and their respective ex-military networks (defined as a group of individuals made up of an ex-commander and those ex-subordinates that the former meets or has contact with at least once a year). While one of the selected ex-commanders (from ex-National Patriotic Front of Liberia (NPFL)) was involved in drug dealing, the remaining four operated in other socio-economic contexts (a broker distributing patronage for governing elites (ex-NPFL), a miner (ex-Liberians United for Reconciliation and Democracy (LURD)), a military recruiter (ex-NPFL), and an MC-taxi driver/farmer (ex-LURD)). While the drug dealer, broker, and military recruiter resided in Monrovia, the remaining two (the miner and MC-taxi driver/famer) lived in two different mid-sized towns.[38] Besides the manner in which these five ex-commanders made their living, they shared a number of similar characteristics with many other Liberian ex-commanders. For instance, even if they cannot be described as poor, they were constantly seeking new economic opportunities and the chance to attach themselves to different elites. In this process, their ex-fighters were seen as a valuable resource. By contrasting the experiences of one drug-dealing ex-commander with that of ex-commanders engaged in other economic activities, it is possible to critically assess assumptions about the relationship between drugs and ex-military networks.

As part of the egocentric analysis, each ex-commander was interviewed on several occasions, while the individual ex-fighters were interviewed once. The ex-commanders assisted the author to get in touch with the ex-combatants. In addition, a number of ex-fighters, who were not on the list compiled by the ex-commanders, but had fought under the latter, were also interviewed (these 'sleepers' were 17 in total). This allowed the author to control the information given by the ex-commander and the other ex-fighters. In total, 158 interviews were conducted, during September 2011, March–April and October–November 2012.

Second, as a compliment to the in-depth egocentric analyses, the author implemented a survey comprised of 56 Liberian ex-commanders and 43 ex-fighters. The latter had fought under one of the surveyed ex-commanders. By also interviewing some of the ex-commanders' ex-fighters, it was possible to control the information provided by the former. The author and seven research assistants[39] conducted the survey during 2011–2012. To ensure a broad geographical spread, work was carried out in Bomi, Bong, Grand Cape Mount, Grand Gedeh, Lofa, Montserrado, and Nimba Counties.

For the purposes of this study, a combatant is held as a person – without military rank – who takes direct part in hostilities on behalf of an armed group. Meanwhile, a commander is defined as the category of military personnel that is situated between rank-and-file combatants and the highest military leadership of an armed group, and who personally lead their subordinates in battle. These two categories of individuals become *ex-combatants* and *ex-commanders* when they have either been discharged from or voluntarily left the military faction they were serving in.[40] Unless otherwise indicated, the empirical material is based on the interviews with ex-commanders and fighters. I only refer to specific interviews when I use direct quotes.

Findings in previous research has highlighted the difficulties of gathering high quality and systematic data on illicit activities such as the drug economy.[41] Even though this study seeks to overcome this problem using source anonymity and data generated from interviews with well over 200 individuals, it is important not to dismiss potential biases. Due to the social stigma attached to drug use, the interviewees have incentives to downplay their own involvement in both using and trading drugs. For these reasons, all numbers should be seen as indications and trends, rather than empirical truths.

War and peace in Liberia

War, command structures, and drugs

When Charles Taylor and his NPFL launched their rebellion in 1989, drug trade and addiction took new dimensions in Liberia. This was due to two reasons. First, from an early start, the war degenerated into warlordism, which made it easier for drug operators to gain a foothold in the country. This development was facilitated by the stationing of Nigerian peacekeepers. In fact, using their connection to Nigerian drug barons, members of the former became key providers of drugs – such as cocaine, marijuana, and amphetamines – in Liberian.[42] Links to the international drug trade also continued after the 1996 Abuja Peace Accord, Taylor's electoral victory in 1997, and during the 1999–2003 civil war (the latter pitted LURD and Movement for Democracy in Liberia (MODEL), against the regime of President Taylor – often referred to as the Government of Liberia (GoL) and primarily composed of ex-NPFL leaders and fighters). As president, Taylor appears to have allied himself with Dutch drug dealers and allowed the country to be used as a transit point for hashish smuggling.[43]

The second reason for why drugs played an increasingly important role during the war, was that the fighting created a large domestic demand for illegal substances. Using drugs became a vital coping mechanism for combatants. A common explanation for taking drugs – such as cocaine and crack-cocaine ('Italian white') – was to become 'brave' and 'feel strong'. The role drugs had in overcoming fear was lucidly expressed by one ex-NPFL combatant:

> Yes, sometimes we smoke, yeah we smoke, drink .... sometime we take something to be active, even fighting ... you can't feel it. Firing at our enemy and to get that way through to capture him. So that we had to take some things to go our way.[44]

Others talked about the need to 'look mad', in order to intimidate opponents. Interestingly, the ex-fighters differed in their narratives concerning whether it was their commanders, or even Taylor, who wanted to make them 'brave' or 'look mad', or whether this was their own wish. Such variations in narratives can probably partly be explained by different coping strategies; by assigning blame to their wartime leaders, it is possible for ex-fighters to distance themselves from violence they have committed against others during episodes of intoxication. Aggressiveness was, however, not the only state of mind that fighters sought to achieve. Just as vital was 'numbness', both vis-à-vis feelings of remorse and physical pain caused by injury. 'Numbness' was particularly attained by taking various sleeping pills ('bubbles' or 'ten-ten').

Of the 142 ex-combatants interviewed in the egocentric analyses, 46% stated that they employed drugs during the war. In reality, this number may have been higher when considering that 21% of the respondents declined to answer. Studies conducted after the first civil war, point to similar levels of substance abuse, where an estimated 50–60% of the ex-fighters were believed to have taken drugs.[45] When looking at which type of substances that were used, marijuana was by far the most popular (taken by 65% of those ex-combatants who stated that they did drugs), followed by sleeping pills (26%), cocaine (22%) and crack-cocaine (20%). An additional 11% referred to 'drugs', without specifying the type.

Interestingly, when asked from where they received the drugs, 65% of the ex-fighters – who stated that they employed drugs – said that it was their commanders who had supplied them. Of these, 55% claimed that the latter, in turn, had received the drugs via supplies that came from the headquarters, while only 4% indicated that their superiors had attained the substances through other means, such as personally purchasing the drugs. An additional 41%, did not provide any information about where their commanders had received the drugs. Irrespective of the original source, the fact that commanders *de facto* controlled such a large portion of the distribution, underlines the central role played by command structures in the creation of wartime drug abuse. Having said this, it is vital to stress that some fighters had their own means to access drugs, such as stealing them from civilian cultivators or traders (13%), buying them from dealers (12%), and capturing them from the enemy (9%).

When disaggregating the empirical data, it becomes clear that there were important factional variations in the above-mentioned trends. For instance, drug use was much more common amongst ex-NPFL fighters. While 63% of the latter declared that they had taken drugs during the war, the corresponding figure for their LURD counterparts was only 22%. One explanation for this is that NPFL had access to a more advanced logistics systems, which could deliver various drugs to the front lines (see below for more information). In addition, ex-NPFL fighters were much more dependent on their commanders in order to gain access to drugs. In fact, all interviewed ex-NPFL combatants stated that at least some of their drugs came from the former. Most of these substances (at least 54%) were distributed by the commanders on behalf of their military leaders via logistical channels. A common narrative amongst ex-NPFL fighters was that the drugs were 'flown in' or 'sent by Taylor', indicating a belief that it was the will of their leader to intoxicate them. For instance, one ex-NPFL fighter explained how Taylor used to send 'whole bags' of marijuana and bubbles to front line troops.[46] The centrality of command structures is further underlined by the fact that the second most common drug source – purchasing – was employed by a mere 15% of the NPFL combatants.

The situation was markedly different for LURD fighters, who were largely compelled to acquire drugs on their own. In fact, parasitical strategies were most central; while 69% of the interviewees (who stated that they used drugs) declared that they obtained drugs by stealing from civilians, 46% indicated that looting enemy supplies was also a common source. Perhaps most interestingly, only 31% of the ex-LURD fighters received drugs from their commanders. The fact that command structures played a much larger role in ex-NPFL fighters' drug acquisition was probably due to the fact that their faction controlled the reins of power. Institutional control and international recognition arguably facilitated efforts by GoL leaders to buy and distribute drugs. This was not an option for LURD, who largely lived off the land and the infrequent supplies provided by their Guinean sponsors.

The Taylor regime's control of state institutions and greater access to international actors also meant that they had an easier time acquiring and distributing heavier drugs. For instance, even if marijuana was the most commonly used substance amongst ex-NPFL fighters (67% of those who said that they used drugs), as many as 27% took crack-cocaine, while 25% used sleeping pills and 25% cocaine. The experiences of the latter were in stark contrast to that of their ex-LURD counterparts. Lacking access to state institutions and with less international connections, it was difficult for the latter to get their hands on more intoxicating drugs. A mere 8% of the ex-LURD fighters – who took drugs – indicated that they had access to cocaine. In fact, within LURD cocaine seems to have been reserved for commanders. In addition, no ex-LURD interviewee said that they used crack-cocaine. The only exception was sleeping pills, which were employed by 30%. However, these were generally captured from government soldiers. Instead, most ex-LURD fighters were confined to marijuana – employed by 92% – which could be more readily acquired from local communities.

Even if evidence suggests that the Taylor regime systematically distributed drugs to its fighters, it is less clear exactly why it did so. Although respondents often referred to Taylor's desire to make them 'brave', it is questionable whether drug use actually increased military efficiency. There is ample of evidence of how 'high' soldiers behaved recklessly. At times, this realisation seems to have forced the regime to rethink its policy towards drugs. According to one ex-NPFL combatant, his unit stopped receiving cocaine when the soldiers were unable to perform. Instead, they were given cane juice – a locally brewed liquor.

Providing drugs should probably rather be seen as part of a larger strategy, where logistic systems were employed to ensure group cohesion. A major challenge for all armed groups was how to prevent combatants from deserting or defecting. One way to ensure loyalty was to provide regular access to goods that fighters demanded, such as food, ammunition, money, and alcohol.[47] Since taking drugs constituted a vital coping mechanism for fighters, it was rational to also provide access to such substances. In these logistic systems, commanders played a key role; it was they who were mandated to distribute goods, including drugs, sent from the headquarters. However, due to the patrimonial character of Liberia's armed factions, all commanders did not receive the same amount or kind of supplies. In fact, there was often a fierce competition between commanders when it came to allocation of goods. The rational for such in-fighting was simple; with more supplies, commanders attracted more fighters, and subsequently increased their chances for social advancement. From this perspective, it was beneficial for commanders to provide drugs to their subordinates in order to be perceived as good providers. There is, however, little evidence suggesting that commanders forced their subordinates to take drugs. In fact, of the ex-fighters who used the latter, only 3% stated that they used drugs under duress. This figure may be higher if one takes into account the evasive phenomenon of peer pressure. It was particularly difficult for child combatants to withstand such pressure, as is indicated in this depiction by one ex-NPFL combatant:

> The war was fought under the influence of drugs .... You take one joint and eat less ... You become brave and hard. I was recruited small ... I was captured when I was still a child. I grew up in that life, taking drugs.[48]

To what extent did military leaders employ command structures to profit from the trade in drugs? Even if there were such tendencies, they were dwarfed by the much more profitable exploitation of natural resources. In fact, a key objective of all factions was to use their manpower to conquer land where diamonds, gold, rubber, and timber could be extracted, as well as ports and border areas from where the latter could be exported. Having said this, evidence suggests that NPFL at least partly financed their struggle by exporting marijuana.[49]

Peace, ex-command structures, and drugs

After the signing of the Comprehensive Peace Agreement (CPA) in 2003, drug trade and abuse continued to thrive in Liberia. Just as during the war, international drug syndicates – especially dealing with cocaine and hashish – had a presence in the country.[50] This was not confined to Nigerian and Dutch nationals; evidence suggests that Latin American smugglers also sought to establish themselves in Liberia.[51] In addition, there was also a booming domestic and regional market for marijuana, prompting farming of the latter in counties such as Bong, Lofa, and Nimba.[52]

These actors had a ready market amongst ex-fighters who had become addicts or socially accustomed to drugs during the wars. In fact, of the ex-fighters interviewed in the egocentric analyses, approximately 28% stated that they were using drugs. This was an 18% drop compared to wartime levels. Perhaps most importantly, there was a shift from heavier drugs to marijuana. In fact, while the vast majority employed the latter, only a small minority abused crack-cocaine.[53] In addition, no one reported taking cocaine or sleeping pills.

Evidence also suggests that there was some correlation between war- and peacetime drug use. Just as during the war, drugs were more prevalent amongst ex-NPFL, than ex-LURD combatants. In fact, while 47% of the former took some sort of drug, the corresponding figure for ex-LURD fighters was only 2%. In reality, the latter figure was probably higher. For instance, one of the ex-LURD commanders studied in the egocentric analyses – the miner – claimed that he had assisted several of his ex-fighters to get clean. This could, however, not be corroborated.

Ex-fighters who employed drugs did not necessarily view it as a problem. This was especially true for those who smoked marijuana, a more socially acceptable and less addictive drug. In fact, a common pastime amongst ex-combatant friends was to 'smoke', 'share fun', and 'lecture'. Even those who used heavier substances, such as crack-cocaine, showed little remorse. The latter was sometimes seen as an important coping mechanism, that helped ex-fighters endure the heavy burden of every-day hustling. When explaining why he smoked crack-cocaine, one ex-NPFL fighter explained:

> Sometimes when I don't take it, I can be feeling .... if you take it gives you power to walk long distances and do things over time. If you don't take it you will not be able to do it over time ... it will take away your power.

Of the interviewed ex-combatants who had used drugs after the war, it was only those who had become sober that talked about their abuse in negative terms. Commonly, these ex-fighters would depict themselves as having lived 'bad' or 'wicked' lives before they changed their ways, often through the help of their families, friends, or religious communities.

With the arrival of peace, drug distribution was largely decentralised. Unlike during the war, when illicit substances – at least for ex-NPFL combatants – constituted an integral part of wartime patronage networks, ex-fighters had to acquire drugs through their own means. This meant buying drugs from a wide spectrum of dealers, ranging from ordinary Liberian civilians and Nigerians, to ex-commanders and other ex-fighters. While buying marijuana was not that expensive – one 'joint' cost around 0.15 USD – financing heavier drug abuse was a major enterprise. In fact, one dose of crack-cocaine cost as much as four USD. What was worse, three or four doses were needed to ensure a continuous 'buzz' throughout the day. For many Liberians, who lived on less than five USD per day, it was subsequently not possible to abuse crack-cocaine without engaging in crime. In fact, some of the interviewed ex-fighters who took the latter substance, made their living through illicit activities, such as pickpocketing or card-hustling ('Three-card Monte'). The post-war transition from heavier drugs to marijuana can probably partially be explained by this commercialisation of drugs. Without access to military elites, who had *de facto* financed ex-fighters' wartime abuse, it was not economically feasible for the latter to take heavier drugs. This is especially true when considering that the very rationale for employing heavy substances – coping with the pressures of war – had disappeared. In addition, ex-commanders appear to have been unwilling or unable to step in and finance their ex-fighters' drug abuse. In this sense, drug consumption reverted to what is more normal in peacetime African societies – use of lighter substances such as marijuana.[54]

Drugs did, however, not only cease to function as a 'glue' that bond ex-commanders and fighters together; evidence suggests that drugs had an outright negative effect on informal command structures. First, many ex-commanders were reluctant to have 'high' ex-fighters around them. The latter constituted a social liability for ex-commanders seeking to carve out a peacetime platform for themselves (community members often frowned upon having such associations) and drug-using ex-fighters were also a security risk. In fact, there was always a risk that frustrated ex-combatant addicts attacked or robbed ex-commanders who refused to help them. This was particularly true for ex-combatants who employed crack-cocaine. The situation was different when it came to marijuana. In fact, several of the interviewed ex-commanders explained how they sometimes smoked marijuana and hung-out with their ex-fighters. Second, there were more efficient ways for ex-commanders to ensure the loyalty of their ex-fighters, than to provide them with drugs. A key strategy was to offer economic patronage, ranging from money, food, and clothes, to medicine and employment. The latter resource was particularly valuable. After the war, many ex-fighters lacked the connections needed to land jobs. Thanks to their links to different elites some ex-commanders could recommend their former subordinates to different employers. Oftentimes, ex-commanders who succeeded in establishing themselves as such broker figures, had a steady stream of ex-combatant callers asking to be 'connected'. Finally, even ex-commanders engaged in the drug trade struggled to keep ex-combatant addicts in their networks. In fact, there was a fierce competition between different dealers, and it was not uncommon that ex-fighters preferred to go to other suppliers who offered a better price.

It was, however, not only drug abuse that had a detrimental effect on ex-command structures. Evidence also suggests that participation in the drug trade had a similar effect. There was, for instance, a social cost associated with befriending ex-commanders working as drug distributers. By merely visiting the house of the latter, community members assumed that ex-fighters were there to purchase illegal substances. To avoid such social stigma, 'clean' ex-fighters often preferred to shun ex-military superiors involved in the drug business. Another factor that put a wedge between such ex-commanders and ex-fighters, was that the former were often reluctant to hire drug addicts – deemed as unreliable – as pushers. This constituted a problem since it was, as previously mentioned, foremost ex-combatant users that continued to befriend drug dealing ex-superiors. With limited employment opportunities to offer their ex-combatant clients, ex-commanders in the drug trade appear to have struggled to uphold their ex-military networks.

A tale of two ex-commanders

To provide a more detailed understanding of the destructive role drug distribution and consumption can have on ex-command structures, the post-war experiences of two ex-commanders is presented in the following – a drug dealer (Adam) and a broker of patronage (Desmond).

The social cost of dealing. By the end of the second civil war, Adam had established himself as a high-ranking Taylor 'general', said to have controlled more than 500 fighters. After demobilising in 2004, Adam settled down in one of Monrovia's less affluent quarters and launched a career in the drug business. Using his relations with a Liberian businessman, Adam distributed crack-cocaine on behalf of the latter. Most of the actual selling was, however, done by three pushers, none of which had fought under him during the war. When asked why he did not employ any of his ex-fighters, Adam explained that: 'I do not want to be bothered with them. I do not want to be in the same habit (drug addiction) like them [...] I do not want them to come very close to me'. Put differently, Adam did not trust his ex-fighters due to their addiction.[55] Many of his customers were, however, ex-fighters from his unit. Although Adam could not afford to give crack-cocaine for free, he did often provide discounts or merchandise on credit. Even if this made him popular amongst some of his ex-subordinates, it was not enough to fend off competition from the upstream of other dealers operating in his community. As a consequence, several of the users in Adam's network preferred to go to other distributors.

The nature of Adam's business enterprise put a limit on the size of his ex-military network. In fact, Adam was only in regular contact (at least once per month), with 12 of his ex-fighters. There are two reasons for why Adam struggled to retain his wartime status. First, due to the social stigma associated with interacting with a drug operator – it was a well-known fact in the community how Adam made his money – 'clean' ex-fighters tended to shy away. In fact, 67% of the ex-fighters in Adam's network took some kind of drug, and half of these abused crack-cocaine. These high usage rates probably explain Adam's response when asked why his ex-fighters continued to befriend him: 'The reason why they still contact me is because of the kind of business that I am doing'.[56] Second, besides access to drugs, Adam had little to offer his ex-fighters. Even if Adam at times provided them with small money, loans, food, clothes, and cigarettes, he could not offer them employment opportunities. This was not only due to his scepticism about hiring his ex-fighters as drug peddlers, but also a function of the limited elite connections that he had. Without the latter, Adam could not broker jobs on behalf of his ex-fighters. As a consequence, the latter had few incentives to continue to pay homage to Adam.

Brokering jobs and retaining wartime loyalties. During the war, Desmond fashioned himself as a 'commanding general' and controlled a pro-Taylor militia unit composed of 150–200 fighters. After his militia was disbanded in 2004, Desmond settled down in a mid-income area of Monrovia. In order to support himself, Desmond engaged in a number of economic activities; he became head of security of the Ministry of Public Works, had a taxi-car that he let one of his ex-fighters drive on his behalf, head-hunted security personnel for businessmen, and at times worked as a body guard/assistant for a senator. Even if Desmond did not personally use drugs, several of his former undermen did. In fact, 38% of the ex-fighters in his network stated that they used drugs after the war. However, none of these employed heavier substances, such as crack-cocaine. Instead, all smoked marijuana.

The fact that drugs did not have an economic or social function for Desmond, did not affect the size of his ex-command structure; the latter was composed of as many as 28 ex-fighters. Of these Desmond met as many as 68% on a weekly basis. Many of the latter made it a habit to pass by his house. During these meetings, gossip and information was shared, and ex-fighters often received small sums of money, food, or used clothes. However, the most important reason for why Desmond's former subordinates continued to pay homage to him, was that he was a well-reputed job-broker. Because Desmond was a respected figure in the community, local businessmen, politicians, and other community members often turned to him when they needed labourers (e.g. security guards, plumbers, shop-keepers). Desmond's brokerage capacity was lucidly articulated by one of his ex-fighters. When asked why he continued to interact with Desmond he declared that 'people know that Desmond is a star, a big man, they usually go to him to ask "Do you have a guy" [somebody that they can employ]'.[57]

Concluding discussion

The point of departure for this article is an apparent lacuna in the study of post-war reconstruction and the drug economy in West Africa. Not only have previous studies assumed that ex-command structures play a key role in the distribution of drugs in post-civil war societies, it is often held that such networks thrive in environments that are heavily penetrated by the trade in and use of drugs. The problem is that such claims have not been assessed using systematically collected empirical data. Experiences from Liberia highlight that such assumptions may not only be incorrect, but also risk generating faulty policy recommendations concerning the benefits of up-rooting lingering ex-military networks. In fact, ex-commanders and fighters were only one of many actors engaged in post-war Liberia's drug economy. Drug trading networks were rather a configuration of divergent actors, including ordinary Liberian civilians who had played a minimal role during the war, police officers,[58] security personnel,[59] foreign citizens (particularly Nigerians), as well as ex-military personnel. What more, ex-command structures associated with the trade and consumption of drugs tended to be weak and faltering. The social stigma attached to drug abuse – especially of heavier types – meant that 'clean' ex-commanders and fighters often shunned former colleagues who were dealers or addicts. As a result, ex-command structures associated with heavier substances tended to disintegrate. This was in sharp contrast to networks where ex-commanders were active in more legitimate economic sectors and where the latter had the capacity to 'broker' jobs on behalf of their former subordinates. Such ex-military networks were often more resilient, since they had a stronger economic function. In addition, drug-dealing ex-commanders were largely unsuccessful in their attempts to retain influence over their ex-fighters by manipulating the wartime drug addition of the latter. For some, the very rational for abusing heavier substances had disappeared with the cessation of hostilities (coping with the pressures of war). For those who continued to employ hard drugs, the decentralisation of the drug economy meant that there was a multitude of suppliers – besides their former superiors – to choose from.

These findings provide important insights for the literature on DDR. It underlines the risks of securitising ex-command structures solely based on the observation that *some* ex-commanders and fighters – operating in marginal spaces – engage in illicit economic activities, such as drug dealing. Even if such depictions are not factually wrong, they risk generating biased assumptions that ex-command structures thrive in spaces of marginality. However, by broadening the scope of enquiry and comparing ex-military networks in different socio-economic milieus, it becomes clear that such structures are often more prosperous in more official settings. This indicates that efforts to uproot strong ex-command structures are unlikely to address the problem of drug trade and addiction in post-civil war societies. On the contrary, such strategies may prove counterproductive due to the role ex-military networks have in providing employment to ex-combatants.

A crucial question is how well these findings travel to other war-afflicted countries, particularly in West Africa. Presumably, similar dynamics are most likely to be observed in societies, such as Liberia, where the trade in drugs had a limited role in financing armed groups and patronage politics plays a key role in sustaining citizens' socio-economic well-being. In such countries, it is arguably less socially acceptable and economic profitable for ex-commanders and fighters to engage in drug business. The latter are, instead, more likely to seek to attach themselves to governing elites who can assist them in gaining access to jobs, money, and schooling. The situation may, however, be different in countries, such as Colombia, where armed groups have a long history of profiting from the drug trade. In such contexts, it may be more economically gainful and socially tolerated for ex-military personnel to engage in the distribution and selling of drugs.

Acknowledgements

The author is grateful to Lotta Themnér and the editors and external reviewers at Third World Thematics for extremely helpful comments and suggestions. I am also thankful to Fofana Abraham, Pindarous Allison, Johnson Borh, Arthur Johnson, Ilmari Käihkö, Mariam Persson, Allan Quee, Mats Utas, and Morlee Zawoo who have all assisted me in various ways. Finally, this article would not have been possible without the generous financial assistance provided by Swedish International Development Cooperation Agency (SIDA).

Disclosure statement

No potential conflict of interest was reported by the author.

Funding

This work was supported by the Swedish International Development Cooperation Agency (SIDA).

Notes

1. Drugs are held as psychoactive substances and their precursors whose production, distribution, sale, and use is forbidden by law or limited to medical and pharmaceutical channels. This definition has been derived from World Health Organization ('Lexicon of Alcohol,' 25, 41). It is important to note that countries vary in which substances are classified as illegal.
2. Bøås, "Castles in the Sand"; Christensen, "Shadow Soldiering"; Ellis, "West Africa's," 194; Lewis, "Casamance Conflict"; Utas, "Sweet Battlefields"; Vigh, "From Warlord."
3. The terms ex-command structures, ex-combatant networks, and ex-military networks are employed interchangeably.
4. Christensen, "Shadow Soldiering"; Themnér, *Violence in Post-Conflict Societies*; Utas, "Sweet Battlefields."
5. Nilsson, "Reintegrating Ex-Combatants."
6. A popular narrative amongst NGO representatives in both Liberia and Sierra Leone was that ex-commanders were able to continue to ensure the loyalty of child ex-combatants by offering them drugs. In turn, this also ensured that they had access to a loyal pool of clients. Observation based on fieldwork by the author in Liberia and Sierra Leone.
7. Christensen, "Shadow Soldiering"; Themnér, *Violence in Post-Conflict Societies*; Utas, "Sweet Battlefields."
8. In this study, I define addiction as 'the repeated use of a psychoactive substance or substances, to the extent that the user is periodically or chronically intoxicated, shows a compulsion to take the preferred substance (or substances), has great difficulty in voluntarily ceasing or modifying substance use, and exhibits determination to obtain psychoactive substances by almost any means' (United Nations, 'Terminology and Information').
9. Carrier and Klantschnig, "Illicit Livelihoods"; Ellis, "West Africa's"; Laudati, "Securing (In)security"; Suckling, "Chain Work"; Vorrath, "From War to Illicit."
10. Cox et al., "Religion, Peacebuilding, and Social."
11. Uppsala Conflict Data Program (UCDP). See http://www.ucdp.uu.se/.
12. Collier and Hoeffler, "Greed and Grievance"; Kaldor, *New and old wars*; Kaplan, "The Coming of Anarchy."
13. Kan, *Drugs and Contemporary Warfare*.
14. Ellis, *The Mask of Anarchy*; Gberie, *A Dirty War*, 137, 149; Peters, "Footpaths to Reintegration," 67, 72; Keen *Conflict and Collusion*.
15. Gberie, *A Dirty War*, 149.
16. Keen, *Conflict and Collusion*, 76, 105, 231; Peters, "Footpaths to Reintegration," 67.
17. Collier and Hoeffler, "Greed and Grievance."
18. Ellis, "West Africa's"; Lewis, "Casamance Conflict"; Vigh, "From Warlord."
19. Lewis, "Casamance Conflict"; Ellis, *The Mask of Anarchy*, 169.
20. Ellis, "West Africa's"; Kan, *Drugs and Contemporary Warfare*; Reno, "Liberia: Durable Illicit Power"; Vorrath, "From War to Illicit."
21. Ellis, "West Africa's"; UNODC, "Cocaine Trafficking"; Vigh, "From Warlord."
22. Ellis, "West Africa's," 173.
23. Vorrath, "From War to Illicit."
24. Christensen, "Shadow Soldiering"; Kan, *Drugs and Contemporary Warfare*; Nussio and Howe, "What if the FARC"; Themnér, *Violence in Post-conflict Societies*.
25. Stratfor, "The Tuaregs."
26. Christensen, "Shadow Soldiering"; Themnér, *Violence in Post-conflict Societies*.

27. Nilsson, "Reintegrating Ex-Combatants."
28. Christensen, "Shadow Soldiering"; Themnér, *Violence in Post-Conflict Societies*; Utas, "Sweet Battledfields."
29. IRIN, "Rehabilitating Child Soldiers"; Keen, *Conflict and Collusion*; Utas, "Sweet Battlefields."
30. Observation based on fieldwork by the author in Liberia and Sierra Leone.
31. See note 6 above.
32. Carrier and Klantschnig, "Illicit Livelihoods."
33. Carrier and Klantschnig, "Illicit Livelihoods"; Laudati, "Securing (In)security"; Suckling, "Chain Work."
34. Ellis, *The Mask of Anarchy*; Utas, "Sweet Battlefields."
35. Utas, "Sweet Battlefields."
36. Ellis, "West Africa's"; Reno, "Liberia: Durable Illicit Power"; Vorrath, "From War to Illicit."
37. This project was conducted in collaboration with Mats Utas.
38. The names of these towns are not mentioned, in order to ensure the anonymity of the informants.
39. The research assistants were Pindarous Allison, Johnson Borh, Arthur Johnson, Ilmari Käihkö, Mariam Persson, Allan Quee, and Morlee Zawoo.
40. Themnér, "Former Mid-Level Commanders."
41. Carrier and Klantschnig, "Illicit Livelihoods"; Laudati, "Securing (In)security."
42. Ellis, "West Africa's," 170, 172, 183; Keen, *Conflict and Collusion*, 130.
43. Ellis, *The Mask of Anarchy*, 170; Utas, "Sweet Battlefields," 11.
44. Interview with ex-NPFL combatant 1, Monrovia, September 15, 2011.
45. Ellis, *The Mask of Anarchy*, 134.
46. Interview with ex-NPFL combatant 2, Monrovia, November 15, 2012.
47. Käihkö, "Taylor Must Go."
48. Interview with ex-NPFL combatant 3, Monrovia, September 6, 2011.
49. Ellis, *The Mask of Anarchy*, 91; "West Africa's," 169.
50. Ellis, "West Africa's," 191; Vorrath, "From War to Illicit," 20, 21.
51. Reno, "Liberia: Durable Illicit Power," 114.
52. Vorrath, "From War to Illicit," 22.
53. It is not always easy to distinguish between marijuana and crack-cocaine. Both substances are generally inhaled via smoking and sometimes crack-cocaine is mixed with marijuana. Complicating things further people often talk about 'smokes', which mostly refers to marijuana, but can sometimes mean cigarettes or crack-cocaine. I am therefore reluctant to use specific percentages when describing the distribution in consumption between marijuana and crack-cocaine.
54. Carrier and Klantschnig, "Illicit Livelihoods," 175.
55. Interview with Adam, Monrovia, Liberia, November 21, 2012.
56. Ibid.
57. Interview with ex-NPFL combatant 4, Monrovia, Liberia, September 7, 2011.
58. Vorrath, "From War to Illicit," 21.
59. Ibid.

Bibliography

Bøås, Morten. "Castles in the Sand: Informal Networks and Power Brokers in the Norther Mali Periphery." In *African Conflicts and Informal Power: Big Men and Networks*, edited by Mats Utas, 205–223. London: Zed Books, 2012.

Carrier, Niel, and Gernot Klantschnig. "Illicit Livelihoods: Drug Crops and Development in Africa." *Review of African Political Economy* 43, no. 148 (2016): 174–189.

Christensen, Maya. "Shadow Soldiering: Mobilisation, Militarisation and the Politics of Global Security in Sierra Leone." PhD diss., Copenhagen University, 2013.

Collier, Paul, and Anke Hoeffler. "Greed and Grievance in Civil War." *Oxford Economic Papers* 56 (2004): 563–595.

Cox, Fletcher D., Catherine R. Osborn, and Timothy Sisk. *Religion, Peacebuilding, and Social Cohesion in Conflict-Affected Countries: Research Report*. Denver, CO: University of Denver and Sié Center, 2015.

Lewis, David. "Casamance Conflict is Unhealed Sore for Senegal." *Reuters*, February 25, 2012.

Ellis, Stephen. *The Mask of Anarchy. The Destruction of Liberia and the Religious Dimension of an African Civil War*. New York, NY: New York University Press, 1999.

Ellis, Stephen. "West Africa's International Drug Trade." *African Affairs* 108, no. 431 (2009): 171–196.

Gberie, Lansana. *A Dirty War in West Africa: The RUF and the Destruction of Sierra Leone*. Bloomington: Indiana University Press, 2005.

IRIN. "Rehabilitating Child Soldiers is a Tough Job." 2004 September 6. http://www.irinnews.org/feature/2004/09/06/rehabilitating-child-soldiers-tough-job.

Käihkö, Ilmari. "'Taylor Must Go': The Strategy of the Liberians United for Reconciliation and Democracy." *Small Wars & Insurgencies* 26, no. 2 (2015): 248–270.

Kaldor, Mary. *New and Old Wars: Organised Violence in a Global Era*. Cambridge: Polity Press, 1999.

Kan, Paul Rexton. *Drugs and Contemporary Warfare*. Dulles, VA: Potomac Books, 2009.

Kaplan, Robert D. "The Coming of Anarchy: How Scarcity, Crime, Overpopulation, Tribalism, and Disease are Rapidly Destroying the Social Fabric of Our Planet." *The Atlantic*, February, 1994.

Keen, David. *Conflict and Collusion in Sierra Leone*. New York: Palgrave, 2005.

Laudati, Ann A. "Securing (in)security: Relinking Violence and the Trade in Cannabis Sativa in Eastern Democratic Republic of Congo." *Review of African Political Economy* 43, no. 148 (2016): 190–205.

Nilsson, Anders. *Reintegrating Ex-combatants in Post-conflict Societies*. Stockholm: Sida, 2005.

Nussio, Enzo, and Kimberly Howe. "What if the FARC Demobilizes?" *Stability* 1, no. 1 (2012): 58–67.

Peters, Krijn. "Footpaths to Reintegration: Armed Conflict, Youth and the Rural Crisis in Sierra Leone." PhD diss., Wageningen University, 2006.

Reno, William. "Liberia: Durable Illicit Power Structures." In *Impunity: Countering Illicit Power in War and Transition*, edited by Michelle Hughes and Michael Miklaucic, 100–124. Washington, DC.: Center for Complex Operations, 2016.

Stratfor. "The Tuaregs: From African Nomads to Smugglers and Mercenaries." *Stratfor Worldview*. February 2, 2012. https://www.stratfor.com/analysis/tuaregs-african-nomads-smugglers-and-mercenaries.

Suckling, Christopher A. "Chain Work: The Cultivation of Hierarchy in Sierra Leone's Cannabis Economy." *Review of African Political Economy* 43, no. 148 (2016): 206–226.

Themnér, Anders. *Violence in Post-conflict Societies: Remarginalization, Remobilizers and Relationships*. Abingdon: Routledge, 2011.

Themnér, Anders. "Former Mid-Level Commanders in Big Man Networks." In *African Conflicts and Informal Power: Big Men and Networks*, edited by Mats Utas, 205–223. London: Zed Books, 2012.

United Nations. *Terminology and Information on Drugs*. New York, 2016.

UNODC. *Cocaine Trafficking in West Africa: The Threat to Stability and Development*. Vienna: UNODC, 2007.

Utas, Mats. "Sweet Battlefields: Youth and the Liberian Civil War." PhD diss., Uppsala University, 2003.

Vigh, Henrik. "From Warlord to Drug Lord: The Life of João Bernardo "Nino" Vieira." In *Warlord Democrats in Africa: Ex-Military Leaders and Electoral Politics*, edited by Anders Themnér, 156–176. London: Zed Publishing, 2017.

Vorrath, Judith. *From War to Illicit Economies: Organized Crime and State-Building in Liberia and Sierra Leone*. Berlin: SWP Research Paper 13, 2014.

World Health Organization. *Lexicon of Alcohol and Drug Terms*. Geneva, 1994.

OPEN ACCESS

Lost in transition: linking war, war economy and post-war crime in Sri Lanka

Shyamika Jayasundara-Smits

ABSTRACT
Scholars continue to draw attention to the link between the war economy and post-war crime. The majority of these studies are about cases of civil war that ended with peace agreements. Sri Lanka's civil war ended with a military victory for the state armed forces; thus, it can help shed new light on the above link. Situated in the war economy perspective, this article investigates the dominant types of crimes reported from post-war Sri Lanka and the mechanisms linking them with the war economy. The culture of impunity, continued militarisation and enduring corruption are identified as key mechanisms through which the war economy and post-war bodily and material crime are linked. It suggests, although the 'victors' peace' achieved by state armed forces was able to successfully dismantle the extra-legal war economy run by the Liberation Tigers of Tamil Eelam, it was responsible for promoting criminality in the post-war period. Overall, this points to the urgency of breaking away from legacies of the state war economy in the post-war period, before introducing programs of longer term political and economic reform.

Introduction

The literature on civil war termination and post-war peacebuilding draws attention to interconnections and continuities between the war economy and post-war crime. They are mainly explained through a rational choice approach to conflict. Often, these studies highlight the role of greed, the resource curse, production of illicit goods, warlords and competition for the monopoly of power and violence by multiple sovereigns as drivers of violent conflicts.[1] Breaking this link has been found to be important for realising positive peace.[2] However, not all civil wars share the same characteristics in terms of their causes and the dynamics, during and after the war.[3] The dynamics in post-war Sri Lanka are quite different from the wars that ended in the post-Cold War period with a peace agreement often facilitated by external intervention. Instead, the dynamics in post-war Sri Lanka are largely set by the military victory by the state armed forces. This allowed the state not only to defeat the Liberation Tigers of Tamil Eelam (LTTE) but also to fully reclaim a monopoly of 'legitimate violence'.[4] Sri Lanka thus presents an opportunity to understand different manifestations of the link between the war economy and post-war crime, in a context of victors' peace.[5]

This article investigates the mechanisms and the relationship between the Sri Lankan war economy and dominant types of post-war crime in Sri Lanka. This article primarily relies on secondary data, including academic literature, newspaper articles, official crime data and policy documents and national and international reports compiled by civil society organisations. The official data related to war, peace and development are all highly contested. Unreliability and manipulation of data are serious issues particularly in societies that have experienced conflict and the war-to-peace transition, like Sri Lanka.[6] For instance, the number of war deaths remains subject to controversy.[7] So do the rosy pictures painted by state authorities about the country's economic performance during and after the war. MacGinty described the latter as the 'state's role in cooking the books'.[8] As observed by UNODC's[9] Global Study on Homicides, Sri Lanka also suffers from incomplete data and non-availability of baseline data on homicides committed during the pre-war period. This makes it difficult to compare and contrast pre-war, war and post-war statistics. Given these limitations, author triangulated official data with limited primary data collected in Colombo at the end of April and mid-November in 2017. They were collected through informal discussions held with members of civil society organisations based in Colombo, a senior Member of Parliament (MP) representing Jaffna District and a senior police officer attached to the South Colombo Police Division.

The rest of this article is organised as follows. First, it offers a brief introduction to the legacies of the war. Next, key aspects of the war economy are presented. In the following section, major developments in post-war crime are analysed by looking at two dominant types of grave crimes (bodily and material) and the main mechanisms through which these crimes are linked with the war economy. The final section summarises these interactions and pleads for tailored strategies to reform the state and the polity.

The end of war

In May 2009, after nearly three decades of fighting, the civil war between the state armed forces (backed by some of the Sinhalese Buddhist majority) and the LTTE (backed by some of the Sri Lankan Tamil minority) came to an end. It was declared a military victory for the state armed forces. The way in which the war ended rekindled a 'give war a chance' thesis, not only in Sri Lanka but elsewhere in the world.[10] It also debunked speculations by military and academic pundits that war could only end with a peace agreement. Against a background of 'peace fatigue', after repeated failed peace negotiations in a fractured political system,[11] the government going for an all-war strategy was not a complete surprise. Also, as expected, military victory came at a huge cost in lives; the number of casualties in the war has been estimated at around 100,000,[12] including at least 40,000 civilian deaths during the last few months of the war alone.[13] On the economic front, the civil war affected Sri Lanka's production and exports, as well as the foreign direct investment (FDI) inflows. It also lowered the country's long-term growth rate. The direct and indirect economic costs of the war were mainly borne by the government. Especially, costs related to the damages to vital physical and social infrastructure are significant. The total costs borne by the government were estimated at 1.7 times the GDP of Sri Lanka in 1996.[14]

The end of the war has been marked by several other problematic legacies. Whilst the international community initially praised President Rajapaksa's government for ending the war, the way the final phase of the war was conducted was heavily criticised. This was followed by repeated calls for an international war crime investigation[15] and probing into critical incidents of human rights violations during the last months of the war.[16] Draconian laws, like the emergency laws and the Prevention of Terrorism Act,[17] are accused of protecting the armed forces from legal prosecution for these crimes. Post-war Sri Lanka also saw an increase in the number of grave crimes recorded.[18] This increase parallels trends reported from other cases of civil war ending, from El Salvador and Guatemala to the Balkans and Colombia.[19] Homicide[20] is a key type of grave crime often reported as increasing in these cases but this was not the case in Sri Lanka. According to the UNODC database, the rate of intentional homicides per 100,000 people fell dramatically in the post-war period from 10.16 during wartime to just 2.79 in 2013. However, as UNODC cautions, the decreasing number of homicides might be due to overlapping records of deaths resulting from intentional homicide and civilian casualties attributed to the conflict during the active years of war.

From the perspective of the 'new war' framework,[21] persistent institutional weaknesses, illicit economies, criminal groups and availability of lootable natural resources are key factors encouraging criminality in the post-war contexts. As studies on Sri Lanka show, post-war crime and violence might be linked with mechanisms including militarisation, low institutional capacity, corruption, youth unemployment or circulation of weapons, either alone or in combination.[22] As a follow-up to previous works, and owing to the dynamics set by the 'victors' peace' in Sri Lanka, this article is framed within the classical state-based war economy perspective to further investigate these links and mechanisms.[23]

Sri Lanka's war economy[24]

The war economy in Sri Lanka can be divided into two parts: the state-based war economy controlled by the government of Sri Lanka (GOSL), and the extra-legal war economy, run by the LTTE.[25] This distinction is analytical rather than empirical. It highlights the key actors who in their main spheres of operation in real life became embedded in one or the other war economy. Both parts of the war economy were aimed at fulfilling the military priority of defeating the enemy. Naturally, the LTTE was the prime target of the state-controlled war economy and vice versa. The state-controlled war economy was sustained by various Sinhalese majority backed governments, which assumed state power from 1983[26]. The state's dedicated efforts to mobilise and allocate valuable resources for winning the war happened in parallel to periodic investments made in pursuing peace talks with the enemy (usually more dependent on donor financial support).[27] As a result, military spending gradually grew to constitute a significant portion of the state's total spending. Much of this was dedicated to bearing the cost of the growing armed forces: in 1985, the number of military service personnel was estimated at 21,600. In 2014, this climbed to more than ten times that, an estimated 223,100. In the same period, Sri Lanka's military expenditure grew in real terms by 29%.[28]

Thus, although the increase in the GOSL armed forces directly fulfils military and combat functions, it also has political and economic expediency.[29] The additional employment opportunities the military offers to the country's young Sinhalese has helped Sinhalese political regimes' social power base in society.[30] The majority of the front-line military positions are filled by the poorer segments of Sinhalese youth, excluded from other, more lucrative white-collar government jobs. As Venugopal's research showed,[31] employment in the military absorbed more than half of young Sinhala men from four poor districts: Ampara, Trincomalee, Polonnaruwa and Moneragala. Since the end of the war, in a fragile political system and an ailing economy, maintaining this massive number of military cadres has become more than necessary. Thus, both post-war governments have devoted a significant portion of the country's national income to the military budget (in 2016, the military budget was approximately US$ 289,160,000).[32] The increase can be seen for instance, in the difference between the 2015 defence appropriation (US$ 2.22 billion) and its military spending in 2016, an estimated US$ 2.89 billion.[33]

A large portion of the military budget has been used to import weapons.[34] Unlike countries at war that are also domestic arms producers, Sri Lanka's war did not give a positive boost to its economy.[35] As a result, a significant portion of the defence budget was met by imposing various war-specific tax schemes, like the 'Defence Levy', 'Save the Nation Levy' and 'Nation Building Levy'.[36] The 'Defence Levy' was introduced in 1992, then renamed as the 'National Security Levy'. This scheme continued until 1997 and was paid by any person who carried out business, whether manufacturing, importing or providing a service. The 'Save the Nation Levy' was imposed on any working person except those in the national police, security and military forces. It was to be paid on a quarterly basis and taxed citizens with an annual income over LKR 45,000 at 2% of their total income, and those who earned over LKR 90,000 at 3% of their total income. In the first half of the year 2000, the National Security Levy helped increase government's earnings by 8%. It was also imposed on the service sector, initially at 5.5% and subsequently increased to 6.5%. Alongside this, it is plausible to argue that the prolonged supply of humanitarian assistance to Sri Lanka by external actors (US$ 74.3 million as of 2013[37]) provided an additional cushion for the government, allowing it to spend more on defence.

Furthermore, corruption in the defence sector by the political and military elites is believed to have contributed to the conception of a parallel-shadow economy. Corruption in the defence sector is difficult to uncover, partly due to the systematic silencing of critical journalists and civil society members.[38] However, there is evidence to suggest that large-scale corruption took place in the defence sector during the war. One prominent example is the uninvestigated scandal of the purchase of MiG-27 aircraft from Ukraine.[39]

In addition to high-level corruption, instances of petty corruption in the defence and security sectors have been reported. They range from members of the defence forces and police receiving bribes from suspected LTTE members to protect them from imprisonment, and bribes to buy support to strengthen military forces' positions in the north and the east. One example is the monetarily significant deal alleged to have been struck in 2004 by the military and the ruling political regime with the breakaway LTTE group led by Colonel Karuna.[40] There are many other examples of corruption linked to the defence establishment.[41]

LTTE and the extra-legal war economy[42]

Creating a separate state was LTTE's main goal. Therefore, additionally to its military activities, LTTE also heavily invested in forming a sophisticated administrative apparatus. This dual strategy allowed the organisation to act as a quasi-state in the north and the east.[42] Over the years, the LTTE has developed a parallel economy of its own, operating outside of the national and the international legal and regulatory frameworks. One of the main modalities of operation was through sophisticated forms of extra-legal transnational networks. As alleged by the former Sri Lankan army commander, General Rohan Daluwatte, the LTTE sustained its de facto rule in the north and some parts in the east by looting the humanitarian supplies sent by the government to the war-affected areas. These supplies include medical supplies, food and other essentials.[43] Later, the LTTE-run war economy was implicated in illegal shipping operations that spanned from South India to other Asian countries and thereafter to Eastern Europe and Africa. Prior to 2005, the organisation itself owned 20 vessels approximately and a considerable number of trawlers.[44] Among other related activities, the establishment of a number of boatyard companies based in East Asia (Indonesia and the Philippines) has been noted. These companies were allegedly used for transporting arms and ammunition under the pretext of cargo deliveries. Sea piracy also brought revenues to the LTTE, posing a considerable threat to the maritime security in the region.[45] The LTTE is also alleged to have engaged in arms and ammunition smuggling from the Far East and Eastern European countries. The bulk of its military hardware was purchased from North Korea with some from Ukraine and Bulgaria. It also developed a parallel tax regime by introducing a range of direct and indirect taxes in the LTTE-controlled areas and in some territories held by the Sri Lankan government.[46] At some point, the Tamil public servants were even asked to contribute a certain percentage of their monthly salary as income tax. Manufacturers and service providers were taxed a percentage of their monthly income. Farmers and those involved in fishing were pressured to contribute a share of their output either in cash or kind. By maximising the opportunities opened up during the intermitted brief phases of ceasefires, the organisation also raised revenues through indirect taxes in the form of customs fees on goods brought into the LTTE-controlled territory. Other sources of income included a vehicle registration tax in the LTTE-controlled areas and a tax on property transactions in Jaffna.

By 2001, the number of Tamils living abroad was estimated at 600,000–800,000. Due to the war, the majority of Sri Lankan Tamils found refuge in Western Europe, India, Australia and North America.[47] According to a report published by the Canadian Security Intelligence Services, members of the Tamil diaspora living in Switzerland, Canada, Australia, the United Kingdom, the United States and the Scandinavian countries have been funding the LTTE financially.[48] According to the US State Department, the LTTE exploited the Tamil diaspora to raise funds and supplies.[49] Propaganda, finance and logistics were the main forms of contribution to the LTTE's war economy from Tamils living abroad. Among the diaspora, some were willingly contributors whereas others were coerced. Approximately 80% of the LTTE's US$ 82 million annual budget was generated from diaspora contributions (and revenues generated from international trade, enterprise and investments).[50] In the late 1990s, the amount of money sent from the Canadian diaspora alone was estimated at between C$ 1 million and more than C$ 12 million a year. In 2005 and 2006, the LTTE used various methods and channels to increase its efforts to raise money for a 'final war'; these included door-to-door collections by overseas members of the LTTE and LTTE-linked organisations. They also devised more targeted methods, such as approaching wealthy businesses and professionals, from whom the organisation demanded significant sums of money. In Canada, ordinary families were typically pressured to give between C$ 2500 and C$ 5000, whereas some wealthy businesses were pressured to give C$ 100,000.

On the home front, the LTTE also put pressure on overseas Tamils visiting their relatives in Sri Lanka to contribute. The assessed 'rate' was often C$ 1, £ 1, or € 1 per day for the length of time each individual has lived in the West. Such visitors were not allowed to leave the country until they produced the requested amount; in some cases, the LTTE also confiscated their passports until the money was paid.[51] Zunzer noted that contradictory to some reports, not all the funds generated by the Tamil Rehabilitation Organisation (TRO) – a frontline LTTE-related humanitarian entity formed by the Tamil diaspora – were used to support military activities. The funds generated by the TRO were mainly used for development work and for paying the overheads to sustain the embryonic institutional structures of the quasi-Tamil state in the north and east of the country.[52]

Following the breakdown of the 2002 ceasefire, the LTTE also stepped up its recruitment drive. By this time the organisation had approximately 30,000 personnel, including both voluntary and involuntary recruits. LTTE recruits included a large number of civilians who had served in the Illapaddei force, an auxiliary force reserve on a LKR 7000 monthly salary, used for both for defensive and offensive operations. In addition, child soldiers constituted a significant number of the LTTE cadres. This is especially noted in the LTTE's eastern faction led by Karuna.[53] Towards the end of 2007, a total of 6,000 children was reported to have joined, although the actual number of child soldiers is believed to be much higher.[54] Similar to the government's military recruits, the LTTE recruits also had functions other than strategic military combat. In particular, they had important legitimating functions in LTTE-controlled areas.[55] LTTE 'recruitment' was not only a mechanism for exploiting the vulnerability of both individuals and groups but also a protective mechanism against the Sri Lankan state. As the war economy literature suggests, the latter proposition usually involved convincing the potential members that they would be safer inside the organisation than outside.[56] Given the controversial laws and practices of the Sri Lankan state – for example the Prevention of Terrorism Act (PTA – operational since 1973) and the Code of Criminal Procedure Act (CCPA), both of which were generously applied against the Tamil youth and the suspected LTTE members (as well as for the anti-state Sinhalese youth-led political group of Janatha Vimukthi Peramuna) – it might not have required much effort for the LTTE leadership to convince Tamil youth in particular to join the organisation, sometimes even without a monetary incentive. Although many of its economic activities were coerced and quasi-voluntary, the LTTE was able to legitimise these by invoking a sense of Tamil nationalism, outside threat and enemy imagery.[57]

Linking the war economy and post-war grave crime

As David Keen observed, post-conflict contexts are unlikely to see a clean break from violence to consent, from theft to production, from repression to democracy, or from impunity to accountability.[58] Peacebuilding also involves transforming war economies into peace economies. Thus, a successful and sustainable transition requires a nuanced understanding of the dynamics in the post-war contexts. To this end, crime-related developments and the identification of possible links of these with the war economy are crucial.[59]

Broadly speaking, post-war Sri Lanka is marked by the intermeshing of crimes committed during and after the war. The crimes committed during the war are mainly the alleged war crimes committed during its last phase. Many reports both locally and internationally implicate the state armed forces and LTTE equally (e.g. UN expert panel report on the direction of the Secretary-General, the UN High Commission for Human Rights and the locally commissioned Udalagama and Paranagama Commission report).[60] So far, the United Nations has passed a number of resolutions calling for cooperation from the Sri Lankan state authorities to conduct a credible investigation into the alleged war crimes committed by both parties.[61] These calls are supported by many Western governments (including the US and the EU) and the majority of the Tamil diaspora. Ironically, the former are accused of selling deadly weapons to the Sri Lankan Government during the last phase of the war. For instance, UK's arms exports were worth more than £13.6 million.[62] It is not only the net value of these weapons that should deserve attention but how these arms deals by-passed the existing 1998 EU Code of Conduct on Arms Export.[63] Like the localised war economy in Sri Lanka, these controversial arms sales point to the importance of the transnational scale, in which Sri Lanka's war economy was firmly embedded and found sustenance.

The official statistics show a gradual increase in grave crimes in the post-war period with minor fluctuations in some sub-categories. The increasing brutality and frequency with which they are committed are noted too.[64] The trend of increasing grave crimes was first reported only in the last few years. It has alluded to various factors such as rapid economic growth, social development and changes in individual lifestyles.[65] Given the unreliability of official data, it is difficult to demonstrate a significant rise in the number of grave crimes just by following the official records. In this regard, one noteworthy revelation by a senior police officer interviewed for this article is the new tendency among various police divisions to downplay and under-report grave crimes. This is mainly done to secure promotions and show better service records to access benefits related to job performance.[66] To garner the fuller picture, it is also necessary to triangulate the official statistics, prevailing social discourses (both mainstream and the marginal) and primary qualitative data. The developments related to the post-war grave crime and their possible links with the war economy are barely acknowledged in local social discourses. However, researchers have begun explaining some of the mechanisms that link the war and some of the developments related to post-war grave crime. These studies are primarily situated in psychosocial,[67] gender,[68] criminology and media-based[69] theories using primary qualitative data. As a follow up to these studies, deriving from a political-economy based analysis, a more nuanced picture of the link between the war economy and the post-war grave crime is presented below.

Bodily crimes

Bodily crime is widely reported from post-war Sri Lanka and between 2009 and 2013 the number of complaints received by the police for investigation of bodily crimes of a sexual nature alone increased by 34%.[70] Since the end of the war, many cases of abductions and disappearances have been reported from the former war zone. A person has been abducted or 'disappeared' roughly once every five days.[71] Women and girls – particularly among the internally displaced people (IDP) – are the main targets of these incidents. Trafficking of women, especially widows and single mothers, and rape have been reported from the war-affected areas. As the regional patterns suggest, at least five incidents of rape have been recorded daily in the north and east of Sri Lanka since 2009. Since most cases are not even reported, the official figure could be even higher.[72] As the Organisation of Women for Rights has highlighted, in the north and the east, the majority of the victims of such crimes (rape, sexual violence, torture, abduction and arbitrary detention) are allegedly connected to the state armed forces. The lack of domestic investigations undertaken with regard to crimes reported in the post-war period is considered a continuing crime against humanity.[73]

A considerable number of sexual crimes have also been reported from districts of Anuradhapura, Polonnaruwa, Kurunegala and Monaragala, which are adjacent to the former war zone. During the war, these areas played an interlocutory role connecting the war in the north with the south by serving as major recruitment hubs for the state armed forces. In these areas, and especially in Anuradhapura, brothels held sex-trafficked women and children. This, the US Department of State said, was linked to the area's role as 'a major transit point for members of the Sri Lankan armed forces heading north'.[74] The former combatants from the state armed forces have been blamed for most of the bodily crimes reported from these areas. Some blame the lack of systematic psycho-social support to the military for the increasing number of bodily crimes committed by the army soldiers.[75]

The possibility of soldiers' involvement in or planning of these criminal activities was also suggested by De Votta.[76] According to him, an estimated 35,000 state armed forces who were stationed in Jaffna (the provincial capital of the Northern Province after the end of the war) could have had a stake in these incidents. A more recent phenomenon called 'grease devil attacks' carried out by naked or semi-naked men smeared in grease sexually assaulting women has also been reported in the post-war north and in the east, suspected as the works of the armed forces.[77] These local accusations also resonate with incidents of the systematic sexual abuse and rape of children reported against the Sri Lanka soldiers who served in the UN peacekeeping missions in Haiti and the Central African Republic. So far, the Sri Lankan authorities have failed to conduct any formal investigation into these incidents.[78]

Material crimes

A higher number of material crimes is also reported from post-war Sri Lanka. Since 2014, the share of material crime has comprised an average of 40% of all grave crimes committed.[79] According to the Police Narcotic Bureau, a majority of these crimes are related to drug trafficking and drug abuse, both criminal offences under law.[80] The exact increase in these crimes is difficult to pin down. Non-comparable data sets following the introduction of the new crime category (minor offences) and politicians' meddling in the reporting[81] and investigation of these crimes partly explains this. However, the relatively high number of material crimes is confirmed by periodic statements issued by the law enforcement authorities. Further, as noted by the police officer interviewed for this study, material crimes such as burglary and theft involving firearms have also been linked with the widespread availability of small arms and light weapons since the end of the war and their frequent use by (ex) members of the Civil Defence Forces. This connection has also been confirmed by the senior superintendent of police, citing a recently compiled set of data collected across the island.[82] Although making an absolute link between material crimes and the war economy requires systematic collection of evidence and further substantiation, there are several mechanisms at play through which the two might be connected.

In general, economic difficulties increase the number of material grave crimes.[83] This raises the contrast between post-war reality and the rhetoric of the Rajapakse regime. The regime boasted of rapid economic growth during its tenure amidst the war and in the post-war period. In 2011, it even forecasted an average of 8.1%[84] economic growth. Based on its own figures, the regime saw no problem in delivering the promised peace-economic dividends. However, real post-war economic growth has been calculated at 2.5%.[85] It showed a gloomy economic scenario with consistently high levels of inflation (6.22% in 2010, 6.74% in 2011, 7.53% in 2012 and 6.94% in 2013). This inflation only started to decrease since 2015.[86]

It is widely believed that the extension of the war economy into the post-war period through further militarisation and high defence expenditure siphoned out resources that would have been available to generate the promised economic dividends related to peace and to address the challenge of widening inequality.[87] Even the claimed rapid economic boom (infrastructure development, improved agricultural productivity) in the north and the east in the post-war period has become a cause of concern since it came with political strings attached. These made inroads for further militarisation and securitisation of the land and the population.[88] The resources dedicated to maintaining a 450,000-strong military force (currently the ratio of military cadre to population is 1:5), in the absence of an active armed conflict or imminent threat of such, are particularly burdensome for the economy.[89]

Further, during the Rajapaksa regime, the military was re-deployed to perform non-military activities. It was assigned a key role in the post-war development strategy. The military was involved in large-scale property development ventures and in state-sponsored mega-infrastructure development projects (such as building roads, bridges, houses and sports stadiums). To facilitate this further, in 2012 the budget of the Defence Ministry was merged with the Urban Development Authority, yielding a combined budget of about 229.9 billion Sri Lankan Rupees. At that time, this combined budget was the largest of any government ministry.[90] All these were justified by highlighting the need for continued securitisation and the need to preserve the high (4.8% figures contested) economic growth achieved during the war.[91]

The regime's new development strategy negatively affected ordinary people's lives.[92] It dismantled the wartime coping economy in the north as a result of pursuing a national security state, which let the military to occupy and even forcibly annex vast amounts of fertile land in the north and east.[93] The military is also accused of driving away impoverished women from their livelihood activities (i.e. small-scale subsistence farming and selling home-grown produce in informal markets). Overall, the might of the military and state patronage military received created unfair conditions and unfair competition for the women in the coping economy.[94]

Although up to 2015 the Rajapakse regime spent massive sums of money borrowed from Chinese banks at a commercial rate, the dividends of these large-scale investments (in the form of large-scale reconstruction and development projects) have not reached average people.[95] Even allocations for essential services such as health and education have experienced a rapid decline, whilst military expenditure continues to rise.[96] Meanwhile, repeating the earlier patterns following failed peace-making efforts, the promised economic dividends of peace also did not reach to the south where most of the Sinhalese live. Some blame this on the workings of the country's electoral system and on unfavourable conditions imposed by the World Bank.[97] In sum, higher military spending, combined with factors like droughts, a deepening budget deficit and a high international debt to GDP ratio, has meant a looming economic crisis. These events suggest a link between the war's entrenching effects on the economy in the post-war period and the increasing number of material crimes.

Increasing unemployment levels is another mechanism that may explain the link between war economy and post-war material crime. Sri Lanka's unemployment rate was 4.4% in 2014, 4.6% in 2015 and 4.9% in 2016.[98] According to national data, youth unemployment is currently as high as 14.2%. Youth unemployment is remarkably similar in areas directly and indirectly hit by the war. For instance, the southern districts of Matara and Kegalle trail only slightly behind the directly war-affected districts of Jaffna, Killinochchi and Ampara.[99] Tragically, as evident in various reports, the post-war economic woes experienced by the youth are manifested in many forms. Among these, the inclination to commit material crimes as well as bodily crimes, such as suicides, are notable. Depression and Post-Traumatic Stress Disorder (PTSD) due to financial hardships and loss of livelihoods have been identified as main causes for the majority of the youth suicides reported from the North.[100]

When probing material crimes, corruption also deserves scrutiny. Under Sri Lankan law, corruption is a criminal offence but it has been a persistent problem in Sri Lanka. Sri Lanka ranks as a highly corrupt country in Transparency International's Corruption Perception Index. As World Governance Indicators show, control of corruption has not improved over the last 15 years. There has been a lack of enforcement of anti-corruption legislation, often leaving powerful political elites who commit such acts unpunished.[101] Political tendencies of the authoritarian style of governance, militarised state and centralisation of powers that emerged and sustained during and after the war and especially during the Rajapaksa regime, have led to enduring corruption.[102] Coupled with the war-related burdens laid on the economy, corruption further reduced the capacity of the state to generate economic growth and a fair redistribution system. As recent literature shows,[103] increasing criminality is one manifestation of the combined effects of inequality, mistrust and corruption. Promises to eradicate corruption (along with other measures of good governance) were the backbone of President Sirisena's election campaign. Sadly, so far the government has been unable to make any satisfactory progress.[104] Neither the end of the war nor the regime change in 2015 has severed the link between structurally rooted corruption, the economy and politics.[105] The continued high level of corruption in the post-war period[106] not only undermines and delays economic recovery but also potentially leaves room for a relapse into violence, criminality and social conflict.

Conclusion

Despite the difficulty of obtaining data, Sri Lanka is an interesting case study for literature on the war economy and post-war crimes. Although it is nearly a decade since the war ended, the legacies of the war continue to manifest in different forms. An increase in post-war grave crime (in terms of bodily and material) is one notable form. In this background, this article examined the dominant types of crimes reported from post-war Sri Lanka and the mechanisms linking them with the war economy. Bodily crime is the most dominant type of crime reported from former war ravaged north and the east. The increased number of bodily crimes mostly reported from these areas in the immediate years after the war links with the dynamics set by a victor's peace and the impunity enjoyed by the state armed forces. This link is further established by the state's continued efforts at the post-war militarisation of the economy and society. The only favourable outcome brought by the victor's peace was the ability to delink the LTTE from Sri Lanka's post-war crime scenario. This was possible due to strong discipline inherited by the former LTTE cadres during their time in the organisation, the government's efforts to demobilise ex-LTTE members, and continued militarisation and pursuit of national security state since the end of the war.

In the post-war period, material crime is the most dominant type of crime reported from the southern part of the country, where majority Sinhalese live. This article also identified the culture of impunity, a lack of progress in generating peace-economic dividends, and uncontrolled corruption as additional mechanisms linking the war economy and the post-war material crimes. This is further intensified by external factors such as continued droughts, the negative trade relationships developed with the West (especially the EU) and the loss of access to important concessionary development aid schemes as Sri Lanka graduated to middle-income status in 2010. However, the inner workings of these mechanisms require further investigation, through more systematic data and evidence gathering.

Overall, the developments noted related to Sri Lanka's post-war grave crime share similarities as well as differences with other post-war contexts. One notable difference is the state's role in the promotion of criminality in the guise of a victor's peace. This was especially observed during the 2009–2015 period. A country's tenuous economic base, destructive political culture (of elites and their supporters alike) and a flawed political system certainly has the ability to produce and reproduce the link between the war economy and post-war grave crime. Thus, a successful post-war transition will require tailor-made strategies targeting reforms to the moral, political and economic edifice of both the state and its polity.

Disclosure statement

No potential conflict of interest was reported by the author.

Acknowledgements

Author would like to thank the two anonymous peer-reviewers for their critical comments and Dr. Sabine Kurtenbach and Désirée Reder for their helpful comments during various stages of writing of this article.

ORCID

Shyamika Jayasundara-Smits http://orcid.org/0000-0002-1022-269X

Notes

1. Reno, *Warlord Politics and African States*; Le Billon, "Diamond Wars?"; Humphreys, "Natural Resources, Conflict, and Conflict Resolution"; Pugh, Cooper and Goodhand, *War Economies in a Regional Context*; and Nordstrom, "Women, Economy, War."

2. Galtung ("Violence, Peace, and Peace Research," 183) defines positive peace as absence of structural violence.
3. Goodhand, "From War Economy to Peace Economy?"; and Sedra "Security sector reform in Afghanistan." In the South Asian region, Afghanistan best demonstrates the close connections between war economy and post-war crime. It is important to note despite the ousting of the Taliban in 2001, conflict is ongoing between the Taliban and the elected government. Thus, the country does not fully present a post-war or post-conflict situation.
4. Defined as violence lawfully exercised by the state under a legitimate civilian authority, where actors conduct themselves in accordance with democratic norms and principles.
5. Understood as peace resulting from a military victory.
6. Mac Ginty, 2013, 425.
7. For different estimates see Mango, *Colombo Telegraph*, 14 February 2014.
8. Holt, "The Limits of Formal Metrics during Conflict and Post-conflict Transition," 9.
9. UNODC, "Global Study on Homicides 2013," 78, 104.
10. Presented by Luttwak "Give War a Chance," making a case for reconsidering a military solution to terminate civil wars and peace through force of arms.
11. The last peace process ran between 2002 and 2008. It was dominated by the international actors, led by Norway, and co-chaired by Japan, the USA and India. The heavy international involvement is attributed to the various shifts that occurred in both the global and local political economies.
12. United Nations, *Report of the Secretary-General's Panel of Experts*, iii.
13. ICANS, *What the Women Say*.
14. Arunatilake et al., *The Economic Cost of the War*.
15. United Nations, *Report of the Secretary-General's Panel of Experts*, 11, 12.
16. ICJ 2012 report on "Authority without Accountability," 13.
17. See ICJ report 2012, *Authority without Accountability*, 42–56 for a fuller picture of the various questionable laws introduced by the State during the war.
18. Grave crimes are crimes that are indictable. There are two main categories of grave crimes: bodily and material. Killing, adduction, rape, incest and other physical forms of harm come under bodily grave crimes. Robbery, theft, house-breaking, drug manufacturing, possession and smuggling, all constitute material grave crime.
19. As cited in Kurtenbach and Rettberg, "Understanding the Political, Economic, and Social System after War Termination," n.p.
20. Homicide is the killing of a human being due to the act or failure to act of another. There are two main types of homicides: Criminal and non-criminal. Criminal homicides include murder and manslaughter. Non-criminal homicides include killing in self-defence, a misadventure or legal (government) execution.
21. Kaldor, *New and Old Wars*.
22. Kurtenbach and Rettberg, "Understanding the Political, Economic, and Social System after War Termination," 1, 3.
23. This framework captures economic activities undertaken by the state to mobilise for the purpose of war, to support the military effort, to protect and defend the home territory, and especially to maintain the physical well-being, solidarity and morale of the people (Galbraith, "The Meaning of a War Economy," 5). During a relatively brief period under the Rajapakse regime, scholars such as Rajasingham-Senanayake attempted to apply the 'Milbus' framework developed by famous Pakistani scholar Ayesha Siddiqa (2007) to explain the rise of the military economy in Sri Lanka. Milbus is defined as military capital used for the personal benefit of military fraternity (1). Siddiqa's main aim was to show how business interests of the military relate to the personal enrichment of the Pakistani military and to the political ambitions of the armed forces. Application of this framework to this study is limited because Milbus does not capture the dynamics of a post-war setting. Unlike Sri Lanka's brief experience with the military economy, Milbus is drawn by analysing a long period of military's role and the interests in Pakistani's economy and conditioned by several long intermittent periods of military rule. Pakistani military elites function as a class or as a political party on their own, whereas in Sri Lanka, the military is not free from civilian rule and only functions as an aide to the flawed

democratic system and to the civil political elites. For these reasons, I have chosen to apply Galbraith's perspective, which allows capturing not only the military economy but also other dimensions of a war economy and the subjective goals that it tries to instil in a population.
24. For an elaboration of different typologies of war economies illustrated by Afghanistan – that is, combat economy, shadow economy, and coping economy – see Goodhand, "From War Economy to Peace Economy?" 168.
25. This typology is used for organising the data based on an actor-centric approach and modelled on the typologies of economies embedded in war economy by Goodhand 2003.
26. 1983 is considered as the official beginning of the civil war.
27. Jayasundara-Smits, "Conflict, War and Peace in Sri Lanka," 3.
28. SIPRI, *Military Expenditure (% of GDP) Yearbook*.
29. Venugopal, "The Politics of Market Reform at a Time of Civil War."
30. Goodhand, "Sri Lanka in 2012," 70.
31. "The Politics of Market Reform at a Time of Civil War," 73.
32. The World Bank website, calculations based on SIPRI Current Military expenditure (LCU).
33. SIPRI, *Military Expenditure by Country, in Local Currency, 1988–2016*.
34. According to the SIPRI database (Arms imports-SPRI trend indicator values) in arms imports reached an all-time high in 2000, featuring close to US$300 million.
35. Goodhand, "Sri Lanka in 2012."
36. The 'nation building tax' rate of 2%. As per the newest regulations, certain services such as telecommunications and electricity supplies and certain petroleum products (such as lubricants) and supplies of goods for a specified building project are exempt (KPMG Sri Lanka 2016 report, "Indirect Tax Alert," 2).
37. Global Humanitarian Assistance Report: A Development Initiative, Sri Lanka Country Profile, 2013 Key Figures. www.globalhumanitarianassistance.org/countryprofile/sri-lanka
38. Lindberg and Orujela, "Corruption and Conflict," 215.
39. http://www.sundaytimes.lk/070812/Columns/sitreport.html.
40. Vinayagamoorthi Muralitharan, widely known as Col. Karuna, was the second-in-command of the LTTE and the leader of the eastern command of the LTTE. In 2004 he defected from the LTTE and joined the government ranks. He is currently facing numerous war crimes charges committed during the war and even after.
41. Lindberg and Orujela, "Corruption and Conflict," 215.
42. Nordstrom (2010, 162) uses the term extra-legal to denote all economic activities that fall outside state-based definitions of legal This encompasses the informal, illicit, illegal, unrecorded and undefined.
42. Stokke, "Building the Tamil Eelam State," 1022.
43. *Business Today*, July 2011.
44. Ibid.
45. Ibid.
46. Stokke, "Building the Tamil Eelam State," 1034.
47. Venugopal, *The Global Dimensions of Conflict in Sri Lanka*, 20.
48. Chalk, *Liberation Tigers of Tamil Eelam's (LTTE) International Organisation and Operations*.
49. Country Reports on Terrorism 2016 – Foreign Terrorist Organisations: Liberation Tigers of Tamil Eelam (LTTE), 19 July 2017.
50. As cited in Venugopal, *The Global Dimensions of Conflict in Sri Lanka*, 22.
51. Human Rights Watch n.d, 2.
52. Zunzer, *Diaspora Communities and Civil Conflict Transformation*, 28.
53. Report by Business Today titled, "Evolution Of The LTTE And International Networking," July 2011.
54. Child Soldiers International, Global Report 2008.
55. Terpstra and Frerks, *Rebel Governance and Legitimacy Civil Wars*.
56. Liebenberg et al., "A Theory of War Economies," 311.
57. Terpstra and Frerks, *Rebel Governance and Legitimacy Civil Wars*.
58. Keen 2007, 10.

59. Goodhand, "From War Economy to Peace Economy?"
60. Deliberations of all these reports are contained in 'Presidential Commission of Inquiry into Complaints of Abductions and Disappearances, Report on the Second Mandate of the Presidential Commission of Inquiry into Complaints of Abductions and Disappearances' (2015). http://media.wix.com/ugd/bd81c0_02a8e91c18ab47359763b405c2d9f89e.pdf.
61. De Votta, "Sri Lanka: From Turmoil to Dynasty," 139.
62. *The Independent*, 18 February 2013.
63. Ibid.
64. Ibid.
65. Niriella, "Thinking of new Horizon in Criminal Justice," 284.
66. As this officer noted, the current official crime statistics are also downplayed due to the introduction of a new softer crime category called 'minor offences', that is, crimes that are non-indictable.
67. YPF, *Nexus between Post War Trauma and Increased Violence*.
68. Guruge et al., "Intimate Partner Violence in the Post-war Context."
69. Siriwardhana, "Post War Media Behavior in Sri Lanka."
70. Report of the Leader of the Opposition's Commission on the Prevention of Violence against Women and the Girl Child noted, 2014, 22.
71. Goodhand, "Sri Lanka in 2012."
72. ICANS, *What the Women Say*, 3.
73. See note 15 above.
74. United States Department of State, *Trafficking in Persons Report*.
75. Jinadasa, "Rate of Crime and the Involvement of Army Soldiers in Post Conflict Society in Sri Lanka," 41; and Colombage, "Crime among Sri Lanka Soldiers on Rise."
76. "Sri Lanka: From Turmoil to Dynasty," 139.
77. ICG East Asia report no. 217 titled, "Sri Lanka: Women's Insecurity in the North and East," 20 December 2011, 30.
78. *Hindustani Times*, 4 June 2017.
79. Presentation by the Crime Intelligence Analysis Bureau of Police 2016.
80. www.police.lk/index.php/narcotic-bureau/145.
81. From the interview with the senior Police official.
82. *Sunday Leader*, 12 December 2012.
83. Webster and Kingston, *Anti-Poverty Strategies*, 10.
84. Goodhand, "Sri Lanka in 2012," 131.
85. Uyangoda, "Sri Lanka in 2009," 110.
86. Based on the Central Bank Data.
87. Nanayakkara, "Can Sri Lanka Eradicate Poverty."
88. Goodhand, "Sri Lanka in 2012," 133.
89. ICG, "The Forever War?"
90. Goodhand, "Sri Lanka in 2012," 70.
91. Wijeweera and Webb, "Military Spending and Economic Growth in Sri Lanka," 506.
92. Goodhand, "Sri Lanka in 2012," 68. Some have described this peculiar development as militarisation and even as military rule.
93. ICG, *Sri Lanka's Transition to Nowhere*, 18.
94. ICANS, *What the Women Say*, 5.
95. Wickramasinghe, "Sri Lanka in 2013," 203.
96. Selvanathan and Selvanathan, "Defence Expenditure and Economic Growth," 70.
97. Mac Ginty, "Bottom up Peace Indicators," 2015.
98. Word Bank Unemployment, total (% of total labour force) (modelled ILO estimate). Compared to the world average (5.748 in 2016), Sri Lanka's unemployment rate seems low. This figure, however, does not include underemployment, which was 2.7% in 2015. Underemployment is defined as when a person's employment is inadequate, in relation to specified norms or alternative employment, account being taken of his occupational skill (training and working experience).
99. Department of Census and Statistics, Ministry of National Policies and Economic Affairs 2016.

100. Based on the analysis of official grave crime data.
101. ICG, *Sri Lanka's Transition to Nowhere*, GAN 2015.
102. Mampilly, "The Nexus of Militarisation and Corruption," 183.
103. Lindberg and Orjuela, "Corruption in the Aftermath of War."
104. ICG, *Sri Lanka's Transition to Nowhere*, II.
105. Lindberg and Orujela, "Corruption and Conflict," 205.
106. In 2016, Sri Lanka ranked 95th out of 176 in the Corruption Perception Index-Transparency International rankings.

Bibliography

AHRC. "Every 90 Minutes a Woman is Raped in Sri Lanka: Rape and Other Crimes against Women on the Increase." *Colombo Telegraph*, July 15, 20. https://www.colombotelegraph.com/index.php/every-90-minutes-a-woman-is-raped-in-sri-lanka-rape-and-other-crimes-against-women-on-the-increase-ahrc/.

Arunatilake, Nisha, Sisira Jayasuriya, and Saman Kelegama. *The Economic Cost of the War in Sri Lanka.* Colombo: Institute of Policy Studies, 2015.

Business Today. *Evolution of the LTTE and International Networking.* 2011. http://www.businesstoday.lk/article.php?article=3481.

Chalk, P. *Liberation Tigers of Tamil Eelam's (LTTE) International Organization and Operations – A Preliminary Analysis.* Commentary. A Canadian Security Intelligence Service Publication, 1999. https://fas.org/irp/world/para/docs/com77e.htm#N_19_.

Colombage, D. "Crime among Sri Lanka Soldiers on Rise." Al Jazeera/Qatar, 2014. Accessed September 25, 2015, from http://www.lankanewspapers.com/news/2014/6/88305_space.html.

Crime Intelligence Analysis Unit of Police. 2016. Presentation by C. S. K. Millawithanachchi. http://www.unodc.org/documents/data-and-analysis/statistics/Activities/seoul-2016-meeting/Supporting_Capacity_Building_Sri_Lanka.pdf.

De Votta, Neil. "Sri Lanka: From Turmoil to Dynasty." *Journal of Democracy* 22, no. 2 (2011): 130–144. doi:10.1353/jod.2011.0019.

Department of Census and Statistics, Ministry of National Policies and Economic Affairs. *Sri Lanka Labour Force Survey, Annual Bulletin*, Colombo, 2016.

Galbraith, James K. "The Meaning of a War Economy." *Challenge* 44, no. 6 (November–December 2001): 5–12.

Galtung, Johan. "Violence, Peace, and Peace Research." *Journal of Peace Research* 6, no. 3 (1969): 167–191 http://www.jstor.org/stable/422690.

GAN. *Sri Lanka Corruption Report.* 2015. http://www.business-anti-corruption.com/country-profiles/sri-lanka.

Global Humanitarian Assistance: A Development Initiative. *Global Humanitarian Assistance: Sri Lanka Country Profile*, 2015. http://www.globalhumanitarianassistance.org/countryprofile/sri-lanka/.

Goodhand, Jonathan. "From War Economy to Peace Economy? Reconstruction and State Building in Afghanistan." *Journal of International Affairs* 58, no. 1 (Fall 2004): 155–174.

Goodhand, Jonathan. "Frontiers and Wars: The Opium Economy in Afghanistan." *Journal of Agrarian Change* 5 (2005): 191–216. doi:10.1111/j.1471-0366.2005.00099.x.

Goodhand, Jonathan. "Sri Lanka in 2012: Securing the State, Enforcing the 'Peace'." *Asian Survey* 53, no. 1 (2012): 64–72. doi:10.1525/as.2013.53.1.64.

Guruge, S., M. Ford-Gilboe, C. Varcoe, V. Jayasuriya-Illesinghe, M. Ganesan, S. Sivayogan, et al. "Intimate Partner Violence in the Post-war Context: Women's Experiences and Community Leaders' Perceptions in the Eastern Province of Sri Lanka", *PLoS ONE* 12, no. 3 (2017): 1–16. doi:10.1371/journal.pone.0174801.

Holt, Sarah. "The Limits of Formal Metrics during Conflict and Post-conflict Transition: Exploring Opportunities for Qualitative Assessment in Sri Lanka." In *Alternative and Bottom-up Peace Indicators*, edited by Roger Mac Ginty, 9–31. Oxon: Routledge, 2015.

Human Rights Watch. *Sri Lanka: Country Summary.* January 2014. https://www.hrw.org/world-report/2014/country.../sri-lanka.

Human Rights Watch. "Funding the 'Final War' – LTTE Intimidation and Extortion in the Tamil Diaspora." 18, no. 1(C), xxxx-b.

Humphreys, M. "Natural Resources, Conflict, and Conflict Resolution: Uncovering the Mechanisms." *Journal of Conflict Resolution* 49 (2005): 508–537.

ICANS. *What the Women Say: Elusive Peace, Pervasive Violence: Sri Lankan Women's Struggle for Security and Justice*. Brief 8: International Civil Society Action Network, 2013. http://www.icanpeacework.org/wp-content/uploads/2017/03/What-the-Women-Say-SriLanka-Brief-Spring-2013.pdf.

ICJ (International Commission of Jurists). *Authority without Accountability: Crisis of Impunity in Sri Lanka*. 2012. http://www.refworld.org/docid/50ae365b2.html.

ICG (International Crisis Group). *The Forever War?: Military Control in Sri Lanka's North*. March 25, 2014. http://blog.crisisgroup.org/asia/2014/03/25/the-forever-war-military-control-in-sri-lankas-north/.

ICG (International Crisis Group). *Sri Lanka's Transition to Nowhere. Asia Report No. 286*, May 16, 2017, Brussels.

Jayasundara-Smits, Shyamika. "Conflict, War and Peace in Sri Lanka – Politics by other means?" Paper presented at the DSA conference Rethinking Development in an Age of Scarcity and Uncertainty, York University, 2011. https://repub.eur.nl/pub/34768/.

Jayasundara-Smits, Shyamika. *In Pursuit of Hegemony: Politics of State Building in Sri Lanka*." PhD thesis, International Institute of Social Studies, Erasmus University Rotterdam, 2013. repub.eur.nl/pub/40137/ThesisPDC[1].pdf.

Jinadasa, Manoj. "Rate of Crime and the Involvement of Army Soldiers in Post Conflict Society in Sri Lanka; Gender Representation in Crime and Lack of the Psycho – Social Awareness in the Army Profession." *Review of Journalism and Mass Communication* 3, no. 2 (2015): 41–57. doi:10.15640/rjmc.v3n2a2.

Kaldor, Mary. *New and Old Wars: Organised Violence in a Global Era*. 3rd ed. Cambridge: Polity, 2012.

Keen, David. "War and Peace: What's the Difference?" *International Peacekeeping* 7, no. 4 (2007): 1–22.

Kurtenbach, Sabine and Angelica Rettberg. "Understanding the Political, Economic, and Social System after War Termination: War Economies and Post-war Crime: A Framework Prepared for the Second War Economies and Post-war Crime Workshop." German Institute for Global and Area Studies (GIGA), Hamburg, Germany, July 4–5, 2016.

Le Billon, P. "Diamond Wars? Conflict Diamonds and Geographies of Resource Wars" *Annals of the Association of American Geographers* 98 (2008): 345–372.

Liebenberg, Sybert, Richard Haines, and Geoff Harris. "A Theory of War Economies." *African Security Review* 24, no. 3 (2015): 307–323. doi:10.1080/10246029.2015.1075412.

Lindberg, Jonas, and Camilla Orjuela. "Corruption and Conflict: Connections and Consequences in War-torn Sri Lanka." *Conflict, Security & Development* 11, no. 2 (2011): 205–233. doi:10.1080/14678802.2011.572455.

Lindberg, Jonas, and Camilla Orjuela. "Corruption in the Aftermath of War: An Introduction." *Third World Quarterly* 35, no. 5 (2014): 723–736. doi:10.1080/01436597.2014.921421.

Luttwak, Edward N. "Give War a Chance." *Foreign Affairs*, July/August (1999).

Mac Ginty, Roger. "Introduction: The Transcripts of Peace: Public, Hidden or Non-obvious?" *Journal of Intervention and Statebuilding* 7, no. 4 (2013): 423–430. doi:10.1080/17502977.2012.727535.

Mac Ginty, Roger, ed. *Alternative and Bottom-up Peacebuilding*. Routledge, 2015.

Mampilly, Zachariah. "The Nexus of Militarization and Corruption in Post-conflict Sri Lanka." In *Corruption and Post-conflict Peacebuilding: Selling the Peace?*, edited by Dominik Zaum and Christine Cheng, 182–200. London: Routledge, 2012.

Nanayakkara, Wimal. "Can Sri Lanka Eradicate Poverty and Reduce Income Inequality by 2030?" *Institute of Policy Studies* June 3, 2016. http://www.ips.lk/talkingeconomics.

Niriella, M. A. D. S. J. S. "Thinking of new Horizon in Criminal Justice: Moving from Retributive to Restorative Justice in the Treatment of the Offenders in Sri Lanka." In *Handbook of Asian Criminology*, edited by Jianhong Liu, Bill Hebenton, and Susyan Jou, 283–296. New York: Springer, 2013.

Nordstrom, C. "Women, Economy, War." *International Review of the Red Cross*. 97, no. 877 (2010): 161–176.

Pugh, M., N. Cooper, and J. Goodhand. *War Economies in a Regional Context: Challenges and Transformations*. Boulder, CO: Lynne Rienner, 2004.

Reno, W. *Warlord Politics and African States*. Boulder, CO: Lynne Rienner, 1998.

Report of the Leader of the Opposition's Commission on the Prevention of Violence against Women and the Girl Child. 2014. http://www.childwomenmin.gov.lk/resources/30/REPORT.pdf.

Sedra, Mark. "Security Sector Reform in Afghanistan: The Slide Towards Expediency." *International Peacekeeping* 13, no. 1 (2006): 94–110. doi:10.1080/13533310500424868.

Selvanathan, Saroja, and E. A. Selvanathan. "Defence Expenditure and Economic Growth: A Case Study of Sri Lanka Using Causality Analysis." *International Journal of Development and Conflict* 4 (2014): 69–76.

Siddiqa, Ayesha. *Military Inc.: Inside Pakistan's Military Economy*. London: Pluto Press, 2007.

SIPRI. *Military Expenditure by Country, in Local Currency, 1988–2016*. https://www.sipri.org/sites/default/files/Milex-local-currency.pdf.

SIPRI. *Military Expenditure (% of GDP) Yearbook: Armaments, Disarmament and International Security*. http://data.worldbank.org/indicator/MS.MIL.XPND.GD.ZS?view=chart.

Siriwardhana, Krishan. "Post War Media Behavior in Sri Lanka." *Journal of Mass Communication and Journalism* 2, no. 9 (2012): 1–3. doi:10.4172/2165-7912.1000127.

Sri Lanka Tax Guide. Washington, DC and Sri Lanka: International Business Publisher USA, 2008.

Stokke, Kristian. "Building the Tamil Eelam State: Emerging State Institutions and Forms of Governance in LTTE-Controlled Areas in Sri Lanka." *Third World Quarterly* 27, no. 6 (2006): 1021–1040. doi:10.1080/01436590600850434.

Terpstra, N. M., and G. E. Frerks. *Rebel Governance and Legitimacy Civil Wars*, 1–29. ISSN: 1743-968X. 2017.

The World Bank. "Unemployment, Total (% of Total Labor Force) (Modelled ILO Estimate)." http://data.worldbank.org/indicator/SL.UEM.TOTL.ZS?end=2016&locations=LK&start=1991&view=chart.

United Nations Advisory Panel. *Report of the Secretary-General's Panel of Experts on Accountability in Sri Lanka*. March 31, 2011. http://www.un.org/News/dh/infocus/Sri_Lanka/POE_Report_Full.pdf.

United Nations Peacebuilding Office. *Peace Dividends and Beyond: Contributions of Administrative and Social Services to Peacebuilding*. New York: UN, 2012.

United States Department of State. *Trafficking in Persons Report – Sri Lanka*. Sri Lanka, June 27, 2011. www.refworld.org/docid/4e12ee4832.html.

United States Department of State, Bureau of Diplomatic Security. "Sri Lanka 2015 Crime and Safety Report." 2015. www.osac.gov/pages.

Uyangoda, Jayadeva. "Sri Lanka in 2009: From Civil War to Political Uncertainties." *Asian Survey* 50, no. 1 (2010): 104–111 http://www.jstor.org/stable/10.1525/as.2010.50.1.104.

Venugopal, Rajesh. *The Global Dimensions of Conflict in Sri Lanka*. QEH Working Paper Series, QEHWPS 99, Oxford: University of Oxford, 2003.

Venugopal, Rajesh. "The Politics of Market Reform at a Time of Civil War: Military Fiscalism in Sri Lanka." *Economic and Political Weekly* 46, no. 49 (2011): 67–75 http://www.jstor.org/stable/41319460.

Walter, Barbara F. "Conflict Relapse and the Sustainability of Post-conflict Peace." *World Development Report Background Papers; 2011*. Washington, DC: World Bank, 2010.

Watchdog. "State Facilitated Colonization of Northern Sri Lanka – 2013." *Groundviews* September 19, 2013.

Webster, Colin, and Sarah Kingston. *Anti-Poverty Strategies for the UK Poverty and Crime Review*. Centre for Applied Social Research (CeASR) Leeds Metropolitan University, Joseph Rowntree Foundation, May 2014.

Wickramasinghe, Nira. "Sri Lanka in 2013: Post-war Oppressive Stability." *Asian Survey* 54, no. 1 (2014): 199–205. doi:10.1525/as.2014.54.1.199.

Wijeweera, Albert and Matthew J. Webb. "Military Spending and Economic Growth in Sri Lanka: A Time Series Analysis", *Defence and Peace Economics* 20, no. 6 (2009): 499–508. doi:10.1080/10242690902868301.

YPF. *Nexus between Post War Trauma and Increased Violence*. Research Department, 2012. http://www.onetext.org/wp-content/uploads/2013/06/Research-on-the-Nexus-between-the-Post-War-Trauma-and-Increased-Violence-in-Sri-Lanka.pdf.

Zunzer, Wolfram. *Diaspora Communities and Civil Conflict Transformation*. Berghof Occasional Paper No. 26. Berghof Research Centre for Constructive Conflict Management, September, 2004.

Peacebuilding and white-collar crime in post-war natural resource sectors

Philippe Le Billon

ABSTRACT
Post-war situations can present an opportune context for white-collar crime in resource sectors – including corruption, tax evasion, land dispossession, and illegal resource exploitation. This paper investigates various forms of white-collar crime and associated human rights abuses, and points at biased processes of 'criminalization'. Whereas white-collar crime is frequently legitimated under the guise of reconstruction and economic growth strategies, the victims of corruption and resource grabs often become 'criminalised'. Such selective forms of criminalisation reflect a securitisation of resource sectors characterised by repressive forms of resource enclosures and increased socio-economic inequalities; putting resource-related white-collar crime at the core of negative peace economies.

The relationship between durable peace and post-war resource governance poses major challenges.[1] On the one hand, resource exploitation is supposed to help with economic recovery and peace consolidation, as resource sectors can boost post-war recovery through jobs, infrastructures, and tax revenues.[2] On the other hand, resource sectors are understood as conflict-prone and potentially violence-ridden, with the opening up of new 'resource frontiers' disrupting war-time livelihoods and informal entitlements over land and resources and some resources remaining under the control of former insurgent or criminal groups.[3] Operating within a neoliberal peace paradigm securitising (under)development, external actors have generally attempted to consolidate the state through increasing Foreign Direct Investments (FDI) into resource sectors and promoting a wide array of reforms to reduce conflicts, corruption, human rights abuses, and environmental impacts.[4] These reforms, however, often face the problem of entrenched modes of clientelist and authoritarian governance, defining illegality in post-conflict states, criminalising already marginalised communities while powerful economic and political actors profit from resource extraction through legal and illegal means, and transforming post-conflict situations offering an attractive business environment to criminal actors.[5]

This paper seeks to better understand post-war crime in resource sectors through a focus on 'white-collar' criminality, as a form of resource-related crime in post-war contexts in part shaped by neoliberal peacebuilding. The concept of 'white-collar crime' is generally understood as a 'non-violent crime' committed by 'a person of respectability and high social status' in the course of their occupation.[6] Much of the attention on post-war crime and violence has been focused on interpersonal physical forms of violence, and in particular homicides, violent petty crimes, and violence against women.[7] Many critics, however, have pointed at the importance of considering violence not only as direct physical *events*, such as homicides, but also as direct and indirect physical, structural and symbolic *processes*.[8] In turn, such broader conceptualisation of violence helps to understand 'white-collar crime' as a violent process injuring the public.[9] First, white-collar crime can lead to and help reproduce *structural violence*, for example, when perpetrators are in a position to pass unfair laws or when white-collar crime exacerbates inequalities. Second, white-collar crime can result in grave *indirect human rights abuses* as a result of the implementation of processes influenced by white-collar criminality, for example, when local communities are violently displaced by a mining project awarded through a corrupt process denying adequate consultation and compensation. Third, white-collar crime can bring about a higher degree of *indirect physical violence* as people resist white-collar criminality, for example, when protesters face heavy-handed state repression or when prominent activists are assassinated for denouncing corrupt officials and abusive corporations. As such, while this paper focuses on white-collar crime defined in part as 'non-violent' crime, it also attempts to demonstrate the violent and injurious dimensions associated with this type of criminality.

Reflecting the 'respectability' and 'high social status' of perpetrators, white-collar crime is also conceptualised as a breach of trust enabling perpetrators 'to rob without violence and burgle without trespass'.[10] In this respect, white-collar crime often takes the form of a breach of entrusted authority for private gain, thereby echoing the classical definition of corruption. Post-war 'respectability', and perhaps more importantly 'social status', is highly political – especially when hostilities come to an end as a result of elite bargaining and negotiations. Whereas belligerents often qualify their opponents as 'criminals' during hostilities (and frequently treat them as such, rather than as armed combatants protected under the laws of war), the post-war context is often characterised by amnesties and 'national unity' governments that in part remove such element of criminality from the public discourse as well as reshape laws and judicial practices.

In addition, criminality also becomes redefined by the legal framework, judicial institutions, and security practices of the dominant post-war political economy. In this respect, a government can stop 'unlicensed' mining and a corporation may be entitled to make use of private security actors to expel 'illegal' artisanal miners. Similarly, massive wastage of government revenues may not necessarily be a criminal act, even if such waste prevents the delivery of vital health services to the population. If 'criminality' remains defined by law, there is thus a risk that activities injurious to the public end up being permitted or even legitimated by the apparatus and logics of post-war reconstruction; while, in contrast, biased processes of criminalisation target individuals resisting dispossession and protecting land and resource-based subsistence livelihoods. This suggests a need to emphasise the injurious character of criminal acts, rather than their legal definition.

Building on this more nuanced understanding of white-collar crime, this paper bridges three literatures: on the post-war control of resource sectors by armed groups;[11] on post-war patterns of corruption and hybrid governance,[12] and on post-war neoliberalism and the uneven outcomes of reconstruction for local populations including human rights abuses and environmental damages.[13] Whereas criminal activities in conflict-affected countries are generally perceived as the result of hasty demobilisation leaving vast numbers of former members of non-state armed groups with few options but petty criminality, this paper thus brings further attention to the criminal dimensions of processes associated with the post-war reshaping of resource sectors. In this regard, it suggests that current post-war resource management regimes focus disproportionately on the dismantling of war economies benefitting armed groups, and tend to overlook white-collar crime by state or corporate actors that damage prospects for a sustainable and positive peace.

Following this introduction, I first briefly examine the crime–conflict nexus, and policy initiatives on resource-related crime and violence in post-war settings. I then survey three post-war countries (Angola, Cambodia, South Sudan) and their resource management practices, with a specific focus on corruption, tax evasion, and repression of petty resource-based livelihoods such as artisanal mining. These cases were selected through three main criteria: first, these cases involved processes ranging from a nearly undisrupted transfer of war-time economies and power structures in the post-war period to extensive reforms of the resource sector unintendedly promoting new forms of white-collar crime, thereby illustrating the variability of paths leading to resource-related post-war crime; second, these cases involved distinct type of resources, enabling cross-sectoral coverage for diamonds (Angola), forested lands (Cambodia), and oil (South Sudan); third, resources figured prominently in the analysis of peacebuilding and post-war reconstruction for each of these countries, thereby providing an illustration of perspectives and resource governance efforts, as well as sources complementing the author's fieldwork. This comparison is not only useful to contrast the forms of violence and criminality involved, but also to demonstrate the major dilemmas presented to policy-makers and difficulties faced by resource-dependent communities in post-war resource areas.[14] I conclude by suggesting that post-war resource management demands a deeper reconceptualisation of violence and criminality.

To this end, I put forward three main arguments. The first is that, while white-collar crime is often considered as 'non-violent' as it generally does not involve direct and physical violence, it does have violent dimensions. The violence of white-collar crime is notably expressed through resource dispossession depriving people of their livelihoods and public revenue losses reducing the delivery of public services. The second argument is that criminalisation is often reworked through the politics of post-war securitisation: white-collar crime becomes legitimated under the guise of neoliberal principles guiding reconstruction and growth strategies, whereas victims and protesters are frequently criminalised by the state. The last, and related, argument is that these selective forms of criminalisation result in repressive forms of resource enclosures and increased socio-economic inequalities, both of which frequently involve human rights abuses. As such, post-war resource management must not stop at dismantling former conflict economies; corruption, tax evasion, resource grabs, forced displacement and the criminalization of petty resource-based livelihoods and dissent must be prevented in order to bring about a positive and sustainable peace. This suggests a new perspective on 'post-war crime' recognising resource-related white-collar crime – and associated human rights and environmental abuses – as core elements of 'negative peace' economies. Moving towards a positive peace thus requires decriminalising the defence of land, resources, and livelihoods by communities and activists facing 'resource grabs' and repression, while ending the impunity of resource-related white-collar crime and associated human rights abuses.

Addressing the crime–conflict nexus in resource sectors

Resource sectors have come under intense scrutiny from conflict studies over the past two decades.[15] Resource sectors figured prominently within the crime–conflict nexus identified in the 2004 report of the UN High-Level Panel on Threats, Challenges and Change, which emphasised the role of organised crime in enabling the illicit trade of conflict commodities.[16] At the risk of reducing insurgency to 'greed-driven' criminality and interpreting the continuation of violence as motivated by and enabled through financial gains,[17] this perspective has motivated interventions to end the plunder and prevent the emergence of a 'criminalised peace'.[18] In this respect, more attention has been devoted to issues of fairness with regard to socio-economic issues, notably with regard to resources, to reduce the continuation of 'greed-driven' practices.[19] Targeting 'post-war crime' can help in bringing a 'positive peace economy' addressing fairness in resource access, revenue distribution, and the reduction of negative socio-environmental impacts.[20]

Conflicts and crime in resource sectors

Resource sectors are widely perceived to attract armed groups and criminal organisations in search of economic opportunities.[21] Former combatants and army units are frequently involved in illegal resource exploitation and extortion schemes targeting resource companies and workers, while corporate-sponsored military units and private militias frequently expel local residents, artisanal miners, and loggers to make way for new resource concessions. Conflict types and forms of violence can range from land dispossession and forced labour to militarisation and armed skirmishes between competing mining or logging groups.[22] Organised crime already involved in wartime resource economies are also expected to scale-up their operations during a transition to peace, with new criminal organisations attracted by resource windfalls and fledgling transition institutions facilitating criminal opportunities, including money laundering.[23] Such violence and criminality, in turn, supposedly deter more 'reputable' companies from investing and contributing to the consolidation of a 'peace economy'.[24] This argument, however, lacks some nuances.

First, while illicit markets are deemed 'inherently more violent than licit markets', many actors linked to illicit markets – including government authorities – often seek to avoid overt physical violence, preferring instead less costly means of accommodation, including corruption and cartelisation.[25] In the DRC, mining concessions granting seems to reduce violent skirmishes in the vicinity of mining concessions and to displace violence to their broader periphery, possibly because mining entrepreneurs need to secure a 'peaceful' context close to the mines to reduce costs; a process also observed for some diamond mining areas in Sierra Leone.[26] Whereas resource access relied in part on the use of force during a conflict, access becomes granted through administrative and legal procedures backed by more subtle forms of violence including land use planning, resource allocation processes, regulatory reforms, court proceeding and policing.[27] The violent dimensions of these interventions mostly reside in livelihood deprivation for artisanal mining communities through loss of access to mining areas and associated displacement. Changes in the *means* of resource control and the *legalities* of resource exploitation, and associated forms of violence and criminality, thus deserve particular attention when considering the evolution of violence and criminality in resource sectors.

Second, post-war crime is often conceived of as *illegal* exploitation, yet plunder can also occur through legal yet abusive forms of exploitation and government corruption. Companies attracted to post-war countries are frequently those willing to use bribery, deploy private armed protection, and take shortcuts in terms of corporate social responsibility.[28] Domestic authorities and donor agencies eager to fast-track FDI may turn a blind eye to the backgrounds and conduct of these companies. As a result, domestic authorities fail to maximise revenue collection in the public interest, while corporate abuse abound and corruption can thrive as a result of the vast revenues often involved and the discretionary power of government officials exercised over 'national' resources.[29] The result of discretionary power is often exacerbated by weak institutional and legal frameworks, financial incentives towards short-term personal gains by politicians facing high uncertainty, and a frequent state of impunity in the face of past abuses.[30]

Third, emphasis is often placed on consolidating state control over resource sectors, with a focus on informal small-scale ventures offering livelihood opportunities for local populations, yet proving difficult for authorities to control and tax.[31] Governments, in turn, often respond through selective legalisation and criminalisation processes, such as licensing requirements for small-scale mining. The costs and bureaucratic hurdles of legalisation processes, however, are often beyond the reach of small-scale actors, whose activities and protests against 'legal' and often large-scale exploitation are thereby criminalised.[32]

Relationships between conflict, crime, and resources thus do not only involve the presence of criminal organisations in resource sectors, and the illicit exploitation and trading of resources, but also the use of physical violence by non-state actors in resource control, and fraudulent or corrupt practices in resource contracting and revenue allocation.

Curtailing links between conflict and crime

Peacekeeping missions mandated with the implementation of a transition to peace have increasingly recognised the importance of curtailing criminal activities, especially criminal proceeds benefiting peace spoilers. Yet, they are also often aware of the difficulties associated with intervention, and of the many entanglements between peacekeeping missions and illicit businesses, including a tolerance for the smuggling of goods benefiting local populations, and the peace reinforcing aspects of some illicit businesses. In this latter respect, the concepts of '*Pax Mafiosa*', 'shadow state', and 'hybrid governance' are frequently applicable, as criminal networks collude with government officials and customary authorities to shape a more 'business friendly' context and move from openly violent and predatory activities like kidnappings to more parasitic and quasi-legal activities such as tax fraud, money laundering, and large-scale corruption on investments schemes.[33]

As economies evolve during the transition to peace, identifying criminal networks and activities often becomes even more challenging, with close ties between politicians, bureaucrats, and business people active in both legal and illegal sectors for the purposes of electoral funding, bribes, business opportunities, and 'fast' licensing. International community actors can draw false dichotomies between 'good guys' and 'bad guys', by condemning the petty plunder of 'greedy rebel leaders' while overlooking massive corruption by 'elected officials'.[34] Emphasising the blurred boundaries and widespread connections between politicians, 'warlords', and illicit sector entrepreneurs in the case of recent West African conflicts, Reno argues that 'it is best to consider a strategy to incorporate selectively some [criminal] networks and target the more disruptive and predatory'.[35] Legal definitions of crime are also questionable as they reflect disparate and contingent customary, colonial, national, and international texts written by lawmakers of dubious legitimacy. As Van Schendel and Abraham note in their discussion of transnational organised crime, 'many transnational movements of people, commodities, and ideas are illegal because they defy the norms and rules of formal political authority, but they are quite acceptable, "licit", in the eyes of participants in these transactions and flows'.[36] In the case of resource sectors, legalities often reproduce colonial logics of dispossession for local populations. In this respect, many post-war legal reforms reflect a dual process of liberalisation attracting foreign investors and formalisation drawing 'informal' local activities within the shaper dichotomies of legality/criminality, with highly unequal effects.[37] As discussed below through the case studies, casting light on the post-war definition, enforcement, and consequences of (il)legalities can help better understand 'white-collar crime' in resource sectors (Table 1).

White-collar crime in post-war resource sectors

This section revisits three emblematic case studies of 'resource-fuelled' war economies, and discusses some of the criminal dimensions of their post-war transformation. In Angola, the diamond sector was presented as the main source of funding for the main rebel group – *União Nacional para a Independência Total de Angola* (UNITA) – and became the subject of UN sanctions, yet the most harmful effects on artisanal diamond miners occurred following the military victory of the government in 2002. Logging was the main source of income for the Khmer Rouge in Cambodia, and the subject of corrupt practices on the part of a wide range of officials, but the greatest impacts on rural households occurred nearly a decade after the official end of the conflict, with large-scale land concessions affecting an estimated 700,000 rural Cambodians. Finally, in South Sudan, oil had been one of the main economic dimensions of the North-South struggle, yet also provided incentives to bring about a negotiated transition towards peace and independence for the South. Corruption and mismanagement not only wasted an oil windfall, but also added to tensions within southern political factions that contributed to a return of civil war within South Sudan in 2013. These cases not only help to point to the various forms of violence and criminality involved in post-war resource sectors, but also to demonstrate the major dilemmas presented to policy-makers and challenges faced by resource-dependent communities.

Table 1. Overview of case studies.

	Angola	Cambodia	South Sudan
Resources	Diamonds	Timber, land	Oil
Conflict outcome	Negotiated settlements (1991, 1994) followed by military victory (2002)	Negotiated settlement (1991) followed by coup (1997)	Negotiated secession (2005), independence (2011) and civil war (2013–2016)
Ruling party	Incumbent (MPLA)	Incumbent (CPP)	Rebel group (SPLM)
Post-war resource-related crimes	Corruption Repression and extortion of small-scale mining	Corruption Land dispossession Repression of protests	Corruption Forced displacement
Resource-related reforms	Legalisation of ASM	Land titling for small-holders	Stronger anti-corruption commission

Angola, diamond mining, and human rights abuses

Diamonds were a major source of finance for UNITA, the main armed opposition movement, especially during the 1990s.[38] The combination of a peace accord in 1991 and a new mining law legalising the possession and sales of diamonds by individuals resulted in a massive rush, including by nationals from neighbouring DRC. Seeking to formalise and better control the sector through its industrialisation, the government of Angola further opened up the sector to foreign mining companies in 1994 through joint ventures with Angolan partners offering a major opportunity for patronage politics in the awarding of concessions. Following its military victory over UNITA in 2002 the Angolan Government awarded new diamond concessions, many of which connected to senior military officers. Following criticisms of its ill-treatment of artisanal miners, the Angolan Government passed a new law to legalise the artisanal mining sector. Yet, many of its provisions remained the same as in previous legislation, and critics argued that in practice the financial and administrative barriers still 'made it impossible for anyone to ever become legal'.[39]

Human rights activists have raised concerns in four main areas, all of which related to the selective application of diamond-related regulations.[40] The first is the violent process of expulsion of irregular migrants working in mostly artisanal and small-scale diamond mines.[41] Conducted between 2003 and early 2005 during, *Operation Brilhante*, Angolan security forces expulsed an estimated 300,000 irregular migrants, with numerous cases of human rights abuses, including looting, beatings, torture, and systematic cases of women being beaten and raped.[42] The second relates to human rights abuses again 'illegal' artisanal miners to facilitate the industrialisation of the sector.[43] The third area relates to a process of dispossession, intimidation, and impoverishment of many local communities, including through inadequate compensation for land reallocated to diamond concessions, curtailment of freedom of movement through strict control of roads, and drastic restrictions on some forms of traditional livelihoods such as farming and husbandry. The fourth area has been with the lack of transparency over the awarding of diamond mining concessions and allegations of patronage politics, as well as conflicts of interests by politically exposed persons.

In the first three areas, Angolan legislation has enabled security forces and companies to take step to control 'illegal' activities, yet these laws also regulate the ways in which such control is to be exercised. The criminal dimension thus resides in the ways these 'legal' processes are being implemented, the level of impunity protecting offenders, and the responsibilities of higher ranking officials and corporate managers who condone or even incite such abusive practices. Criminal dimensions in the fourth area include corrupt practices and conflict of interest among politically exposed persons, including high ranking military officers. Finally, critiques of abuses in the diamond sector have themselves been to some extent criminalised. Initially facing the threat of a nine-year prison sentence and $1.2 million dollar fine for allegedly defaming army generals for their connection to grave human abuses in the diamond sector, the most prominent journalist working on these issues – Raphael Marques – was given instead a six-month suspended jail sentence after a shortened trial; probably because the incriminated generals preferred not to appear in court. In contrast, very limited efforts have been made to bring about accountability for resource-based white-collar crime and associated human rights abuses. Domestic elites' and foreign governments' interest to access Angolan resources explains in part these abuses and impunity.[44]

Cambodia, land concessions, and dispossession

Cambodia's war economy in the early 1990s was in large part dominated by the logging sector.[45] The selective awarding of concessions and export permits was typical of patronage politics and marred by allegations of corruption, kickbacks, and crony-capitalism.[46] The post-war era saw a diversification of land-based resource sectors from logging concessions to 'economic land concessions' (ELCs) supposed to put to productive use the lands degraded by logging activities, but saw renewed logging (in part to clear land for agricultural purposes) and more permanent forms of land dispossession for local communities. The Land Law passed in 2001 further extended private ownership rights to agricultural lands while nullifying 'temporary possession' and 'acquisition by the plough' – the most widespread forms of ownership among the rural poor as a result of wartime displacements and the loss of records – and requiring a government-issued 'title certificate'.[47] Dispossessed peasants received very little or no compensation, with government leases generally amounting to $1–10 per hectare, compared to about $200 per hectare for leasing between farmers.

In practice, community-level ownership recognition and a largely egalitarian post-war land tenure among rural poor were superseded by 'formal' land titling and large-scale acquisitions backed by violent evictions carried out by police and private militias. Characterised by widespread corruption and nepotism, the Land Law drastically exacerbated power imbalances within society, while the control of the judiciary by the ruling elite conferred a further degree of impunity for wealthy and well-connected groups benefiting from the new system.[48] Seeking to hold on their lands, peasants have relied on a hybrid form of tenure, obtaining titles from the central government when the opportunity for a low-cost transaction arises, but maintaining their informal tenure through community-based social networks and the support of local-level authorities. Such form of tenure, however, is riddled with uncertainty and insecurity, making farmers vulnerable to corrupt and often coercive forms of dispossession. By 2012, ELCs covered an estimated 2.6 million hectares, or 65% of arable lands in the country. About 90 companies, many of them regional investors working in partnership with ruling party-aligned Cambodian politicians and entrepreneurs, controlled about a million hectares.[49] In contrast, only about 100,000 hectares had been allocated to communities through 'social land concessions' (SLCs), prompting critics to argue that the social land concession scheme was a 'deliberate strategy deployed by the Cambodian ruling elite to instrumentalise international aid agencies in formalising displacement and distributional injustices, in smoothing the adverse social impacts of their very own land policies and in minimising resistance by dispossessed rural people'.[50] Between 2000 and 2013, an estimated 77,00,000 people were negatively affected by ELCs, while rural landlessness was estimated to have doubled since the late 1990s.[51] A land titling operation in 2012 was tainted by nepotism, with a study examining a former Khmer Rouge stronghold concluding that titling mostly 'reinforce[d] the patterns of social differentiation initiated by land rent capture practices of early migrants and pushe[d] more vulnerable peasants into seeking wage labor and resorting to job migration'.[52]

Land reforms in Cambodia constituted a violent and criminal form of dispossession as it purposively exploited the (legal) vulnerability of its victims, redistributed (land) assets through coercive means, involved corrupt practices, and harmed individuals dispossessed from their land (both current and future generations) as well as a large part of society since leased land was often turned from food production for local consumption to cash crops for exports. Land concession enforcement also involved a high degree of repression by state security and the militias of politicians and business interests, including the assassination of community activists and shooting of protesters.[53] Beyond pointing out at the lack of judicial redress for farmers losing their land and denouncing the criminalisation of 'land defenders', critics are pushing for the International Criminal Court to investigate and prosecute actors responsible for abuses associated with the land-grabbing crisis in Cambodia.[54]

South Sudan, oil production, and kleptocratic rule

Oil has been embroiled in many of the recurring wars that have devastated South Sudan. The history of oil investments in South(ern) Sudan stems in part from the Yom Kippur war and the oil crisis of 1973, which led western oil companies to look for new reserves outside Organisation of Petroleum Exporting Countries and the US Government to reach for new allies in 'broader Middle East'.[55] Following Chevron's oil find in the southern province of Upper Nile in 1978, the government in Khartoum placed the oil sector under its control by reworking administrative boundaries and built oil-related infrastructure in the north, contrary to demands by southern politicians.[56] Having secured investment partnerships with Canadian and Chinese companies, Khartoum struck agreements with Sudan People's Liberation Movement/Army (SPLM/A) splinter groups from the oil areas and brutally 'cleared out' the area to develop the oil fields and complete a northward pipeline to the Red Sea by 1999.[57] Fast-rising oil revenues consolidated the GoS's security apparatus but created new vulnerabilities associated with the possibility of sabotage, and provided incentives for peace negotiations between North and South. GoS and the SPLM signed a Comprehensive Peace Agreement (CPA) in 2005, establishing a 'joint' government, equally sharing oil revenues, and enabling South Sudanese to vote for independence in 2011.[58] While Khartoum may have distorted the allocation of oil revenues during the CPA-period, the South still received about $12.7 billion in oil revenues between 2005 and 2011, or $192 per person annually, a major cash inflow in this very poor country.[59] Loosing 75% of production and 70% of proven reserves located within South Sudan, Khartoum began charging the Government of South Sudan (GoSS) high-level 'transit fees' and oil-loss compensation payments. In response, GoSS temporarily shut down production in 2012. The shutdown of oil production and mismanagement of prior oil revenues exacerbated tensions within a clientelist South Sudanese Government, contributing to its breaking apart in December 2013 and renewed civil war between factions around President Kiir and Vice-President Machar.[60] Despite resumption of production and exports, South Sudanese payments to Khartoum became unaffordable as oil prices tumbled in 2014 and GoSS started to borrow against future oil revenues.

The criminal dimension of oil governance in South Sudan mostly related to human rights abuses but also the mismanagement and embezzlement of oil revenues generating about 98% of South Sudanese revenues (excluding foreign aid).[61] White-collar crime mostly took place through corruption (including ghost workers salaries and rigged public contracts).[62] In light of the many allegations of corruption, absence of prosecution for corrupt practices, widespread nepotism within civil service recruitment, and poor progress of major infrastructure projects despite massive expenditures, several observers characterised the regime as a kleptocracy.[63] The costs has been immense for the population, with the wastage of billions of US$ in oil windfalls, entrenchment of a corrupt elite, and renewed civil war. International donors are now much more aware of the deadly consequences such 'criminal' practices, and the 2015 peace deal between Kiir and Marchar provides the Anti-Corruption Commission with a mandate to prosecute offenders, but there remains much doubt about its effectiveness as long as the logic of supposedly maintaining political stability through impunity continues to prevail.[64]

Discussion

These three case studies illustrate some of the criminal dimensions arising from post-war transitions in resource sectors. In all cases, the implementation of changes within resource access regimes during the post-war period was characterised by what should be qualified as criminal behaviour. In Angola, a violent crackdown on illegal migrants and artisanal diamond mining combined with an attempt to draw in FDI in the industrial diamond mining within a context marred by conflicts of interests among politically exposed persons. In Cambodia, a new Land Law enabled the allocation of vast economic concessions dispossessing many rural households of their land, while crony capitalism and personal gains from senior politicians seemed widespread. In South Sudan, a peace agreement with the government in Khartoum enabled a more direct access to oil revenues, but governance failures resulted in a massive wastage, widespread allegations of corruption, and aggravated tensions among competing South Sudanese elites once revenues collapsed.

In each case, some measures were taken to address criticisms, but they operated within challenging institutional contexts and were reported to have been often ineffective or even counterproductive. In Angola, critiques of the crackdown, and a realisation that artisanal mining could not be 'eradicated', in part because of the protection of security officials, led to a partial legalisation of artisanal mining. Yet abuses against artisanal miners continued, while the legalisation appeared to act as a barrier for legalised access given the difficulty of obtaining a licence. In Cambodia, critiques of the massive allocation and rising protests led to a rushed land titling that was often biased in favour of companies or exacerbated local-level inequalities in land-holding. In South Sudan, a toughening of anti-corruption measures seemed ineffective, especially given the continued politics of power-sharing and accommodation following the brief return of Riek Machar to the Vice-Presidency in April 2016. All cases involved high levels of impunity, with only minor ranking security officials being put on trial and most of them being acquitted, in contrast with criminalised human rights and community activists, as well as journalists, some of whom faced prison sentences or were murdered.

As mentioned above, the international community has recently given more attention to the crime–conflict nexus, with the UN Security Council seeking to prevent the participation of criminal organisations in resource sectors, the illicit exploitation and trading of resources by non-state armed groups, abusive forms of violence associated with resource control, and fraudulent or corrupt practices in resource contracting and revenue allocation. Greater awareness and funding support have propelled a mainstreaming of counter-crime initiatives in peace operations.[65] Much of this attention, however, has been focused on petty and organised crime, rather than the white-collar criminal dimensions of legal reforms and resource development projects. This focus is understandable from the perspective of immediate and violent threats to peace, and to peacekeepers. Yet, not only does white-collar crime result in serious forms of violence, including physical abuses and dramatic loss of livelihoods among affected populations. It can also result in politically destabilising protests and loss of legitimacy for local authorities, potentially creating a context prone to renewed conflict.

Moreover, the long-term consequences of white-collar crime can include an erosion of the tax base, and thus the long-term welfare of the broad population. Corruption, illegal exploitation, tax evasion, resource dispossession, and the repression of local resource-based livelihoods and community activists thus arguably deserve more attention. National-level efforts in post-war countries are often insufficient given the incentives involved and a frequent lack of capacity. These efforts thus need to be combined with regional and international initiatives to control the assets and conflicts of interests of politically exposed persons; conduct due diligence and fiscal audits of major resource companies and disclose their beneficiary ownership; recognise dispossession and repression as serious human rights abuses under commodity certification schemes; protect local livelihoods and resource access for poor rural households; and end the criminalisation of dissent and impunity of white-collar criminalities.

Conclusion

Post-war transition provides a challenging context for resource governance. New resource regulations, increased investments, and greater market access coming out of the post-war transition can help generate a welcomed peace dividend. Yet, these transformations often entail more restrictive rules and stringent enforcement of resource access, as well as a consolidation of resource sectors by dominant companies, which in turn can undermine the interests of the poor, who lose their land and lack access to the employment and revenues generated by large-scale resource-based activities promoted for mainstream resource-based growth. Among the specific challenges of post-war resource governance figure the dismantling of war economies benefitting armed groups, the transformation of clientelistic modes of resource entitlement and revenue allocation, and the balancing of large-scale investments, informal local livelihoods, and environmental concerns.

Preventing white-collar crime and holding perpetrators accountable require a wide range of reforms and implementation mechanisms ranging from anti-corruption tools to tax evasion prevention measures.[66] Recognising and protecting the rights to land, resources and livelihoods of populations in post-war 'resource frontiers' regions may be among the most effective pre-emptive measures, including through the creation of 'no-go' areas for mining and agro-industrial projects. Legislating and enforcing such measures requires broad coalitions challenging the vested interests of domestic elites and commercial agendas of international actors. Enforcement, in this regard, is particularly challenging as post-war demilitarisation of resource economies is often partial or biased. Not only are public security forces often ordered to protect corporate interests rather than the public, but security officers also frequently provide privatised security services to resource concessionaires, obtain stakes in large-scale ventures in exchange for 'pacifying' resource areas, or expropriate land and set up their own resource companies. In contrast, insurgent groups that may have played a role in 'protecting' the informal livelihoods and land entitlements of local communities have been disbanded or co-opted. Such situations can leave local population at the mercy of white-collar crime, especially when more peaceful means of community protection such as civil society organisations and peasant associations face repressive measures ranging from restrictive laws to targeted assassinations.[67] In this respect, a major but still debated dimension of peacebuilding rests on the mobilisation of 'popular resistance to all forms of violence', including those associated with white-collar criminality.[68] Rising opposition against corruption, tax evasion, and 'resource grabs' forms part of the register of this growing resistance.

The post-war securitisation of resource sector, however, often threatens resistance through the criminalisation of dissent and coping economies, including repression of aggrieved peasants, informal resource users, and critical civil society members. As noted by the International Criminal Court's Office of the Prosecutor, the pattern of impunity often associated with grave human rights abuses against rural communities and their environment demand that consideration be given to 'prosecuting Rome Statute crimes that are committed by means of, or that result in, *inter alia*, the destruction of the environment, the illegal exploitation of natural resources or the illegal dispossession of land'.[69] Overlooking white-collar crime not only undermines a 'just' post-war recovery, but also the prospects of a sustainable positive peace.

Disclosure statement

No potential conflict of interest was reported by the author.

Funding

This work was supported by SSHRC and CIRDI.

Notes

1. Bannon and Collier, *Natural Resources*; Grzybowski, *Toolkit and Guidance*; Lujala and Rustad, *High-value Natural Resources*.
2. Lujala and Rustad, "A Price Worth Fighting."
3. Tsing, "Natural Resources and Capitalist Frontiers"; Le Billon, *Wars of Plunders*; Reno, "Understanding Criminality"; Baird and Le Billon, "Landscapes of Political Memories"; Bayer and Pabst, "Heroes and Victims."
4. Duffield, *Global Governance*; Cooper, "Picking out the Pieces"; Roy, "Stabilize, Rebuild." The bulk of these initiatives have targeted extractive sectors, including logging, mining, oil and gas, with renewed attention to large-scale land acquisition and agro-businesses.
5. Unruh and Williams, *Land and Post-conflict*; Van Leeuwen and Van Der Haar, "Theorizing the Land–Violent Conflict Nexus."
6. The term white-collar crime was coined and defined by sociologist Edwin Sutherland in 1949, see Sutherland, *White Collar Crime*. The FBI defines it as 'those illegal acts which are characterized by deceit, concealment, or violation of trust and which are not dependent upon the application or threat of physical force or violence'. White-collar crime is not necessarily illegal, as it might not be prohibited by law or can even be legalized by vested interests. This can particularly be the case in post-conflict settings awaiting progressive legal reforms. See also Payne, *White-collar Crime*.

7. Berdal and Suhrke, *The Peace in Between*; Tsing, "Natural Resources and Capitalist Frontiers."
8. Tyner and Inwood, "Violence as fetish Geography."
9. On white-collar crimes on the environment, see Payne, *White-collar Crime*.
10. Shapiro, "Collaring the Crime," 346.
11. See notably, Le Billon, *Wars of Plunders*; Lujala and Rustad, *High-value Natural Resources*.
12. See, Belloni and Strazzari, "Corruption in Post-conflict"; Cheng and Zaum, *Corruption and Post-conflict*; Meagher, "Smuggling Ideologies"; Reno, *Corruption and State Politics*.
13. Cooper, "Picking Out the Pieces"; Maconachie, "The Extractive Industries"; Vogel and Raeymaekers, "Terr (it) or (ies) of Peace."
14. Le Billon, *Wars of Plunders*; for a statistical analysis of resource-related peacebuilding initiatives, see Rustad et al. "Do Resource-related Peacebuilding."
15. Koubi et al., "Do Natural Resources Matter."
16. de Boer and Bosetti, "The Crime-conflict"; United Nations, *A More Secured World*.
17. Collier and Hoeffler, "Greed and Grievance"; Keen, *The Economic Functions of Violence*; Autesserre, "Dangerous Tales"; Le Billon, *Wars of Plunders*.
18. Ballentine and Nitzschke, *Profiting from Peace*; Le Billon and Nicholls, "Ending Resource Wars"; Cockayne, "Winning Haiti's Protection."
19. Matthew et al., *From Conflict to Peacebuilding*.
20. On the concept of 'positive peace economy' addressing some of these issues, and more generally 'whereby economic relationships not only have no obvious association with direct/physical violence, but also are free of structural violence and support just and sustainable peace', see Peterson, *Building a Peace Economy*.
21. Koubi et al., "Do natural Resources Matter for Interstate and Intrastate Armed Conflict?"; Caxaj et al., "Promises of Peace"; Drohan, *Making a Killing*; de Morais, *Diamond Extraction*.
22. Zhukov, "Roads and the Diffusion"; Massé and Le Billon, "Gold Mining in Colombia"; Le Billon, *Wars of Plunders*.
23. Bergenas and Knight, "Green Terror."
24. Interest by resource companies will depend on a host of factors, including political risks, including security and reputational risks, as well as commercial considerations, including reserve characteristics, resource prices, exploration and development costs, financing opportunities, competing resource projects and the broad economic conjuncture. For a discussion, see Bray, "Attracting Reputable Companies."
25. Andreas and Wallman, "Illicit Markets"; Naylor, "Violence and Illegal Economic Activity."
26. Maystadt et al., "Mineral Resources"; Le Billon, "Diamond Wars."
27. Blomley, "Law, Property."
28. While some of these practices may not constitute white-collar crime, they can act as destabilizing factors resulting in conflicts and further repression, see Conde and Le Billon, "Why Do Some Communities Resist."
29. Kolstad and Soreide, "Corruption in Natural Resource"; Le Billon, *Extractive Sectors*.
30. Cheng and Zaum, "Corruption and Post-conflict."
31. Snyder, "Does Lootable Wealth."
32. Tschakert, "Recognizing and Nurturing"; Geenen, "A Dangerous Bet"; Jackson, "Making a Killing."
33. Andreas, "Symbiosis Between Peace"; Reno, *Corruption*; for a critique of hybrid political orders, see Mac Ginty and Richmond, "The Fallacy of Constructing."
34. Marchal, "Peace Operations."
35. Reno, "Understanding Criminality," 49.
36. Van Schendel and Abraham, *Illicit Flows*, 4.
37. Putzel et al., "Formalization," 453.
38. Cleveland, *Diamonds in the Rough*; Dietrich, "Power Struggle."
39. PAC, *Diamonds and Human Security*.
40. de Morais, *Diamond Extraction*; Human Rights Watch, *If You Come Back*.
41. De Boeck, "Garimpeiro Worlds."
42. Human Rights Watch, *If You Come Back*; MSF, *Les femmes témoignent*.
43. De Boeck, "Diamonds and Disputes"; de Morais, *Diamond Extraction*.

44. Pérez Nino and Le Billon, "Foreign Aid"; Malca and Skaar, "Negative Peace."
45. Global Witness, *Forests, Famine and War*.
46. Global Witness, *Deforestation Without Limits*; Le Billon, "The Political Ecology."
47. Springer, "Illegal Evictions."
48. Oldenburg and Neef, "Reversing Land Grabs."
49. ADHOC, *A Turning Point*.
50. Neef et al., "The Politics and Ethics," 1085.
51. ADHOC, *Land Situation in 2013*.
52. Global Witness, *Hostile Takeover*; Diepart and Sem, "Fragmented Territories," 1.
53. Human Rights Watch, *Cambodia*.
54. Tat and Bagshaw, "A Search for Justice"; Embree, "Criminalizing Land-grabbing"; Oehm, "Land Grabbing."
55. Ayers, "Sudan's Uncivil War"; Patey, *The New Kings of Crude*.
56. Ayers, "Sudan's Uncivil War"; Kok, "Adding Fuel"; Hutchinson, *Nuer Dilemmas*.
57. Rone, *Sudan, Oil, and Human Rights*.
58. Rolandsen, "A Quick Fix."
59. Data collated by author from GoSS Ministry of Finance and IMF 'South Sudan' country reports.
60. Pinaud, "South Sudan"; Le Billon and Savage, "Binding Pipelines."
61. James, *Fields of Control*.
62. Sentry, *The Nexus of Corruption*.
63. De Waal, "When Kleptocracy"; Pinaud, "South Sudan."
64. Mayai, *Assessing Anti-corruption*.
65. Hansen, "The Organized Crime-peace."
66. Le Billon, *Extractive Sectors and Illicit Financial Flows*.
67. Global Witness, *How Many More?*
68. Luckham, "Whose Violence, Whose Security?"
69. ICC, *Policy Paper*, 14.

Bibliography

ADHOC. *A Turning Point? Land, Housing and Natural Resources Rights in Cambodia in 2012*. Phnom Penh: ADHOC, 2013.

ADHOC. *Land Situation in 2013*. Phnom Penh: ADHOC, 2014.

Andreas, P. "Symbiosis between Peace Operations and Illicit Business in Bosnia." *International Peacekeeping* 16, no. 1 (2009): 33–46.

Andreas, P., and J. Wallman. "Illicit Markets and Violence: What is the Relationship?" *Crime, Law and Social Change* 52, no. 3 (2009): 225–229.

Autesserre, S. "Dangerous Tales: Dominant Narratives on the Congo and Their Unintended Consequences." *African Affairs* 111, no. 443 (2012): 202–222.

Ayers, A. J. "Sudan's Uncivil War: The Global Historical Constitution of Political Violence." *Review of African Political Economy* 37, no. 124 (2010): 153–171.

Baird, Ian G., and Philippe Le Billon. "Landscapes of Political Memories: War Legacies and Land Negotiations in Laos." *Political Geography* 31, no. 5 (2012): 290–300.

Ballentine, K., and H. Nitzschke. *Profiting from Peace: Managing the Resource Dimensions of Civil War*. Boulder, CO: Lynne Rienner, 2004.

Bannon, I., and P. Collier. *Natural Resources and Violent Conflict: Options and Actions*. Washington, DC: World Bank, 2003.

Basanisi, M. 2008. "Who Will Watch the Peacekeepers?" *New York Times*, May 23.

Bayer, Markus, and Andrea Pabst. "Heroes and Victims: Economies of Entitlement after Violent Pasts." *Peacebuilding* (2017): 1–16.

Belloni, R., and F. Strazzari. "Corruption in Post-conflict Bosnia-Herzegovina and Kosovo: A Deal among Friends." *Third World Quarterly* 35, no. 5 (2014): 855–871.

Berdal, M., and A. Suhrke. *The Peace in between: Post-war Violence and Peacebuilding*. Abingdon: Routledge, 2013.

Bergenas, J., and A. Knight. "Green Terror: Environmental Crime and Illicit Financing." *SAIS Review of International Affairs* 35, no. 1 (2015): 119–131.

Blomley, N. "Law, Property, and the Geography of Violence: The Frontier, the Survey, and the Grid." *Annals of the Association of American Geographers* 93, no. 1 (2003): 121–141.

Bray, J. "Attracting Reputable Companies to Risky Environments: Petroleum and Mining Companies." In *Natural Resources and Armed Conflicts: Options and Actions*, edited by I. Bannon and P. Collier, 287–352. Washington, DC: World Bank, 2003.

Brisman, A., N. South, and R. White. *Environmental Crime and Social Conflict: Contemporary and Emerging Issues*. London: Routledge, 2015.

Caxaj, C. S., H. Berman, J.-P. Restoule, C. Varcoe, and S.L. Ray. "Promises of Peace and Development: Mining and Violence in Guatemala." *Advances in Nursing Science* 36, no. 3 (2013): 213–228.

Cheng, C., and D. Zaum. *Corruption and Post-conflict Peacebuilding*. London: Routledge, 2012.

Cleveland, T. *Diamonds in the Rough: Corporate Paternalism and African Professionalism on the Mines of Colonial Angola, 1917–1975*. Athens: Ohio University Press, 2015.

Cockayne, J. "Winning Haiti's Protection Competition: Organized Crime and Peace Operations past, Present and Future." *International Peacekeeping* 16, no. 1 (2009): 77–99.

Cockayne, J., and A. Lupel. *Peace Operations and Organized Crime: Enemies or Allies?*. London: Routledge, 2011.

Collier, P., and A. Hoeffler. "Greed and Grievance in Civil War." *Oxford Economic Papers* 56, no. 4 (2004): 563–595.

Conde, M., and P. Le Billon. 2017. "Why Do Some Communities Resist Mining Projects While Others Do Not?" *The Extractive Industries and Society*.

Cooper, N. "Picking out the Pieces of the Liberal Peaces: Representations of Conflict Economies and the Implications for Policy." *Security Dialogue* 36, no. 4 (2005): 463–478.

De Boeck, F. "Garimpeiro Worlds: Digging, Dying & 'Hunting' for Diamonds in Angola." *Review of African Political Economy* 28, no. 90 (2001): 549–562.

de Boer, J., and L. Bosetti. "The Crime-conflict 'Nexus': State of the Evidence." *Occasional Paper* 5 (2015): 9.

de Morais, R. M. *Diamond Extraction and Crimes against Humanity in Northeastern Angola*. Luanda: Maka Angola, 2012.

De Waal, A. "When Kleptocracy Becomes Insolvent: Brute Causes of the Civil War in South Sudan." *African Affairs* 113, no. 452 (2014): 347–369.

Diepart, J. C., and T. Sem. "Fragmented Territories: Incomplete Enclosures and Agrarian Change on the Agricultural Frontier of Samlaut District, North-West Cambodia." *Journal of Agrarian Change* (2016): doi:10.1111/joac.12155.

Dietrich, C. "Power Struggle in the Diamond Fields." In *Angola's War Economy*, edited by J. Cilliers and C. Dietrich. Pretoria: Institute for Security Studies, 2000.

Drohan, M. *Making a Killing: How and Why Corporations Use Armed Force to Do Business*. Toronto: Random House, 2003.

Duffield, M. *Global Governance and the New Wars: The Merging of Development and Security*. London: Zed Books, 2001.

Embree, J. "Criminalizing Land-grabbing: Arguing for ICC Involvement in the Cambodian Land Concession Crisis." *Fla. J. Int'l L.* 27 (2015): 399–420.

Gleick, P. H. "Water, Drought, Climate Change, and Conflict in Syria." *Weather, Climate, and Society* 6, no. 3 (2014): 331–340.

Global Witness. *Forests, Famine and War: The Key to Cambodia's Future*. London: Global Witness, 1995.

Witness, Global. *Deforestation without Limits: How the Cambodian Government Failed to Tackle the Untouchables*. London: Global Witness, 2002.

Witness, Global. *Hostile Takeover: The Corporate Empire of Cambodia's Ruling Family*. London: Global Witness, 2016.

Witness, Global. *How Many More?*. London: Global Witness, 2015.

Goodhand, J. "From War Economy to Peace Economy? Reconstruction and State Building in Afghanistan." *Journal of International Affairs* (2004): 155–174.

Grzybowski, A. *Toolkit and Guidance for Preventing and Managing Land Natural Resources Conflict. Extractive Industries and Conflict*. New York: United Nations Interagency Framework Team for Preventive Action, 2012.

Guidolin, M., and E. La Ferrara. "Diamonds Are Forever, Wars Are Not: Is Conflict Bad for Private Firms?" *American Economic Review* 97, no. 5 (2007): 1978–1993.

Hansen, W. "The Organized Crime-peace Operations Nexus." *Prism: A Journal of the Center for Complex Operations* 5, no. 1 (2014): 62.

Human Rights Watch. *If You Come Back We Will Kill You: Sexual Violence and Other Abuses against Congolese Migrants during Expulsions from Angola*, New York, 2012.

Human Rights Watch. *Cambodia: Land Titling Campaign Open to Abuse*, 2013.

Humphreys, M., J. D. Sachs, and J. E. Stiglitz. *Escaping the Resource Curse*. New York: Columbia University Press, 2007.

Hutchinson, S. E. *Nuer Dilemmas: Coping with Money, War, and the State*. Berkeley: University of California Press, 1996.

ICC. *Policy Paper on Case Selection and Prioritisation*. The Hague: Office of the Prosecutor. International Criminal Court, 2016.

Jackson, S. "Making a Killing: Criminality & Coping in the Kivu War Economy." *Review of African Political Economy* 29, no. 93–94 (2002): 517–536.

James, L. M. *Fields of Control: Oil and (in)Security in Sudan and South Sudan*. Small Arms Survey, 2015.

Keen, D. *The Economic Functions of Violence in Civil Wars*. London: International Institute of Strategic Studies, 1998.

Klare, M. *Rising Powers, Shrinking Planet: The New Geopolitics of Energy*. New York: Metropolitan Books, 2008.

Kok, P. N. "Adding Fuel to the Conflict: Oil, War and Peace in the Sudan." In *Beyond Conflict in the Horn*, edited by L. Cliffe, M. A. Abdel Ghaffar, and M. Doornbos, 104–111. London: James Currey, 1992.

Kolstad, I., and T. Soreide. "Corruption in Natural Resource Management: Implications for Policy Makers." *Resources Policy* 34, no. 4 (2009): 214–226.

Korf, B. "War, Livelihoods and Vulnerability in Sri Lanka." *Development and Change* 35, no. 2 (2004): 275–295.

Koubi, V., G. Spilker, T. Bohmelt, and T. Bernauer "Do Natural Resources Matter for Interstate and Intrastate Armed Conflict?" *Journal of Peace Research* 51, no. 2 (2014): 227–243.

Le Billon, P. "The Political Ecology of Transition in Cambodia 1989–1999: War, Peace and Forest Exploitation." *Development & Change* 31, no. 4 (2000): 784–805.

Le Billon, P. "Diamond Wars? Conflict Diamonds and Geographies of Resource Wars." *Annals of the Association of American Geographers* 98, no. 2 (2008): 345–372.

Le Billon, P. *Extractive Sectors and Illicit Financial Flows: What Role for Revenue Governance Initiatives?* Bergen: U4 Anti-Corruption Centre, 2011.

Le Billon, P. "Bankrupting Peace Spoilers: Can Peacekeepers Curtail Belligerents' Access to Resource Revenues." In *High-value Natural Resources and Post-conflict Peacebuilding*, 25–48. London: EarthScan, 2012.

Le Billon, P. *Wars of Plunders: Conflicts, Profits and the Politics of Resources*. New York: Oxford University Press, 2013.

Le Billon, P., and E. Nicholls. "Ending 'Resource Wars': Revenue Sharing, Economic Sanction or Military Intervention?" *International Peacekeeping* 14, no. 5 (2007): 613–632.

Le Billon, P., and E. Savage. "Binding Pipelines? Oil, Civil Wars, and Economic Rationales for Peace in the Two Sudans." *African Geographical Review* 35 (2016): 134–150. doi:10.1080/19376812.2015.1113551.

Luckham, R. "Whose Violence, Whose Security? Can Violence Reduction and Security Work for Poor, Excluded and Vulnerable People?" *Peacebuilding* 5, no. 2 (2017): 1–19.

Lujala, P., and S. A. Rustad, eds. *High-value Natural Resources and Post-Conflict Peacebuilding*. Abingdon: Routledge, 2011.

Lujala, P., and S. A. Rustad. "A Price Worth Fighting for? Natural Resources and Conflict Recurrence." *Journal of Peace Research* 49, no. 4 (2012): 531–546.

Mac Ginty, R., and O. Richmond. "The Fallacy of Constructing Hybrid Political Orders: A Reappraisal of the Hybrid Turn in Peacebuilding." *International Peacekeeping* 23, no. 2 (2016): 219–239.

Maconachie, R. "The Extractive Industries, Mineral Sector Reform and Post-conflict Reconstruction in Developing Countries." *The Extractive Industries and Society* 3, no. 2 (2016): 313–315.

Malca, C. G., and E. Skaar. "Negative Peace and Autocracy in the Shadow of Impunity. In *After Violence: Transitional Justice, Peace, and Democracy*, edited by Elin Skaar, E., C. Gianella, and T. Eide, 149–173. London: Routledge, 2015.

Marchal, R. "Peace Operations and International Crime: The Case of Somalia." In *Peace Operations and Organized Crime: Enemies or Allies*, edited by J. Cockayne, and A. Lupel, 84–98. London: Routledge, 2011.

Massé, F., and P. Le Billon. "Gold Mining in Colombia, Post-war Crime and the Peace Agreement with the FARC." *Third World Thematics* (2017).

Matthew, R. A., O. Brown, and D. Jensen. *From Conflict to Peacebuilding: The Role of Natural Resources and the Environment* (no. 1). UNEP/Earthprint, 2009.

Mayai, A. T. *Assessing Anti-corruption, Accountability, and Transparency Measures in South Sudan*. Juba: Sudd Institute, 2015.

Maystadt, J.-F., G. De Luca, P. G. Sekeris, and J. M. Ulimwengu. "Mineral Resources and Conflicts in DRC: A Case of Ecological Fallacy?" *Oxford Economic Papers* 66, no. 3 (2014): 721–749.

Meagher, K. "Smuggling Ideologies: From Criminalization to Hybrid Governance in African Clandestine Economies." *African Affairs* 113, no. 453 (2014): 497–517.

Montague, D. "The Business of War and the Prospects for Peace in Sierra Leone." *Brown Journal of World Affairs* 9, no. 1 (2002): 229–237.

Montague, D. "Stolen Goods: Coltan and Conflict in the Democratic Republic of Congo." *SAIS Review* 22, no. 1 (2002): 103–118.

MSF. *Les femmes témoignent: Cent femmes racontent leur calvaire Angolais*. Médecins Sans Frontières, 2007, December.

Naylor, R. T. "Violence and Illegal Economic Activity: A Deconstruction." *Crime, Law and Social Change* 52, no. 3 (2009): 231–242.

Neef, A., S. Touch, and J. Chiengthong. "The Politics and Ethics of Land Concessions in Rural Cambodia." *Journal of Agricultural and Environmental Ethics* 26, no. 6 (2013): 1085–1103.

Oehm, F. M. "Land Grabbing in Cambodia as a Crime against Humanity-approaches in International Criminal Law." *VRÜ Verfassung in Recht Und Übersee* 48, no. 4 (2016): 469–490.

Oldenburg, C., and A. Neef. "Reversing Land Grabs or Aggravating Tenure Insecurity? Competing Perspectives on Economic Land Concessions and Land Titling in Cambodia." *Law and Development Review* 7, no. 1 (2014): 49–77.

PAC. *Diamonds and Human Security. Annual Review 2009*. Ottawa: Partnership Africa Canada, 2009.

Payne, B. K. *White-collar Crime: The Essentials*. Thousand Oaks, CA: Sage, 2016.

Patey, L. *The New Kings of Crude: China, India, and the Global Struggle for Oil in Sudan and South Sudan*. Oxford: Oxford University Press, 2014.

Pérez Niño, H., and P. Le Billon. "Foreign Aid, Resource Rents, and State Fragility in Mozambique and Angola." *The ANNALS of the American Academy of Political and Social Science* 656, no. 1 (2014): 79–96.

Peterson, J. *Building a Peace Economy? Liberal Peacebuilding and the Development-security Industry*. Oxford: Oxford University Press, 2014.

Pinaud, C. "South Sudan: Civil War, Predation and the Making of a Military Aristocracy." *African Affairs* 113, no. 451 (2014): 192–211.

Putzel, L., A. B. Kelly, P. O. Cerutti, and Y. Artati. "Formalization as Development in Land and Natural Resource Policy." *Society and Natural Resources* 28, no. 5 (2015): 453–472.

Reno, W. *Corruption and State Politics in Sierra Leone*. Cambridge: Cambridge University Press, 1995.

Reno, W. "Understanding Criminality in West African Conflicts." *International Peacekeeping* 16, no. 1 (2009): 47–61.

Rolandsen, ò. H. "A Quick Fix? A Retrospective Analysis of the Sudan Comprehensive Peace Agreement." *Review of African Political Economy* 38, no. 130 (2011): 551–564.

Rone, J. *Sudan, Oil, and Human Rights*. Washington, DC: Human Rights Watch, 2003.

Roy, Vita. "Stabilize, Rebuild, Prevent?: An Overview of Post-conflict Resource Management Tools." *The Extractive Industries and Society* 4, no. 1 (2017): 227–234.

Rustad, S. A., H. Binningsbø, and P. Le Billon. "Do Resource-related Peacebuilding Initiatives Build Peace." Paper Presented at the Annual Convention for the International Studies Association, 2009.
Schouten, P. *Extractive Orders: A Political Geography of Public Authority in Ituri, DR Congo*. London: JSRP/LSE, 2016.
Shapiro, S. P. "Collaring the Crime, Not the Criminal: Reconsidering the Concept of White-collar Crime." *American Sociological Review* (1990): 346–365.
Smith, D. 2015. "Angolan Journalist given Suspended Jail Term over Blood Diamonds Book." *The Guardian*, May 28.
Snyder, R. "Does Lootable Wealth Breed Disorder? A Political Economy of Extraction Framework." *Comparative Political Studies* 39, no. 8 (2006): 943–968.
Springer, S. "Illegal Evictions? Overwriting Possession and Orality with Law's Violence in Cambodia." *Journal of Agrarian Change* 13, no. 4 (2013): 520–546.
Sutherland, E. H. *White Collar Crime – The Uncut Version*. New Haven, CT: Yale University Press, 1949/1983.
Tat, P., and D. M. Bagshaw. "A Search for Justice and Rights in Land Dispute Resolution in Cambodia." *Conflict Resolution Quarterly* 32, no. 2 (2014): 203–229.
The Sentry. *The Nexus of Corruption and Conflict in South Sudan*. Washington, DC: The Sentry, 2015.
The Sentry. *War Crimes Shouldn't Pay. Stopping the Looting and Destruction in South Sudan*. Washington, DC: The Sentry, 2016.
Tschakert, P. "Recognizing and Nurturing Artisanal Mining as a Viable Livelihood." *Resources Policy* 34, no. 1 (2009): 24–31.
Tsing, A. L. "Natural Resources and Capitalist Frontiers." *Economic and Political Weekly* 38, no. 48 (2003): 5100–5106.
Tyner, J., and J. Inwood. "Violence as Fetish: Geography, Marxism, and Dialectics." *Progress in Human Geography* 38, no. 6 (2014): 771–784.
United Nations. *A More Secured World: Our Shared Responsibility*. Report of the High-level Panel on Threats, Challenges and Change. A/59/565, 2004.
Unruh, J., and R. Williams. *Land and Post-conflict Peacebuilding*. London: Routledge, 2013.
Van Leeuwen, M., and G. Van Der Haar. "Theorizing the Land-violent Conflict Nexus." *World Development* 78 (2016): 94–104.
Van Schendel, W., and I. Abraham, eds. *Illicit Flows and Criminal Things: States, Borders, and the Other Side of Globalization*. Bloomington: Indiana University Press, 2005.
Weinstein, J. M. *Inside Rebellion: The Politics of Insurgent Violence*. Cambridge: Cambridge University Press, 2007.
Williams, A., and P. Le Billon. *Corruption, Natural Resources and Development: From Resource Curse to Political Ecology*. Cheltenham: Elgar, 2017.
Zhukov, Y. M. "Roads and the Diffusion of Insurgent Violence: The Logistics of Conflict in Russia's North Caucasus." *Political Geography* 31, no. 3 (2012): 144–156.

Large-scale land acquisitions and violence in post-war societies

Annegret Kuhn

ABSTRACT
Integrating theoretical assumptions from peace and conflict research and insights from development and agricultural studies, the paper scrutinises the specific mechanisms linking large-scale land acquisitions (LSLAs) and different types of violence and crime in post-war societies. The case study of Cambodia is used to demonstrate how the particular mechanisms work and interact. Insights from the paper indicate that, under the given post-war context conditions, LSLAs contribute to the perpetuation and consolidation of an illegal and violence-inducing entanglement of political power and economic interests among agro-investors, state actors and military forces. This nexus can be traced back to the historical legacy of civil war through various mechanisms – notably, the interplay of weak political institutions, widespread corruption and extreme power asymmetries. The legacy of war also continues through the persistence of war economy structures such as illegal logging, which is becoming intertwined with large-scale agricultural investments.

Introduction

There has been a new wave of large-scale land acquisitions (LSLAs) since the beginning of the twenty-first century.[1] Due to the secrecy surrounding most LSLAs, their exact number is highly disputed. The Land Matrix Global Observatory – currently the most comprehensive database available – records that 1549 large-scale land deals or about 86 million hectares of land were acquired in the Global South and eastern Europe by foreign investors alone from 2000 until April 2016.[2] LSLAs predominantly take place in the countries of the Global South and the top 10 target countries are shown in Table 1.

Four of the listed countries experienced a major internal armed conflict prior to the LSLAs-boom according to the commonly used definition and data of the Correlates of War Project.[3] The high prevalence of LSLAs in post-war settings has also been confirmed by various other empirical studies.[4]

This is partly due to the fact that foreign investment in the form of large-scale land acquisitions (LSLAs) is often highly welcomed by the governments of post-war countries[5] in the Global South. These land acquisitions are considered able to provide (local) development

Table 1. Number of Land Deals Worldwide (as of 2016).

Country:	Number of land deals (between 2000 and April 2016)
Indonesia	123
Cambodia	95
Ethiopia	61
Mozambique	60
Laos	49
Brazil	45
Papua New Guinea	34
Argentina	26
Zambia	26
Russia	25

Source: Nolte, Chamberlain and Giger 2016, 18.

opportunities and may, thus, indirectly also act as a catalyst for the consolidation of peace. Numerous empirical examples have shown, however, that this is not always actually the case. In fact, such land deals can exacerbate different types of internal violence[6], thereby preventing a stable transition process from war to peace as well as spurring social conflict, human rights violations and other forms of interrelated post-war crimes such as the forceful displacement of local peasants, the threatening or killing of land restitution claimants and endemic corruption.

There is a growing number of publications on local resistance, conflict and violence in the context of LSLAs. [7] However, studies systematically analysing the historical trajectories of violence in the specific context of LSLAs in post-war societies are still rare – despite the fact that these societies are generally considered to be particularly prone to a resurgence of internal violent conflict and crime.[8] To address this research gap, the paper scrutinises specific context conditions and especially potential mechanisms linking LSLAs and different, interacting types of violence and crime in post-war countries. Special focus is placed on the historical legacies of war economies and how they shape land-related violence. The case study of Cambodia is used as an example to demonstrate how the theoretically derived mechanisms work on the ground.

As post-war societies differ with regard to historical, political, and socio-economic contextual settings and, not least, the nature of the internal violent conflict, the findings of this paper are not automatically transferable to all other post-war settings with LSLAs. However, there are a number of crucial characteristics present in a wide range of post-war societies to a substantially higher degree than in other countries, and which seem to have a pronounced and distinct impact on internal violence in the context of LSLAs.

The paper proceeds as follows: the following section briefly summarises the global dynamics of LSLAs, highlighting their enhanced presence in post-war societies. The third section then discusses the more general opportunities and especially the risks of LSLAs for the dynamics of local conflict and different types of violence, and presents an overview of the existing literature thereon. In the fourth section, more specific focus is placed on the underlying mechanisms linking LSLAs and local violence and crime in post-war societies. The theoretically derived assumptions are subsequently illustrated and further refined through a case study of Cambodia, one of the leading target countries of LSLAs in the Global South.[9] The last section brings the paper to a close by summarising and discussing findings, and by highlighting possible avenues for further research.

Large-scale land acquisitions and dynamics of violence

Principally, LSLAs entail both diverse risks and opportunities for socio-economic development, internal stability and peace within the target countries – or more particularly in the affected local communities. Empirical insights derived from existing studies – mostly within Development and Agricultural Studies – are far from being conclusive however, and the overall consequences of LSLAs are hence still controversial.

On the local level, LSLAs imply economic development opportunities and potential subsequent poverty alleviation effects through the provision of public goods and infrastructure – or through the creation of new both direct and indirect employment prospects.[10] Local socio-economic development opportunities, in the sense of spillover effects, also emerge through the agricultural and processing technology transfer facilitated by investors.[11]

Conversely, LSLAs also carry numerous risks for the target country's local population. For example, they can endanger local food security and water supplies by fostering an increase in land competition that itself leads to the supplanting of local (subsistence) food production methods.[12] More indirectly, negative welfare effects for the local population also occur as a result of the induction of rising land and food prices.[13]

LSLAs, not least, increase the risk of new conflicts and different types of internal violence occurring. Thus in numerous cases massive violations of political, socio-economic, and cultural human rights – including the forced displacement and resettlement of local populations in the context of LSLAs – have been documented; some of them spurring local counter-violence in turn.[14] In some cases, these human rights violations, mostly perpetrated by state security forces, have been supplemented with rising forms of structural violence in the sense of a formal and informal bundling of the power of state actors and economic elites together with common private interests in the land sector.[15] On the other hand, and partly due to the above-depicted types of violence, increasing local resistance to LSLAs can be observed in numerous African, Latin American, and Asian countries.[16] These kinds of protest range from completely non-violent campaigning – demonstrations, protest marches, land occupations, road blockades and incendiary incidents – to outright riots.[17] New conflict lines may, moreover, also occur or proliferate within local groups, when for example certain ones support the land investments while others oppose them.[18]

There is a growing both academic and non-academic literature about conflicts and further types of violence in the context of LSLAs.[19] Existing insights about key context conditions and central forces at stake seem to indicate that a lack of participation by the local population in decision-making processes increases the risks of local protest occurring.[20] Baird has, moreover, shown the central importance of the contextual factors of specific histories, ethnic belonging, local and national politics as well as geographical factors on site, which can all influence the dynamics of local contestation of LSLAs.[21] At the same time, Monsalve Suárez and other authors have shown that international human rights instruments can decrease violence related to LSLAs – but only where the local population has access to justice and legal remedies.[22]

There are, however, only a few studies systematically scrutinising the particular mechanisms linking LSLAs and different types of violence and crime in the specific context of post-war societies. This is especially true for the analysis of the historical legacies of existing war economies and their potential influence on post-war land-related violence.

To address this research gap, the following analysis will scrutinise through which potential mechanisms the central contextual settings of post-war societies – including the trajectories of war economies – might influence different types of violence in the context of LSLAs. This is done by integrating theoretical assumptions from peace and conflict research on post-war societies with existing empirical insights from development and agricultural studies on the general consequences of LSLAs.

Mechanisms of LSLAs in post-war societies

Post-war societies are, of course, not a homogenous group of countries. Still, there are a number of crucial characteristics that most post-war societies do nevertheless have in common, and exhibit the concurrence of these characteristics to a substantially higher degree than in other countries. These characteristics are hence likely to have a pronounced and distinct impact on the dynamics of LSLAs-related violence – when compared to LSLAs in non-post-war settings.

To begin with, most post-war societies are characterised by high socio-economic inequalities and intertwined power asymmetries between different social groups.[23] This holds true not least for land tenure relations, which often mean a high concentration of land tenure in the hands of political and economic coalitions formed by the winners of the internal conflict.[24] In this context, it is likely that LSLAs in post-war settings additionally exacerbate existing land inequalities when specific groups of the population, ones not counted among the winners, are excluded from negotiations over land deals as well as from the potential benefits thereof. By this, local protests and uprisings are spurred mainly through the relative deprivation mechanism[25]: frustration and protest are likely to arise when people experience a significant or growing discrepancy between their own socio-economic situation and that of a specific reference group. The likelihood of (violent) conflict will, moreover, be particularly pronounced when inequality of land tenure concurs with horizontal inequalities, meaning ethnic or other identity-based cleavages on site – which often become politicised during times of war.[26]

Existing power asymmetries also contribute to shaping dominant national discourses about the meaning of 'development' – and what the central pillars of it are to be.[27] When the political elites of post-war countries declare LSLAs to be beneficial for the national interest and the development of the country, any subsequent resistance to LSLAs can be more easily marginalised or even criminalised. This implies that the violent repression of local resistance by the military, the police or private security forces thereby becomes more easily legitimised.[28]

Most post-war societies, second, demonstrate an especially low effectivity of state capacity, which goes hand-in-hand with low levels of rule of law, rampant corruption and high levels of impunity.[29] These circumstances additionally reinforce the fact that powerful social groups disproportionally profit from post-war land deals. A further consequence may be the commonplace bribing of politicians so as to bypass national regulations vis-à-vis the awarding of LSLA concessions. On the other hand, the prevalent weak rule of law can, furthermore, foster the choosing of violent means for acquiring land, for example when investors hire private actors to enforce their interests through threatening, injuring, and/or assassinating those local peasants who refuse to sell their land.[30] In the case of past resource wars[31], the weak rule of law can more specifically also be exploited using land deals for the continuation of war economies – such as drug cultivation and dealing, or illegal logging.[32] This perpetuates or even further reinforces the dominant economic and political influence of former war entrepreneurs, the maintenance of criminal networks and associated violence.

Finally, in almost all major internal violent conflicts massive forced displacement takes place – with many people fleeing their homes due to the violence.[33] While the resolving of related housing, land and property rights poses an enormous challenge in all post-war societies[34], the situation might further sharpen in the context of LSLAs: during lengthy resettlement processes following the termination of conflict, land that has officially been declared 'unused' or 'abandoned' can be sold to land investors.[35] Local peasants returning home thus find their land occupied, and are, consequently, not only deprived of their homeland but also of previous possibilities regarding food, water, and housing self-subsistence. This, in turn, engenders local resistance and conflicts mainly through the absolute deprivation mechanism, which in a nutshell can be defined as the discrepancy between what people need and what they have concerning minimum living standards such as food, clean water, sanitation facilities, and health care.[36] Conflict potential may be especially high when there are no or only weak legal mechanisms in place regarding the rights of returning people. On the other hand, here again physical violence may be exerted by land investors and their allies against returning local people as well as against trade unionists trying to advocate for local peasants' interests.

As outlined above, the presented characteristics of post-war societies link LSLAs and different types of violence and crime in post-war countries through various – interacting – mechanisms (see Figure 1).[37] Theoretically, the probability of post-war violence occurring in the context of LSLAs can be assumed to be especially high in countries that previously experienced a resource war. This is a result of the subsequent intertwining of war economy structures, such as drug cultivation or illegal logging, with LSLAs made by former war entrepreneurs, which results in the promotion of criminal networks and associated violence.

In the following section, the case study of Cambodia illustrates how the mechanisms work and interact with each other. This is done using the method of process tracing, which is especially well suited for the study of complex interaction effects and for the identification of the (historical) sequences of a process.[38]

Cambodia, large-scale land acquisitions and post-war violence

The country case of Cambodia has been chosen as it represents, on the one hand, the crucial characteristics of a post-war state, including the legacy of an armed conflict partly financed by illegal resource trading, which has been identified as particularly conducive to post-war LSLAs-related violence. Cambodia is also a major target country of LSLAs. It can thus be considered an emblematic case to further uncover the complex links between LSLAs and the dynamics of violence and crime in post-war societies.

The case study analysis is based on the assessment of multiple data sources: secondary literature, existing databases, organisational reports, grey literature, and newspaper articles comprising fine-grained local empirical insights. To be able to comprehensively capture the historical trajectories of violence, and especially the legacies of the internal armed conflict and existing war economies, the following section will start by providing an overview of the internal armed conflict in Cambodia.

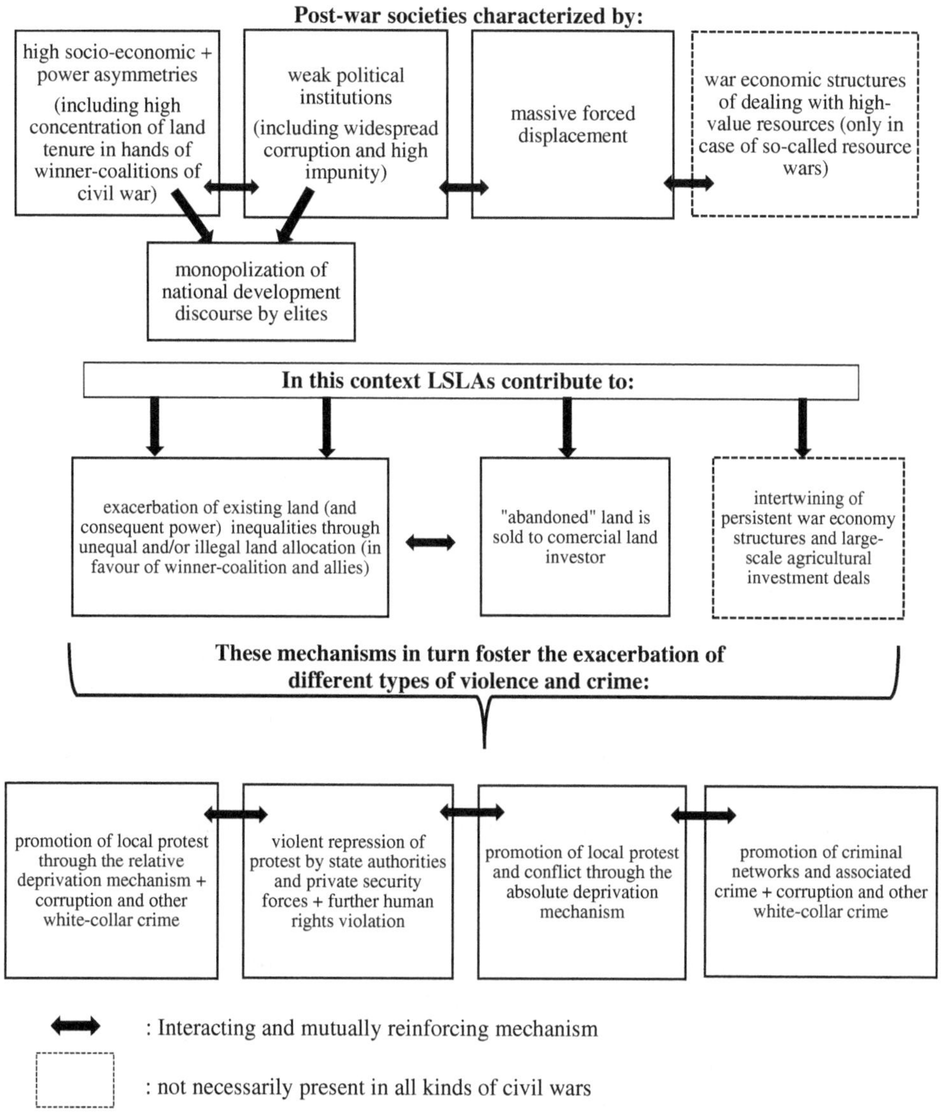

Figure 1. Potential mechanisms linking LSLAs and different types of violence in post-war societies.

The internal armed conflict in cambodia and its post-war legacies

Cambodia's recent history was marked by decades of a prolonged – partly internationalised – internal armed conflict, which originally began in 1970. After the invasion of Vietnamese troops and the fall of the brutal Khmer Rouge regime in January 1979, the latter continued to fight the pro-Vietnamese communist government in the form of a guerrilla movement.[39] The internal conflict only ended in 1998, when the last factions of the weakened Khmer Rouge finally surrendered their weapons. The intra-state violence caused internal displacements and made two million people international refugees.[40]

In 1991, a temporary peace agreement between the ruling Cambodian People's Party (CPP), the Khmer Rouge and two further non-communist rebel groups had been reached

Table 2. Political Terror Scale Data for Cambodia (PTS).

Year	1985	1990	1995	2000	2005	2010	2014
Amnesty International	3	3	3	3	3	3	3
US State Department	4	4	4	2	3	3	3

Source: politicalterrorscale.org (Wood and Gibney 2015). PTS 5 = widespread terror, 1 = no state repression.

under the mediation of the United Nations. This peace process was subverted, however, when in 1993 the Khmer Rouge boycotted national elections and withdrew from the peace process. The guerrilla war of the Khmer Rouge continued, as noted, until 1998, although during that decade an increasing number of its leaders would surrender to the state – a choice driven by generous amnesty offers and material incentives from the Cambodian Government.[41] The loss of financial resources and the death of Pol Pot, the long-time strongman of the Khmer Rouge, were also key factors herein.[42] The Khmer Rouge had partly funded their fight by the illegal trading of timber, a practice that had also been taken up by the Cambodian military as well as state and private allies.[43] The logging and timber export ban of 1995, implemented by the government and endorsed by international actors, hit the Khmer Rouge more than the latter still enduring and flourishing networks.

In the late 1990s, numerous Khmer Rouge leaders were granted continued control over land and (unofficial) logging rights by the Cambodian Government in exchange for defecting.[44] After the end of the internal conflict, the majority of the Khmer Rouge combatants were integrated into the national army – including most of the group's erstwhile leaders. The prosecution of former Khmer Rouge leaders only took place very belatedly and in a piecemeal fashion.

While Cambodia's increasingly liberal economy has recovered since the end of the internal conflict and has featured overall strong growth rates[45], even until today the country still suffers from the legacy of war. It can be characterised by the continued existence of weak political institutions – especially a highly deficient rule of law with accompanying endemic corruption, as well as widespread human rights violations by the state.[46] Moreover, there are high socio-economic asymmetries in Cambodian society: according to a report by the Asian Development Bank socio-economic inequality has risen strongly there since the middle of the 1990s, including increasingly unequal land distribution.[47]

The historically entrenched entanglement of economic and political power has – since the end of the internal violent conflict – centred around the leadership ranks of the dominant political party, the CPP, with its strongman and still going Prime Minister Hun Sen. Thus, the inner circles around Hun Sen in large part constitute not only the political but also the economic elite of the country.[48] In the context of a low post-war state capacity, Hun Sen has managed to gradually establish a powerful system of rule based on clientelism and patronage.[49]

One of the central pillars of economic and political power in Cambodia remains until today the continuation of the former war economy of illegal timber trading. Key actors in these illegal logging activities are the military as well as various police units – with them either being directly involved or protecting logging activities by others, namely Cambodian politicians and their family members. These logging activities are increasingly complemented by – and closely entrenched with – dealings over LSLAs for the purpose of building agro-industrialised plantations (Table 2).[50]

Land politics and dimension of LSLAs in Cambodia

Historically speaking, during the rule of the Khmer Rouge regime (1975–1979) private ownership of land was abolished and land titles documents were destroyed. Private land ownership was only re-established in 1992.[51] Until today the vast majority of the country's territory is in the possession of the Cambodian Government. The government at first primarily assigned forest concessions[52]; since the mid-2000s these have been increasingly replaced by economic land concessions (ELCs) for agro-industrial plantations.[53] The awarding of land concessions is essentially regulated by the Land Law of 2001, as well as by various follow-up sub-decrees. This land law defines two categories of state land: 'state public land' and 'state private land'. Concessions are only given for the latter. Land concessions can be granted for up to 99 years and for areas up to 10,000 hectares in size per person. According to the law, social, and environmental impact assessments are obligatory – as is compensation for affected populations.[54] Cambodian land laws also include communal land titling and social land concessions (SLCs) for poor families, disabled soldiers, and the families of deceased soldiers.[55] While the Land Law of 2001 and its sub-decrees can in theory be considered comprehensive and progressive, many sources have underlined that their actual realisation is often inadequate.[56]

Thus in practice only a few SLCs have actually been awarded – most of them to (former) military affiliates.[57] Communal and titles are even more rarely granted.[58] Moreover, the whole process of land allocation is in large part characterised by 'selective and uneven property rights formalization'[59], which unilaterally favours large agro-business concessions. As of the end of 2013, about 1.1 million hectares of land had been awarded for the purpose of rubber plantations, 150,000 hectares for sugar plantations and 100,000 hectares for pulp and paper.[60] The majority of investors are Vietnamese and Chinese, but also from large Cambodian investor groups.[61]

While the national moratorium on new ELCs declared by the Cambodian Government in 2012 has begun to address the imbalance in land allocation and misplacement of titles, the implementation of the moratorium is characterised by major shortcomings and has in practice thus far not resulted in major changes with regard to the dynamics of LSLAs (Cismas and Paramita 2016).[62] As confirmed by a variety of analysts, these large-scale land concessions have seemingly become – and remain – the 'central pillar of national development efforts'.[63] According to the Sub-Decree on ELCs (2005), they are considered to 'increase employment in rural areas' – including the 'intensification and diversification of livelihood opportunities' (Royal Government of Cambodia, 2005, Article 3). This official development discourse concerning ELCs for agro-industrial production, which are only ever positively depicted, is also very prominent in public statements made by Cambodian politicians, including by Prime Minister Hun Sen himself.[64] The establishment of the dominance of this discourse is facilitated by , in large part, politically controlled or victimised Khmer-language media.[65]

LSLAs and post-war violence in Cambodia

There are a large number of reports, data sources and media statements available about the negative impacts of LSLAs on local communities in Cambodia.[66] Numerous analyses have listed the multitude of local land conflicts, human rights violations (from the destruction of houses, over physical violence to forced displacement) and cases of corruption and bribery occurring in the context of LSLAs in Cambodia. Land disputes and local protests against LSLAs have risen in tandem with the increasing governmental awarding of ELCs.[67] Local forms of protest usually range from public campaigns to streets marches, land occupations, and road blockades.[68] These protests are often met with brutality by the police and military actors. Moreover, there have been numerous cases of the arbitrary arrest of protesters, of intimidation and infringement as well as of the killing of environmental and land activists and other protesters.[69] Local forms of protest are often violently repressed by security forces. Thus, cases like the following one reported by the Cambodian NGO ADHOC can be considered exemplary. In Snuol District, security guards opened fire against villagers protesting against the awarding of land to the Cambodian TTY Company and injured four people – two of them seriously.[70] While the case was brought to court, sentences were suspended afterwards.

LSLAs have, furthermore, engendered the renewed massive forced and partly violent displacement of local people – often without (adequate) compensation.[71] The majority of those evicted migrate to the suburbs of urban centres, or even to neighbouring countries – especially Thailand, where many of them work illegally.[72] In both cases, these migrants suffer from the non-existence of institutional and official safety nets, and as undocumented foreign workers they are disproportionally exposed to 'less favourable terms for wages and conditions of work, long hours, confinement to the workplace, physical violence, sexual abuse [...]'.[73]

The often excessive use of physical violence by the military and police officers as well as forced displacement are frequently endorsed by political actors, including Prime Minister Hun Sen himself, either actively or at least passively in the sense of silent acquiescence. In the case of the murdered 14-year-old girl, Heng Chantha, Hun Sen 'instead of launching a criminal investigation into police conduct, [...] accused protesters of organizing a 'secessionist movement' and then ordered the arrest of its leaders'.[74] Simultaneously, in public declarations and statements Hun Sen has repeatedly praised the various heads of large-scale agro-industrial companies for generously contributing to the country's development.[75] The informal alliances that form with regard to land allocation, which manifest themselves in these propositions and practices, can be traced back to the historically entrenched entanglement of economic and political power in Cambodia. While this entanglement dates back to the pre-civil war period, it was further strengthened by the prevalent war economic structures.[76] Since the end of the internal armed conflict, the informal alliances have especially centred around the leadership ranks of the CPP and Prime Minister Hun Sen.[77]

The following examples of a LSLA by the Phnom Penh Sugar Company in the province of Kampong Speu and by the Pheapimex Company in Pursat Province unpick in more detail the multiple consequences of this specific land-related 'convergence of the state apparatus with private business interests'[78] for the different forms of local violence and crime – and their mutual reinforcement. The Phnom Penh Sugar Company is owned by the CPP senator and business tycoon Ly Yong Phat. In 2010, the company was granted an ELC for industrial sugar cane cultivation covering 8,343 hectares in Thpong District, Kampong Speu Province. According to the database of the Environmental Justice Atlas (EJOLT), the concessions were granted without prior consultation or environmental and social impact assessments being done.[79]

Around 1,500 families are reported to have been affected by the new plantations. Several hundred local people were evicted and resettled in areas without adequate infrastructure or productive land. Moreover, the environmental impacts have been devastating, including from the dumping of waste into community streams – which has caused fish to die, and led to the sickness of both villagers and their livestock. Local communities responded to forced displacement with different types of resistance, which ranged from protests and small-scale arson to highway barricades. A number of community members who took part in these protests have since been arbitrarily arrested. Protests were, moreover, repressed through a massive police and military presence, with the company in question additionally employing Battalion 313 – a private army of former Khmer Rouge combatants – to intimidate villagers, to force them to accept inadequate compensation and to protect the land concessions.[80]

The second case is centred around Pheapimex, one of Cambodia's largest companies. It is owned by Lau Men Khing, a CPP senator, and his wife (who is, according to Global Witness, a close friend of Hun Sen's wife).[81] In 2000, Pheapimex was granted a land concession for eucalyptus plantations in Pursat Province – without an environmental impact assessment being done and without any prior consultation of local land owners.[82] As the new plantations brought with them numerous negative social, economic, and environmental consequences for the local communities – and the announced employment opportunities were barely provided in reality – there were numerous local protests against them. Protests escalated in 2004, when local activists were arrested. Moreover, in November 2004 several protesters were severely wounded in a hand grenade attack – an incident that has never been investigated by the government in the years since.[83] Instead, Prime Minister Hun Sen defended the company by publicly defaming the protesters and arguing that: 'The grenade attack was only aimed at blaming the government or the local authorities, because [...] the purpose of the grenade attack (in which some people were injured and nobody died) was just aimed to make their propaganda voices louder'.[84]

It has furthermore repeatedly been reported that Pheapimex as well as Phnom Penh Sugar Company have in numerous cases also undertaken illegal logging activities on their ELCs, which were officially acquired for agricultural investment only. These illegal activities are covered up by employing (para-)military units (including members of Brigade 70, which acts as a bodyguard unit for Prime Minister Hun Sen) for transportation and further adjunct services.[85]

Discussion of results and conclusion

The example of Cambodia demonstrates how LSLAs – both directly on site and more indirectly – engender and intensify different, interacting types of violence and crime. Under the given post-war context conditions, the potentially violence-mitigating effects of LSLAs – through the provision of new employment opportunities in the agricultural business and infrastructural endowment, or in a broader sense through the contribution to local economic development – seem to materialise very thinly and then exclusively for a small minority within the target country. In contrast, apart from spurring local conflicts in the sense of contentious collective action by resisting local populations, LSLAs have especially facilitated the perpetuation and consolidation of an informal and often illegal entanglement of political and economic power among agro-investors, state actors and military forces in post-war Cambodia. While numerous actors of these informal alliances are drivers of physical violence and other human rights violations, the entanglement more generally also promotes the proliferation of corruption and further white-collar crime, and concurrently fosters the maintenance of criminal networks related to illegal resource trade.

As has been shown, this nexus can be traced back to multiple historical legacies from the internal armed conflict era: first of all, the banning of private land ownership and its appropriation by the state under the Khmer Rouge regime (1975–1979) represented 'fruitful' foundations for this later entanglement in the context of LSLAs. Based on that, the reality of war-torn, weak political institutions – including the highly deficient rule of law – alongside extreme power asymmetries have induced the continued existence and politico-economic power of actors' constellations or networks. Herein, the above-mentioned groups of actors build alliances that advocate for concurrent political and private interests of rent-seeking. The role of the state thereby is a multiple one: first, state actors are directly involved in land deals when officials (or their family members) own the companies that are purchasing ELCs. Second, government actors from the local to the national level are breaking the law in awarding land concessions exceeding the legal limits, in making concessions without the prior consultation of local people and in not conducting prior environmental and social impact assessments. Moreover, the political elite, with Prime Minister Hun Sen leading the way, are also more indirectly involved by advocating a liberal market-oriented national economic strategy – which aggressively promotes the expansion of agro-industrial plantations.

In this context, the government is also quite successfully monopolising the national discourse about LSLAs in terms of 'Economic Land Concessions for Development', thus defaming and even criminalising resistance to them. These practices facilitate a violent – crackdown on local protest against LSLAs by a politicised military, the police and private security units. Human rights violations by security forces – ranging from forced eviction, intimidation and physical injury to assassination – are consequently promoted in the context of LSLAs, and themselves provoke renewed protest by local villagers.

A further legacy of the internal conflict era is, second, the perpetuation of war economy structures like illegal logging and associated crime and violence, which is becoming increasingly intertwined with large-scale agricultural investment deals. This war economy, generating extensive natural resource rents, has not only continued since the end of internal conflict but actually further proliferated, due to the prevalence of LSLAs: As such, on the one hand, LSLAs serve as a pretext for acquiring land with valuable forests, and illegal logging is then carried out on land officially obtained via an ELC. On the other hand, illegal logging also paves the way for the future awarding of ELCs to agro-industrial plantations. Key actors in these illegal logging activities are the military as well as various police units, with them either being directly involved or protecting logging activities by others – namely Cambodian politicians, their family members and further individuals from the national business elite. These are, in short, the same group of actors who figure prominently in the context of LSLAs.

Finally, there also seem to be more indirect, frequently disregarded risks of potential violence ensuing from LSLAs. The growing number of them has reinforced forced displacement, which in turn spurs the migration of displaced people to the outskirts of the urban centres of the country and to neighbouring countries – where many of them are forced to work illegally. In both cases, these migrants are heavily exposed to human rights violations and crime.

While the individual mechanisms linking LSLAs and different forms of violence are not exclusively bound to post-war societies, the case study of Cambodia has further corroborated that their manifestation and concurrence seem to be particularly pronounced in such settings – when compared to LSLAs in non-post-war settings. Thus, they may make these countries especially vulnerable to multiple forms of violence in the context of LSLAs. To actually prove the causality of this assumption and the particular mechanisms at work, future research will have to conduct broader comparative studies of different cases so as to conclusively confirm or refute the findings of this paper.

Historical circumstances such as the banning of private land ownership under the Khmer Rouge regime in the 1970s are rather case-specific factors. However, the reciprocal enhancement of enduring war economy structures like illegal resource trading and of large-scale land investments, which substantially contributes to the promotion of various types of physical violence, other human rights violation, and crime, seems to indeed be transferable to many other country settings that previously experienced a so-called resource war.

The same holds true for the interacting mechanisms linking weak political institutions, extreme power asymmetries and high impunity with the proliferation of land-related violence. These interactions further empower an informal entanglement of power among agro-investors, state actors, and military forces, which fosters corruption and further white-collar crime as well as numerous forms of human rights violations.

Disclosure statement

No potential conflict of interest was reported by the author.

Acknowledgements

I thank Madeleine Hatfield along with two anonymous reviewers for their very helpful comments on my article. I am also grateful for the highly useful feedback I received from Sabine Kurtenbach, Angelika Rettberg, and other researchers of the "War Economies and Postwar Crime" project funded by the Alexander von Humboldt Foundation.

Notes

1. In accordance with prevailing notions about the phenomenon, LSLAs can be provisionally defined as transactions that entail a transfer through sale or concession of the right to use

or own large amounts of arable land for commercial purposes (see also Anseeuwe et al., *Transnational Land Deals*, VI).

2. Nolte, Chamberlain and Giger, *International Land Deals*, 7. Some sources indicate much higher numbers besides (see for example Deininger et al., *Rising Global Interest*).
3. The definition of an internal armed conflict used in this article is based on the commonly used definition and data of the Correlates of War Project. The Correlates of War Project defines an internal armed conflict as an 'intra-state war' if it involves organized armed forces, and results in a minimum of 1000 battle-related deaths in one calendar year (Sarkees and Wayman, *Resort to War*).
4. Such as those of Geuder-Jilg, *Land Acquisitions and Impact*; Nolte, Chamberlain and Giger, *International Land Deals;* and Thaler, *Large-Scale Land Acquisitions*. For a discussion of the reasons for this tendency, see, for example, Nolte, Chamberlain and Giger, *International Land Deals*, or Sturgess and Flower, *Land and Conflict*.
5. In this paper the concepts of 'post-war' and 'post-conflict' are used synonymously. The definition of an internal armed conflict employed in this paper is based on the definition of intra-state wars by the widely used Correlates of War (COW) Project (see endnote 3).
6. Following Tilly (2003) within this article the term 'violence' is used in the sense of collective violence, excluding purely individual actions, nonmaterial damage, and accidents (Tilly, *Politics of Collective Violence*, 4).
7. For example, Bottazi, Goguen and Rist, "Conflicts of Customary Land"; Hall et al., "Resistance, Acquiescence"; Martiniello, "Social Struggle"; and Oberlack et al., "Sustainable Livelihoods."
8. Collier and Hoeffler, "Greed and Grievance"; and Suhrke and Berdal, *The Peace in Between*.
9. Nolte, Chamberlain and Giger, *International Land Deals*, 18.
10. Collier and Venables, *Greening Africa*; Deininger et al., *Rising Global Interest*; Kleemann et al., *Rural Welfare Implications*; and Rist et al., "Livelihood Impacts."
11. Görg and Greenaway, "Much Ado about Nothing"; see also Hennings, *Resistance against Large-Scale*.
12. Lund, Odgaard and Sjaastad, *Land Rights*; and Rulli, Saviori and D'Odorico, "Global Land and Water."
13. DeSchutter, "How Not to Think"; and Kleemann and Thiele, *Rural Welfare*.
14. Álvaro Roa, "Expansion des Ölpalmanbaus"; Bues, *Increasing Pressure*; Hennings, "Das Konfliktpotenzial"; Hornung, *Zucker für den EU-Markt*; Siagian et al., *The Loss of Reason*; Springer, "Articulated Neoliberalism"; and Thorburn, "The Plot Thickens."
15. Hennings, "Das Konfliktpotenzial."
16. See for example Baird, "Resistance and Contingent"; Geuder-Jilg, *Land Acquisitions*; Sändig and Schramm, "Protest und Widerstand"; and Sturgess and Flower, *Land and Conflict*.
17. Gerber, "Conflicts over Industrial"; Hall et al., "Resistance, Acquiescence"; and Temper et al., "Mapping the Frontiers."
18. Bottazzi, Goguen and Rist, "Conflicts over Customary."
19. Baird, "Resistance and Contingent"; Hall et al., "Resistance, Acquiescence"; Martiniello, "Social Struggle"; and Overbeek, Kröger and Gerber, *An Overview*.
20. Sändig and Schramm, "Protest und Widerstand".
21. Baird, "Resistance and Contingent."
22. Suárez, "The Human Rights Framework"; and De Schutter, "The Role of Property Rights."
23. Bircan et al., *Violent Conflict and Inequality*; and Licklider, "Obstacles to Peace."
24. Sturgess and Flower, *Land and Conflict*.
25. Gurr, *People* versus *States*.
26. Østby, "Polarization, Horizontal."
27. Hall et al., *Powers of Exclusion*.
28. Hennings, "Das Konfliktpotenzial"; see also, *other author* within this special issue.
29. Hendrix, "Measuring State Capacity"; Rettberg, Leiteritz and Nasi, *Different Resources;* Cheng and Zaum, "Introduction – Peacebuilding"; and Lujala and Rustad, *High-Value Natural Resources*.
30. Alonso-Fradejas, "Anything but a Story"; and Siagian et al., *The Loss of Reason*.

31. While the term 'resource war' might imply several other dimensions, it is in the following used in the sense of wars, which are significantly caused, sustained or prolonged through the funding by illegal trade of valuable natural resources (see also Le Billon, "The Geopolitical Economy").
32. Grajales, "Land Grabbing," 541; see also, *other author* in this special issue.
33. Chimni, "Refugees Return."
34. Lecki, *Housing, Land and Property*.
35. Sturgess and Flower, *Land and Conflict*, 10.
36. Gurr, *Peoples* versus *States*.
37. Due to the unavailability of comprehensive data thus far, it is beyond the scope of this paper to conclusively test all of the assumptions about the mechanisms at work. This may be an important further step for future research, once the preliminary conceptual framework has been conclusively elaborated.
38. George and Bennett, *Case Studies*.
39. For details, see for example: Chandler, *The Tragedy*; and Keller, "UNTAC in Cambodia."
40. Mullenbach, "Reconstructing Strive-Torn," 62.
41. Kirsten, "Transitional Justice," 18; and Small Arms Survey, "Stabilizing Cambodia," 121.
42. Le Billon, "Getting it Done," 150.
43. Ross, "Oil, Drugs, and Diamonds"; and Global Witness, *Cambodia's Family Trees*, 12.
44. Le Billon, "Getting it Done," 219.
45. Hill, Hal and Menon, *Cambodia's Rapid Growth*, 7.
46. MacInnes, *Land is Life*; see also Table 2.
47. Hill, Hal and Menon, *Cambodia's Rapid Growth*, 5.
48. MacInnes, *Land is Life*.
49. Global Witness, *Cambodia's Family Trees*; and Small Arms Survey, "Stabilizing Cambodia," 122.
50. Global Witness, *Cambodia's Family Trees*; and Neef and Touch, *Land Grabbing*, 1–2.
51. Thyl de Lopez, "Natural Resource," 38.
52. Touch and Neef, *Resistance to Land Grabbing*, 1.
53. Neef and Touch, *Land Grabbing*, 2.
54. ADHOC, *A Turning Point*, 6.
55. Bues, *Increasing Pressure*, 8–9.
56. ADHOC, *A Turning Point*; Bues, *Increasing Pressure*; Dwyer, "The Formalization Fix"; MacInnes, *Land is Life*; and Touch and Neef, *Land Grabbing*.
57. Bues, *Increasing Pressure*, 9.
58. Dwyer, "The Formalization Fix," 914.
59. Ibid., 924.
60. Forest Trends, *Conversion Timber*, ii.
61. Ibid., iv.
62. Cismas and Paramita, "Land Acquisitions in Cambodia."
63. Dwyer, "The Formalization Fix," 910.
64. Global Witness, *Cambodia's Family Trees*; Neef and Touch, *Land Grabbing*; and Bues, *Increasing Pressure*.
65. Freedom House, *Freedom of Press*; and Springer, "Articulated Neoliberalism."
66. ADHOC, *A Turning Point*; Baird, "Resistance and Contingent"; Cismas and Paramita, "Land Acquisitions in Cambodia"; MacInnes, *Land is Life*; and Neef, Touch and Chiengthong, "The Politics and Ethics."
67. Baird, "Resistance and Contingent"; and Bues, *Increasing Pressure*, 9.
68. ADHOC, *A Turning Point*; and Temper et al., "Mapping the Frontiers."
69. ADHOC, *A Turning Point*; and Subedi, *Report of the Special*.
70. ADHOC, *A Turning Point*, 12–13.
71. MacInnes, *Land is Life*; Subedi, *Report of the Special*; Springer, "Articulated Neoliberalism"; and Mgbako et al., *Forced Eviction*.
72. ADHOC, *A Turning Point*; and Sophal, *Review of Labor*.
73. Sophal, *Review of Labor*, iii.
74. Human Rights Watch, *Human Rights Watch Report*, 294.

75. Global Witness, *Cambodia's Family Trees.*
76. Hensengerth, *Social and Political.*
77. Global Witness, *Cambodia's Family Trees*; and Hensengerth, *Social and Political.*
78. Subedi, *Report of the Special*, 6.
79. Accessed January 15, 2017. http://www.inclusivedevelopment.net/campaign/cambodia-sugarcane-land-grabs
80. Accessed January 15, 2017. https://ejatlas.org/conflict/blood-sugar-land-grab-by-phnom-penh-sugar-company-kampong-speu-cambodia
81. Global Witness, *Cambodia's Family Trees.*
82. MacInnes, *Land is Life*, 10.
83. Global Witness, *Cambodia's Family Trees*, 10; and EJOLT: https://ejatlas.org/conflict/pheapimex-fuchan-conflict-cambodia.
84. Global Witness, *Cambodia's Family Trees*, 77.
85. MacInnes, *Land is Life*, 10; and Titthara, "Memories of a Land."

Bibliography

ADHOC. *A Turning Point? Land, Housing and Natural Resources Rights in Cambodia in 2012*. Phnom Penh: ADHOC, 2013.

Alonso-Fradejas, Alberto. "Anything but a Story Foretold: Multiple Politics of Resistance to the Agrarian Extractivist Project in Guatemala." *Journal of Peasant Studies* 42, no. 3–4 (2015): 489–515. doi:10.1080/03066150.2015.1013468.

Álvaro Roa, Paula. "The Expansion of Oil Palm Cultivation." In: *Land Means Life: The Grabbing of Farmland by Investors*, edited by Brot für die Welt, EED, and FCSL, 18–19. Frankfurt: Brot für die Welt, 2011.

Amnesty International. *Amnesty International Report 2013. the State of the World's Human Rights*. London: AI, 2013.

Anseeuw, Ward, Mathieu Boche, Thomas Breu, Markus Giger, Jann Lay, Peter Messerli, and Kerstin Nolte. *Transnational Land Deals for Agriculture in the Global South. Analytical Report Based on the Land Matrix Database*. Bern: CDE/CIRAD/GIGA, 2012.

Baird, Ian G. "Resistance and Contingent Contestations to Large-Scale Land Concessions in Southern Laos and Northeastern Cambodia." *Land* 6, no. 16 (2017): 1–19. doi:10.3390/land6010016.

Bircan, Cagatay, Tilman Brück, and Marc Vothknecht. *Violent Conflict and Inequality*. Brooks World Policy Institute Working Paper, No. 129 (2010).

Bottazzi, Patrick, Adam Goguen and Stephan Rist. "Conflicts of Customary Land Tenure in Rural Africa: Is Large-Scale Land Acquisition a Driver of 'Institutional Innovation'?." *Journal of Peasant Studies* 43, no. 5 (2016): 971–988.

Bruce, John. *Legal Empowerment of the Poor: From Concepts to Assessment*. Washington, DC: USAID, 2007.

Bues, Andrea. *Increasing Pressure for Land – Implications for Rural Livelihoods in Developing Countries: The Case of Cambodia*. Welthungerhilfe, 2011. http://www.welthungerhilfe.de/fileadmin/media/pdf/Studien/Cambodia_Increasing_Pressure_final_Nov11.pdf.

Chandler, David. *The Tragedy of Cambodian History: Politics War and Revolution since 1945*. New Haven, CT: Yale University Press, 1991.

Cheng, Christine, and Dominik Zaum. "Introduction – Key Themes in Peacebuilding and Corruption." *International Peacekeeping* 15, no. 3 (2008): 301–309. doi:10.1080/13533310802058752.

Chimni, Bupinder. "Refugees, Return and Reconstruction of 'Post-Conflict' Societies: A Critical Perspective." *International Peacekeeping* 9, no. 2010 (2010): 163–180. doi:10.1080/714002734.

Cismas, Ioana, and Patricia Paramita. "Large-Scale Land Acquisitions in Cambodia. Where Do (Human Rights) Law and Practice Meet?" In *Large-Scale Land Acquisitions*. edited by Christophe Gironde, Christophe Golay, and Peter Messerli, 249–272. Leiden: Brill, 2016.

Collier, Paul, and Anke Hoeffler. "Greed and Grievance in Civil War." *Oxford Economic Papers* 56 (2004): 563–595. doi:10.1093/oep/gpf064.

Collier, Paul, and Anthony Venables. *Greening Africa? Technologies, Endowments and the Latecomer Effect.* OxCarre Working Papers, No. 089, Oxford: University of Oxford, 2012.

De Schutter, Olivier. "The Role of Property Rights in the Debate on Large-Scale Land Acquisitions". In *Large-Scale Land Acquisitions, Livelihoods and Human Rights in South-East Asia*, edited by Christophe Gironde and Christophe Golay53–77. Leiden: Brill Nijhoff, 2016.

Deininger, Klaus, Derek Byerlee, Jonathan Lindsay, Andrew Norton, Harris Selod, and Merced Stickler. *Rising Global Interest in Farmland. Can It Yield Sustainable and Equitable Benefits?*. Washington, DC: World Bank, 2011.

DeSchutter, Olivier. *Large-Scale Land Acquisitions and Leases. a Set of Minimum Principals and Measures to Address the Human Rights Challenge*. UN Report: A/HRC/13/33/Add.2, 2009. http://www.srfood.org/images/stories/pdf/officialreports/20100305_a-hrc-13-33-add2_land-principles_en.pdf..

DeSchutter, Olivier. "How Not to Think of Land-Grabbing: Three Critiques of Large-Scale Investments in Farmland." *Journal of Peasant Studies* 38, no. 2 (2011): 249–279.

Dwyer, Michael B. "The Formalization Fix: Land Titling, Land Concessions, and the Politics of Spatial Transparency in Cambodia." *Journal of Peasant Studies* 42, no. 5 (2015): 903–928.

Environmental Justice Atlas (EJOLT). Accessed April 1, 2017. https://ejatlas.org/

Forest Trends. *Conversion Timber, Forest Monitoring*, and Land-Use Governance in Cambodia. 2015. http://www.forest-trends.org/documents/index.php?pubID=4944.

Freedom House. *Freedom of Press 2005. Discarding Democracy: Return to the Iron Fist.* Washington, DC: Freedom House, 2005. https://freedomhouse.org/report/freedom-press/2015/cambodia.

George, Alexander L., and Andrew Bennett. *Case Studies and Theory Development in the Social Sciences*. Cambridge: MIT Press, 2006.

Gerber, Julien-Francois. "Conflicts over Industrial Tree Plantations in the South: Who, How and Why?" *Global Environmental Change* 21, no. 1 (2011): 165–176.

Gertel, Jörg, Sandra Calkins, and Richard Rottenburg. "Disrupting Territories: Commodification and Its Consequences." *Disrupting Territories: Land, Commodification & Conflict in Sudan*, edited by Jörg Gertel, Richard Rottenburg, and Sandra Calkins, 1–30. Woodbridge: Currey, 2014.

Geuder-Jilg, Erwin. *Land Acquisitions and Their Impacts on Peace, Security and Stability*. Berlin: Brot für die Welt, 2014.

Gironde, Christophe and Christophe Golay. "Large-Scale Land Acquisitions, Livelihoods and Human Rights in South-East Asia." In *Large-Scale Land Acquisitions*, edited by Christophe Gironde, Christophe Golay, and Peter Messerli, 275–292. Leiden: Brill.

Global Witness. *Cambodia's Family Trees: Illegal Logging and the Stripping of Public Assets by Cambodia's Elite*. London: Global Witness, 2007.

Görg, Holger, and David Greenaway. "Much Ado about Nothing? Do Domestic Firms Really Benefit from Foreign Direct Investment?" *The World Bank Research Observer* 19 (2004): 171–197.

Grajales, Jacobo. "Land Grabbing, Legal Contention and Institutional Change in Colombia." *Journal of Peasant Studies* 42, no. 3–4 (2015): 541–560.

Gurr, Ted. *Peoples* versus *States: Minorities at Risk in the New Century*. Washington, DC: U.S. Institute of Peace Press, 2000.

Hall, Derek, Philip Philip Hirsch, and Tanja Li. *Powers of Exclusion: Land Dilemmas in Southeast Asia.* Singapore: NUS Press, 2011.

Hall, Ruth, Marc Edelman, Saturnino M. Borras Jr., Ian Scoones, Ben White, and Wendy Wolford. "Resistance, Acquiescence or Incorporation? An Introduction to Land Grabbing and Political Reactions 'from Below'." *Journal of Peasant Studies* 42, no. 3–4 (2015): 467–488.

Hendrix, Cullen. "Measuring State Capacity: Theoretical and Empirical Implications for the Study of Civil Conflict." *Journal of Peace Research* 47, no. 3 (2010): 273–285.

Hennings, Anne. *Resistance against Large-Scale Land Acquisitions: Bougainville's Peace Process under Threat?* Conference Paper, No. 49, BICAS et al., 2015.

Hennings, Anne. "Das Konfliktpotenzial exklusiver Landgrabbing-Praktiken: Eine Herausforderung für den regionalen Frieden." *ZeFKo – Zeitschrift für Friedens- und Konfliktforschung* 5, no. 2 (2016): 221–248. doi:10.5771/2192-1741-2016-2-221.

Hensengerth, Oliver. *Social and Political Factures after War. the Role of Youth Violence in Post-1993 Cambodia.* Project WP, No. 4, INEF: Duisburg, 2008.

Hill, Hal, and Menon, Jayant. *Cambodia*: Rapid *Growth* with Institutional Constraints. Asian Development Bank Economics. Working Paper Series, No. 331, 2013.

Hornung, Manfred. *Zucker für den EU-Markt. Landraub in Kambodscha.* 2011. https://www.boell.de/de/oekologie/asien-zucker-fuer-eu-landraub-in-kambodscha-11975.html.

Human Rights Watch. *Human Rights Watch Report 2013*. New York, NY: HRW, 2013.

Keller, Lucy. "UNTAC in Cambodia – from Occupation, Civil War and Genocide to Peace." *Max Planck Yearbook of United Nations Law,* 9 (2005): 1–52.

Kirsten, Ainley. "Transitional Justice in Cambodia: The Coincidence of Power and Principle." In *Transitional Justice in the Asia Pacific*, edited by Renée Jeffery and Hun Joon Kim. New York, NY: Cambridge University Press, 2014.

Kleemann, Linda, and Rainer Thiele. *Rural Welfare Implications of Large-Scale Land Acquisitions in Africa: A Theoretical Framework*. Kiel Working Paper, 1921, Kiel: Kiel Institute for the World Economy, 2014.

Land Matrix. *The Online Public Database on Land Deals*, 2015. Accessed October 4, 2015. www.landmatrix.org

Le Billon, Philippe. "The Geopolitical Economy of 'Resource Wars'". In: *Geopolitics*, (published online June 4, 2010), 1–28. doi: 10.1080/14650040412331307812.

Le Billon, Philippe. "Getting It Done: Instruments of Enforcements." In *Natural Resources and Violent Conflict*, edited by Ian Bannon and Paul Collier, 216–286. Washington, DC: World Bank, 2003.

Lecki, Scott. *Housing, Land and Property Rights in Post-Conflict Societies: Proposals for a New United Nations Institutional and Policy Framework*. Genova: UNHCR, 2005.

LICADHO. *Static Maps & Spatial Data. Land Concessions: Overview*, 2016. http://www.licadho-cambodia.org/land_concessions/maps/map-overview-small.jpg.

Licklider, Roy. 2001. "Obstacles to Peace Settlements." In: *Turbulent Peace. the Challenges of Managing International Conflict*, edited by Chester A. Crocker, Fen Osler Hampson, and Pamela Aal, 697–718. Washington, DC: US Institute of Peace Press, 2001.

Lijphart, Arend. "Comparative Politics and the Comparative Method." *American Political Science Review* 65 (1971): 682–693.

Lujala, Päivi, and Siri Aas Rustad, eds. *High-Value Natural Resources and Post-Conflict Peacebuilding*. London: Earthscan, 2011.

Lund, Christian, Rie Odgaard, and Espen Sjaastad. *Land Rights and Land Conflicts in Africa: A Review of Issues and Experiences*. Copenhagen: Danish Institute for International Studies, 2006.

Mamonova, Natalia. "Resistance or Adaptation? Ukrainian Peasants' Responses to Large-Scale Land Acquisitions." *Journal of Peasant Studies* 42, no. 3–4 (2015): 607–634.

Markwitz, Lawrence. "The Resource Curse Reconsidered: Cash Crops and Local Violence in Kyrgyzstan." *Terrorism and Political Violence* 29, no. 2 (2015): 342–358.

Martiniello, Giuliano. "Social Struggles in Uganda's Acholiland: Understanding Responses and Resistance to Amuru Sugar Works." *Journal of Peasant Studies* 42, no. 3–4 (2015): 653–669.

Martiniello, Giuliano. "Social Struggles in Uganda's Acholiland: Understanding Responses and Resistance to Amuru Sugar Works." *The Journal of Peasant Studies* 42, no. 3–4 (2015): 653–669.

Megan, Mac Innes. *Land is Life: An Analysis of the Role 'Grand Corruption' Plays in Enabling Elite Grabbing of Land in Cambodia*. London: Global Witness, 2015.

Mgbako, Chi, Rijie Ernie Gao, Elizabeth Joynes, Anna Cave, and Jessica Mikhailevich. "Forced Eviction and Resettlement in Cambodia: Case Studies from Phnom Penh." *Washington University Global Studies Law Review*, 9, no. 1 (2010):39–76. http://openscholarship.wustl.edu/law_globalstudies/vol9/iss1/3.

Mullenbach, Mark J. "Reconstructing Strife-Torn Societies: Third Party Peacebuilding in Intrastate Disputes." In *Conflict Prevention and Peace-Building in Post-War Societies: Sustaining the Peace*, edited by T. David Mason and James D. Meernik, 53–80. London: Routledge, 2006.

Neef, Andreas, and Siphat Touch. *Land Grabbing in Cambodia. Mechanisms, Narratives, Resistance*. Paper presented at the Global Land Grabbing Conference II at Cornell University: Ithaca, 17–19 October, 2012.

Neef, Andreas, Siphat Touch, and Jamaree Chiengthong. "The Politics and Ethics of Land Concessions in Rural Cambodia." *Journal Agricultural and Environmental Ethics* 26, no. 6 (2013): 1085–1103.

Nolte, Kerstin, Wytske Chamberlain, and Markus Giger. *International Land Deals of Agriculture: Fresh Insights from the Land Matrix: Analytical Report II* (2016): doi:10.7892/boris.85304.

Oberlack, Christoph, Laura Tejada, Peter Messerli, Stephan Rist, and Markus Giger. "Sustainable Livelihoods in the Global Land Rush? Archetypes of Livelihood Vulnerability and Sustainability

Potentials." *Global Environmental Change,* 41 (2015): 153–171. http://www.sciencedirect.com/science/article/pii/S0959378016302928

Østby, Gudrun. "Polarization, Horizontal Inequalities and Violent Civil Conflict." *Journal of Peace Research* 45, no. 2 (2008): 143–162.

Overbeek, Winfridus, Markus Kröger, and Julien-Francois Gerber. *An Overview of Industrial Tree Plantation Conflicts in the Global South. Conflicts, Trends, and Resistance Struggles.* Ejolt Report: 3, 2012.

Peluso, Nancy, and Christian Lund. "New Frontiers of Land Control: Introduction." *Journal of Peasant Studies* 38, no. 4 (2011): 667–681.

Rettberg, Angelika, Ralf Leiteritz, and Carlo Nasi. *"Different Resources, Different Conflicts?" A Framework for Understanding the Political Economy of Armed Conflict and Criminality in Colombian Regions* (2014): doi:10.2139/ssrn.2499580.

Rist, Lucy, Laurence Feintrenie, and Patrice Levang. "The Livelihood Impacts of Oil Palm: Smallholders in Indonesia." *Biodiversity Conservation* 19, no. 4 (2010): 1009–1024.

Ross, Michael. "Oil, Drugs, and Diamonds: How Do Natural Resources Vary in Their Impact on Civil War?" In *Beyond Greed and Grievance: The Political Economy of Armed Conflict*, edited by Karen Ballentine and Jake Sherman, 47–70. Boulder: Lynne Rienner, 2003.

Rulli, Maria Cristina, Antonio Saviori, and Paolo D'Odorico. "Global Land and Water Grabbing." *Proceeding of the National Academy of Science* 110, no. 3 (2013): 892–897.

Sändig, Jan, and Annette Schramm. "Protest Und Widerstand Gegen Großinvestitionen Im Globalen Süden." *Zeitschrift Für Friedens- Und Konfliktforschung* 5 (2016): 252–266.

Sarkees, Meredith Reid, and Frank Wayman. *Resort to War: 1816–2007.* Washington, DC: CQ Press, 2010.

Siagian, Saurlin, Amin Siahaan and Buyung Nur Khairani. *The Loss of Reason. Facts on Human Rights Violations in the Oil Palm Related Plantations in Indonesia.* A Report Paper from Case Studies at Labuhan Batu, 2011.

Small Arms Survey. "Stabilizing Cambodia: Small Arms Control and Security Sector Reform." Chap. 5 in: *Small Arms Survey 2006. Unfinished Business*, edited by Small Arms Survey, 2006. http://www.smallarmssurvey.org/fileadmin/docs/A-Yearbook/2006/en/Small-Arms-Survey-2006-Chapter-05-EN.pdf.

Sophal, Chan. *Review of Labor Migration Management: Policies and Legal Framework in Cambodia.* Working Paper 11, Bangkok: ILO, 2009.

Springer, Simon. "Articulated Neoliberalism: The Specificity of Patronage, Kleptocracy, and Violence in Cambodia's Neoliberalization"." *Environment and Planning* 43 (2011): 2554–2570.

Sturgess, Patricia and Christopher Flower. *Land and Conflict in Sierra Leone: A Rapid Desk-Based Study*, 2013. http://www.evidenceondemand.info/land-and-conflict-in-sierra-leone-a-rapid-desk-based-study.

Suárez, Sofía Monsalve. "The Human Rights Framework in Contemporary Agrarian Struggles." *Journal of Peasant Studies,* 1 (2013): 239–290. doi:10.1080/03066150.2011.652950.

Subedi, Surya. *Report of the Special Rapporteur on the Situation of* Human Rights in Cambodia. UN Human Rights Council, 2011. http://www.refworld.org/docid/4e7331222.html.

Suhrke, Astri, and Mats Berdal. *The Peace in between.* London: Routledge, 2013.

Temper, Leah, Daniela Del Bene, and Joan Martinez-Alier. "Mapping the Frontiers and Front Lines of Global Environmental Justice: The EJAtlas." *Journal of Political Ecology* 22 (2015): 255–278.

Thaler, Kai. *Large-Scale Land Acquisitions and Social Conflict in Africa.* Conference Paper for Discussion at: Food Sovereignty: A Critical Dialogue International Conference September 14–15, 2013.

Thorburn, Craig. "The Plot Thickens: Land Administration and Policy in Post New Order Indonesia." *Asia Pacific Viewpoint* 45, no. 1 (2004): 33–49.

Thyl de Lopez, Thanakvao. "Natural Resource Exploitation in Cambodia: An Examination of Use, Appropriation, and Exclusion." *The Journal of Environment & Development* 11, no. 4 (2002): 355–379.

Tilly, Charles. *The Politics of Collective Violence.* Cambridge: Cambridge University Press, 2003.

Titthara, May. "Memories of a Land Unspoiled". In *The Pnom Penh Post.* December 20, 2013. http://www.phnompenhpost.com/national/memories-land-unspoiled.

Touch, Siphat, and Andreas Neef. *Resistance to Land Grabbing and Displacement in Rural Cambodia.* Conference Paper, No. 16, Chiang Mai, 2015.

Wood, Reed, and Marc Gibney. "Political Terror Scale, 1976-2012." *Human Rights Quarterly* 35, no. 2 (2015): 367–400.

Gold mining in Colombia, post-war crime and the peace agreement with the FARC

Frédéric Massé and Philippe Le Billon

ABSTRACT

Peace negotiations with left-wing insurgent groups have brought hope for a reduction in illegal economic activities in Colombia, including gold mining. We consider the impact of a transition to peace on possible trajectories of post-war crime in the gold sector, focusing on its major conflict-crime connections and responses by government authorities. We suggest that illegalities will likely persist, if not increase, in the post-war period given the challenges of consolidating Colombian state presence in mining areas, rapidly incentivising and assisting gold miners to formalise, and implementing stricter and more comprehensive due diligence measures in the mineral supply chain.

Introduction

Numerous studies have demonstrated a link between extractive sectors and armed conflicts, and notably a risk of renewed violence and criminalisation in resource-rich post-war transition contexts.[1] Given these concerns, policy interventions have included the prolongation of commodity sanctions, the demobilisation of insurgents and policing of resources areas, the formalisation and certification of resource extraction actors and activities, as well as the promotion of foreign direct investment into large-scale extractive projects and the repression of related social-environmental opposition.[2] Much attention has also been devoted to establish 'clean supply chains' able to bring 'conflict-free' minerals to market. Here, we look at the case of gold in Colombia and the likelihood of producing 'crime-free gold' following the peace agreement with the main left-wing guerrilla.

The attractiveness of gold for insurgents and criminal organisations in Colombia came to both domestic and international attention around 2010, in the midst of a global gold rush triggered by sharply rising gold prices.[3] Whereas much attention has been devoted to diamonds and coltan, gold has taken a prominent place in this international agenda given its widespread geographical occurrence, long-established use in illicit financial flows, and massive environmental impacts.[4] As a legal commodity mostly produced by an informal sector long tolerated by the Colombian state, gold also presented fewer risks than narcotics for producers and traffickers, thereby attracting a wide array of criminal entrepreneurs but also many coca workers seeking alternative livelihoods.[5] The remote location of many gold deposits and relatively low capital requirements made gold mining attractive to leftist insurgent groups, like the *Fuerzas Armadas Revolucionarias de Colombia-Ejército del Pueblo* (FARC-EP, thereafter FARC). Interest in gold also extended to money laundering, as gold's high price to weight ratio, wide market, and difficult traceability make it a convenient financial instrument to launder large revenues from drug trafficking and other illegal activities. Besides money laundering and alternative employment source for *cocaleros*, illegal gold mining has entertained complex relationships with the coca sector – including reinvestments across the two sectors and land purchases – often as part of a diversified portfolio of criminal activities, with gold and coca being more complementary than substitute activities.

In short, illegal armed groups and criminal organisations easily tapped into the gold sector through extortion, direct exploitation, and money laundering; a situation that became of significant concern for Colombian authorities. By 2014, President Santos declared a 'war against criminal mining'.[6] This position not only reflected Colombian security issues, but also growing concerns for the social and environmental impacts of mining, and the reputation of the Colombian gold sector. Although mining issues were not officially part of the peace negotiations with the FARC – though it is assumed to be part of the agenda of the other leftist insurgent group, the *Ejército de Liberación Nacional* (ELN) – the government expects that the end of the armed conflict will allow for both a 'clean-up' of the gold sector and a boosting of mining investments.

Drawing from primary and secondary sources, as well as interviews conducted in Colombia with representatives from companies, mining organisations, public security agents, prosecutors, and members of illegal armed groups between January 2015 and December 2016, we briefly present in the second section the characteristics of Colombia's gold sector, its illegal and criminal dimensions, as well as its relative importance to the FARC. We then examine in the third section the responses by the Colombian Government and the effects that some policies and implementation challenges have had on the illegalisation and growing criminalisation of the informal sector. The fourth section outlines the three main options for the post-war gold sector, including a 'pax mafiosa' through which criminal continue to permeate the sector but with little armed violence. We then discuss in the fifth section, the likely implication of the transition to peace, suggesting that it will have limited effects on the criminalities involved in the gold sector, and could even contribute to a breakdown of social order in some former FARC-controlled mining communities and aggravate criminal practices within legalised mining activities. We conclude with a brief discussion of the difficulties of bringing about a 'crime-free' gold production as compared to 'conflict-free' gold, and outline both further research needs and some practical implications for Colombia's transition period out of a five decades long conflict with the FARC.

Gold mining, illegalities and armed actors in Colombia

Mining for gold in Colombia has a long history rooted in both indigenous and colonial practices.[7] The Colombian gold sector experienced a major boom between 2008 and 2012 as a result of fast rising gold prices, but also a more effective fight against narcotics production and trafficking, and high levels of poverty, unemployment and displacement creating an abundant workforce (see Figure 1). By 2016, Colombia produced about 61 tons of gold and had become a mid-size producer ranking as the sixth largest Latin American gold

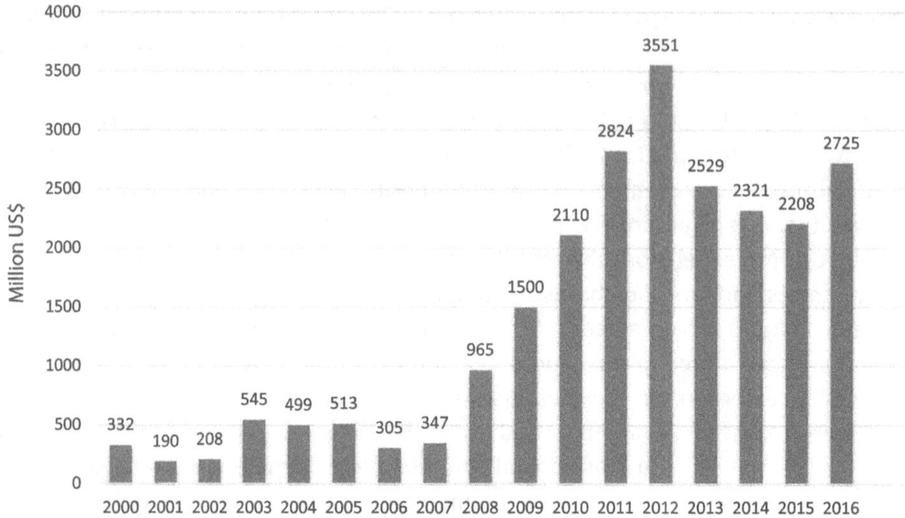

Figure 1. Colombia gold production value (2000–2016). Source: MinMinas and industry sources.

producer, and twentieth in the world. Accounting for about 0.8% of GDP, gold represented Colombia's fourth major export product, after oil, coal, and coffee.[8]

Gold mining is widely dispersed around the country, with about 20% of municipalities showing geological prospects and mining activities occurring in at least 12 of Colombia's 32 departments. Yet, as seen in Figure 2, most of the current mining areas are located in the departments of Antioquía, Chocó and Bolivar, of which have a presence of left-wing guerrilla groups (esp. FARC, but also the ELN) and heirs of paramilitary groups or 'criminal organisations' (Bacrim). In late 2012, the Attorney General's Office estimated that out of the 489 municipalities with presence of illegal mining in general (out of a total of 1123 in Colombia), almost 40% had presence of the FARC, the ELN and/or the Bacrim. Today several FARC demobilisation camps remain relatively close to gold mining areas, most notably in Antioquia (especially Fronts 9, 18, 34, 36, 58), and to a lesser extent in Cauca (Fronts 6, 29, 30) and Chocó (Fronts 34, 57), and the presence of the ELN and Criminal Organisations (CO) near gold mining areas remains particularly strong in Antioquia, Chocó, Nariño and South Bolivar. From this overview, the risk profile of continued links between gold and illegal armed groups seems highest in Antioquia (from ELN, CO and possibly demobilised FARC units), followed by Chocó (from ELN and CO), and Cauca (from CO and possibly demobilised FARC units).

Colombia experienced a large inflow of foreign direct investment into mining as a result of the liberalisation of the mining code in 2001, rising commodity prices, and relative improvement of the security situation.[9] Such investments, in turn, increased the market for quasi-extortionary private security and other service provision by criminal organisations.[10] Yet, the gold boom in Colombia does not owe much to foreign direct investments, especially when compared to other extractive sectors such as oil and coal. By 2011, large-scale gold mining operations (*gran mineria*) complying with the complex legal requirements accounted for less than 12% of total production. In short, the boom mostly resulted from the growth of the informal sector, with only 13.3% of the 4133 gold mining production units identified by the 2011 Mining Census having a mining title.[11] The informal sector includes two main categories of gold production. The first consists of subsistence ancestral or artisanal mining

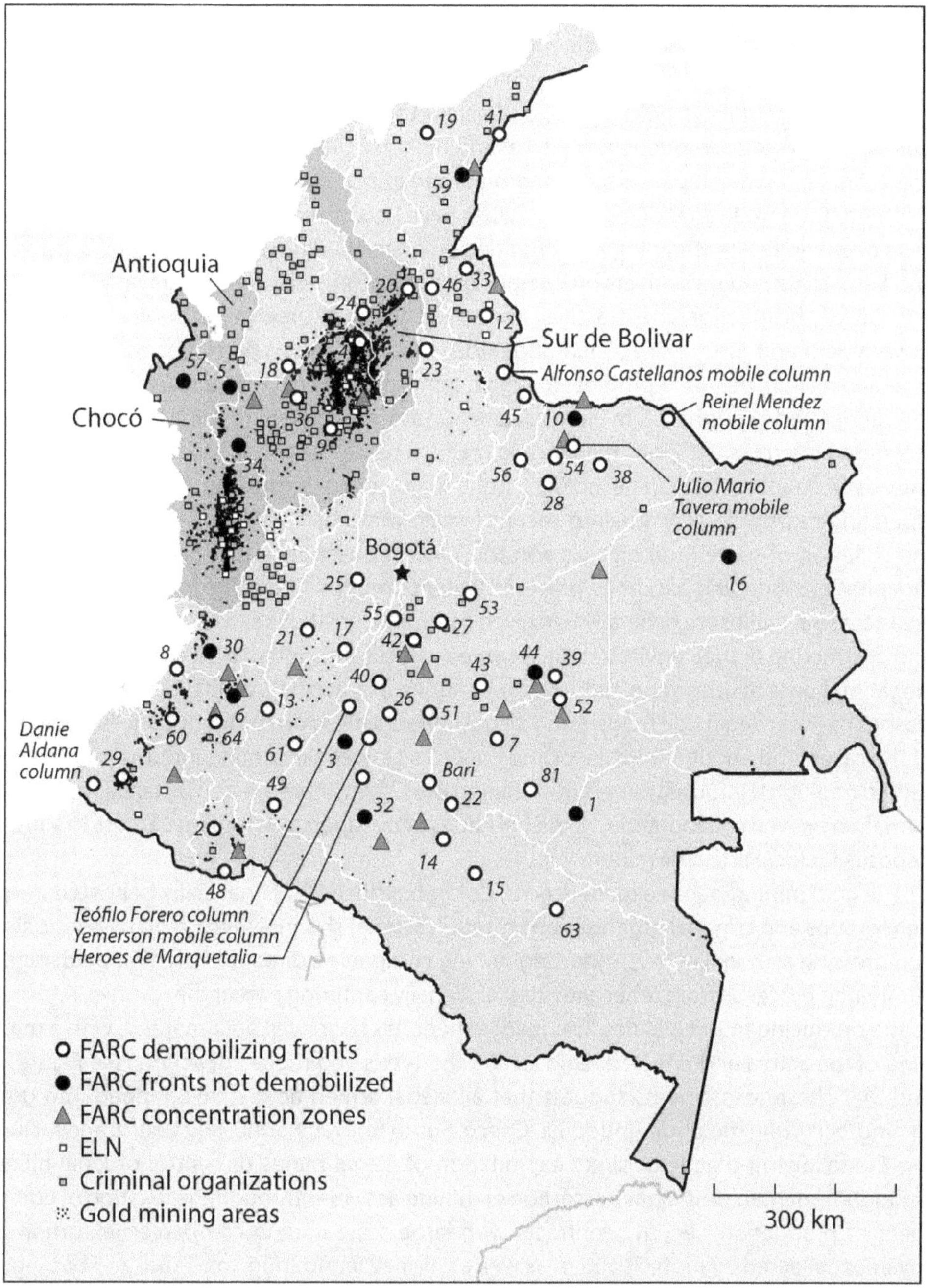

Figure 2. Gold mining areas, insurgent groups and criminal organisations. Source: Güiza and Aristizabal, "Mercury and Gold Mining"; data communicated by UNODC and UNIMIC; Accessed 11 March 2017. https://colombia2020.elespectador.com/pais/el-mapa-final-para-la-concentracion-de-las-farc.

Notes: Symbols for illegal armed groups represent the approximate location of the epicentre of their operations, with areas of presence being generally much larger, especially for the FARC in the eastern part of the country.

(*barequero*) using hand-panning and some rudimentary mechanical tools (pumps, crushers), part of which is conducted by indigenous populations and Afro-Colombians.[12] The second consists of small-to-medium scale mechanised operations using backhoes and dredgers (*pequeña y mediana mineria*). As discussed below, the latter category has provided both the bulk of 'illegal' gold production as well as the most profitable opportunities for extortion, protection, or ownership by insurgent groups and criminal organisations.

These three categories of mining activities have had mixed relations, with frequent conflicts between resident mining communities, small-to-medium scale mining by 'outsiders', and large-scale mining projects by foreign companies. Tensions were aggravated in part as a result of the neoliberal extractivist model legally instituted in 2001 by the Pastrana Government and further deepened under the Uribe and Santos presidencies.[13] Mobilising legal and military means to promote foreign mining investment under a low taxation regime, the model had brought 4.8 million hectares under concessionary mining titles by 2010, increasing overlaps with informal mining areas. Tensions also resulted from the arrival of 'outsiders' financed by capital holders from major cities (especially Medellin and Cali). Operating mostly illegally, small-to-medium scale ventures have generally benefited from the collusion of some local officials and the 'protection' of insurgent groups and criminal organisations. Bringing backhoes, powerful water pumps or dredgers into traditional mining areas, these activities are generally perceived by local populations as a looting of their savings and destruction of their environment. A survey of local authorities in 18 municipalities with illegal mining activities reported large migrations of informal miners in nearly all cases, clashes between legal title holders and illegal miners settled on company concession in half of the cases, and about a third reporting conflicts between incoming informal miners and settled traditional informal miners over mining sites.[14] Yet, there are also instances of accommodation or even collaboration, as the backhoes of 'outsiders' can facilitate access to alluvial deposits for local artisanal miners.[15]

The gold mining boom experienced in Colombia since 2008 financially benefited insurgent groups and criminal organisations through several channels, including by controlling and pressing artisanal miners, extorting mining companies, directly exploiting gold mines, laundering proceeds from other activities, or illegally capturing part of the royalties returned to the producing municipalities. This involvement has been well documented, with a mapping of the actors and affected regions, and the types and modes of action (see Figures 2 and 3).[16] These assessments suggest that all illegal armed actors have tapped into gold mining, occurring mostly in Antioquia, Chocó, South Bolivar, Nariño, and Cauca, and including the following practices: direct exploitation of illegal mines or control of legal mines through 'front men' (*testaferos*); extortion of mining activities through the taxation of equipment or production; security contracts with large-scale mining companies; extortion of royalties collected by municipalities; as well as money laundering, tax fraud, and bribing.[17]

It is much more difficult, however, to know the amount and distribution of revenues generated by illegal mining. Revenue estimates for the FARC have varied from one to twenty million dollars per year prior to 2014,[18] but had possibly increased to US$40 million by 2015, in part as FARC and ELN leadership would have requested their commanders to raise further revenues from this sector.[19] In Antioquia alone, FARC's income from extortion of illegal miners could have been as high as US$2 million a month.[20]

Several factors make estimations difficult. The first one has to do with the structure of the sector and its various degrees of (il)legality and permeability to insurgent groups and criminal

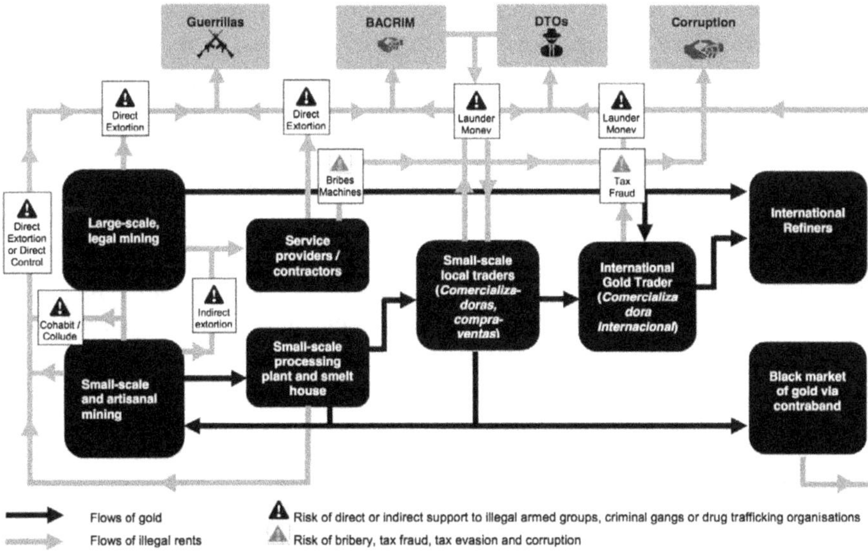

Figure 3. Relations of illegal armed groups to the gold sector. (See note 17 above. DTOs stand for Drug Trafficking Organizations.) Source: Massé and Munevar, OECD, 2016.

Table 1. Criminal dimensions in the gold sector.

- Extortion of mining activities by insurgent groups and criminal organisations
- Protection of illegal activities against authorities and local communities
- Participation and capital holding in mining ventures by insurgent groups and criminal organisations
- Money laundering, especially from drug trafficking, via mining activities
- Corruption of authorities to allow for (illegal) mining and retrocede royalties associated with money laundering through fake gold production
- Interpersonal violence, including homicides, within mining populations
- Abusive and dangerous labour conditions resulting in death and injuries
- Major environmental damages

Source: Colombian legislation and policies, OECD Due Diligence Guidance (Annex II).

organisations. As mentioned above, only 10–15% of gold production complies with *all* legal processes (e.g. mining title, environmental licenses, royalties payments). The rest is broadly considered 'illegal', but includes *informal* subsistence-level artisanal mining that is widely considered to be licit (or legitimate), including by authorities. By March 2017, about 120,000 gold panners had officially registered throughout the country.[21] A more narrowly defined *illegal* category consists of all operations that do not comply with legal requirements. Although illegal mining is not necessarily considered as a criminal offence, it used to be rhetorically described as such by the government until recently, for various reasons (see Table 1).

Second, the involvement of criminal organisations in the gold sector has *not* only to do with the profits generated by illegal exploitation or extortion, but also with the role served by gold in laundering the proceeds from other criminal activities, especially the sale of illicit drugs. As noted earlier, gold is widely traded and difficult to trace, especially once smelted. Gold bullion bought on the international market with drug money and illegally imported into Colombia is smelted and then falsely declared as produced from local mines. A scheme all the more attractive as criminal organisations were often able to recover a share of the royalties (*regalias*) retroceded to the municipalities where gold was supposedly produced (see below). Interestingly enough, between 2003 and 2011 gold export figures exceeded production figures, some of it bought from abroad illegally with drug money and re-exported legally.[22] Not only did leftist guerrillas, paramilitaries and criminal organisations exercise armed and political control over many of the country's gold mining areas, but in some regions, gold processing and trading became even easier to the extent that these actors had set up their own local gold buying shops (*compra-venta*), processing plants, smelters, and gold sales offices.[23] Drug money is also laundered through the gold sector via payments for the acquisition of mining equipment and supplies through front companies for insurgent groups or criminal organisations, in effect subsidising the mining sector as part of the laundered money go into buying machinery, especially backhoes.[24] Finally, fake gold exports are also declared to fraudulently recover false VAT claims.[25]

Government responses against illegal mining

Colombian public authorities did not initially consider the boom in 'illegal' mining as a prominent issue since gold had long been mined at artisanal and small scales, and production kept flowing through official export channels. By 2010, however, illegal gold mining started receiving increasing media attention and some Colombian government agencies began perceiving it as a serious concern and even a matter of national security. In October 2012, the Andean Council of Ministers of Foreign Affairs approved decision 774 in order to formalise or regularise small-scale mining, or artisanal and traditional mining; authorise the destruction of machinery if it cannot be confiscated; control and tax the importation of machinery; and combat the laundering of assets and related crimes products of illegal mining. The Colombian Government progressively incorporated these decisions into its domestic legislation and adopted new ones, including on gold traceability, intensifying and militarising police interventions, improving detection, facilitating formalisation, and reforming some fiscal dimensions.

In December 2012, Decree 2637 created the Single Register of Mineral Marketers (RUCOM) requiring that all the gold sold by marketers comes from miners who hold title and comply with environmental standards.[26] Yet, illegally mined gold can still be laundered through the production quota of 107,000 panners officially registered, representing nearly 50 tons per year or about 90% of the Colombian production. To reduce the mechanisation of informal and illegal mining, the decree also authorised the *in situ* destruction of heavy machinery used in illegal mining (dredgers, backhoes, etc.), rather than simply their confiscation, and the Colombian Government increased controls on heavy machinery imports and interventions against mechanised illegal mining. In parallel, a dedicated unit against natural resources and environmental crimes within the Attorney's General Office was created and investigated more than 6000 mining projects, among which 484 related to criminal investigations against illegal gold mining; yet, less than 50 cases ended with indictments and convictions.[27] Therefore, several legislations were being considered to allow for judicial and security forces to prosecute cases of illegal mining with charges of money laundering or illicit enrichment, rather than only for environmental damages.[28] In order to reinforce its inter-agency collaboration, the government created the Unit Against Criminal Mining (UNIMIC) in January 2014, and developed early detection of alluvial illegal mining through the satellite imagery system used for illegal crops detection, in cooperation with UNODC.

Finally, royalties reallocated to municipalities have been reduced and mayors can no longer decide how to use them.

The impact of increasing repression against illegal gold mining, together with slightly downward prices in gold and the suspension of aerial fumigation and reduction in manual eradication against coca, may have contributed a little to an increase in coca production given past patterns of balancing between coca and gold mining activities. Such possible impact, however, should be treated with caution given that coca farm-gate prices also declined, that the price of gold in Colombian pesos remained about the same given its depreciation against the US dollar, and that the effectiveness of repressive measures seem to be undermined by a 'balloon effect' whereby increased government pressure in one region simply moves activities to other geographical areas.[29]

Repressive approaches have been complemented by attempts to formalise and legalise gold mining activities, but stringent requirements and lengthy processes have left many miners within the informal sector. Even among legally-titled operations, many were not compliant with fiscal, environmental and labour regulations.[30] In response to critiques, President Santos launched a new plan to legalise and formalise 'illegal' miners during his first mandate, with the new policy going into operation in mid 2014.[31] Yet by 2015, close to 20,000 demands for mining titles from artisanal and small-scale miners were still awaiting a response.[32]

To sum-up, the Colombian Government has taken many measures over the past five years to curb down illegal mining and the involvement of illegal armed groups and criminal organisations. Yet, government interventions have faced many difficulties due to the high number of mining sites, their remote location, the relative absence of the state, threats against government officials, the adaptation of illegal practices to new measures, and arduous legalisation and formalisation processes motivating many miners to remain illegal.

Golden peace, mining wars, or *pax mafiosa*?

Post-war transitions generally involve a change in the logics of hostilities, generally understood as a shift from politically motivated violence to criminal violence driven by economic motives.[33] Such changes, in turn, call into question the benefits of a peace agreement, as some forms of violence persist or become aggravated.[34] Beyond optimist depictions a fair and peaceful gold sector and pessimist predictions of widespread 'post-war' violence around gold mining, another option is that the sector will come under a *pax mafiosa* whereby criminal interests continue permeating the sector but with little overt physical violence.[35] We briefly discuss each below.

Golden peace

On 10 December 2016, the Nobel Peace Prize committee awarded a gold medal to Colombian President Juan Manuel Santos in recognition of his efforts to bring about a negotiated peace with the FARC. Minted from Colombian gold extracted from two *Fairmined* certified mines, the medal was not only symbolic of a hard-won prize, but also aspirations for a conflict-free and fair mining sector in Colombia. The post-war transition could bring a 'golden peace', one not only ending criminal practices within mining, but also decriminalising and improving legitimate ASM practices. The final peace agreement between the FARC and the Colombian

Government does include a brief mention of this, with both parties agreeing on the need to confront criminal mining and to ensure a tax monopoly of the public treasury, but also recognising that artisanal mining does not constitute criminal mining.[36]

In the optimistic perspective of a 'Golden Peace', the most conflict-affected gold-bearing regions would benefit from the demobilisation of the guerrillas, with large-scale companies been less at risk of being blackmailed and facing security risks for their facilities and personnel, thereby helping to reduce demand for generous tax breaks and costly military protection. Artisanal and small-scale miners trapped by the logics of armed conflicts could work with less fear or pressure of being threatened, extorted, arrested or their equipment destroyed because of their presumed association with the FARC. Such post-war context could also facilitate ASM formalisation in mining areas under FARC control or influence and development outreach processes, not to mention improving the delivery of government services. In other words, on paper, a 'golden peace' would bring a safer, and fairer context for the gold mining sector to operate, and for communities in gold-mining regions to prosper.

As a *Fairmined* staff notes, however, 'this will depend mostly on the measures taken by the government and the implementation of the agreements'.[37] So far, and as discussed above, the measures taken by the government have shown their limits. In the absence of stronger due diligence initiatives to implement responsible gold production and trade, current policies are likely to sustain the laundering of 'illegal and criminal' gold through artisanal production quotas, to confine many small-scale entrepreneurs to the realm of the illegal and to predation from the criminal organisations, and to contribute to an escalation of social conflicts over large-scale mining projects disposing local communities. Failing to positively transform the sector, the 'golden peace' is likely to be superseded by 'mining war' pitting local mining communities, social movements, criminal organisations, public forces and large mining companies.

Mining wars

In a remote corner of Colombia, a low flying military aircraft drops a bomb on a bright orange backhoe seemingly lost on a denuded patch of tropical forest. This bombardment, though rare, illustrates the rise of militarised confrontations between public forces and illegal mining operations since first launched in 2012. Pessimist perspectives generally see high levels of violence affecting the 'post-war' mining sector, along three main types of 'mining war'. The first type pits public forces against criminal networks, with a Colombian Government engaging into a long war of attrition against an increasingly militarised and criminalised sector shaped by the profitability of illegal operations, a sense of legitimacy among many miners, as well as the poverty and lack of alternative among many workers. In this scenario, FARC's demobilisation has no significant effect. As a UNIMIC police colonel remarked, 'Did the war on drugs end with the capture of Pablo Escobar? No … and in the mining sector, we don't even have a Pablo Escobar to arrest'.[38] Indeed despite been the largest guerrilla group in the country, FARC certainly did not have a monopoly on illegal mining. By early 2017, there was every indication that the demobilisation of the FARC would neither result in the end of illegal mining, nor in the end of militarised operations against it.[39]

A second type of 'mining war' pits criminal networks and remaining insurgent groups against each other for the control of the most lucrative mining mine sites and transportation corridors. In this respect, there is widespread concern that FARC's demobilisation will open up its former mining areas to increased violent competition against the remaining non-state armed groups and criminal organisations. Again, by early 2017, there were some signs of such violent competition, in Chocó, Bajo Cauca Antioqueño, Cauca, Catatumbo and Nariño.[40]

A third type of 'mining war' relates to tensions between groups supporting large-scale mining and social movements opposing such projects. High-level government officials often reassert the imperative of resource extraction for Colombia's development in a post-war transition. For the Colombia minister of defense,

> The exploitation of our natural resources is absolutely necessary for the future of the country, and for post-conflict. We need to do so with the greatest social and environmental responsibility, but these are incomes that are required for the financing of the coming programs.[41]

Despite seeing the logic of public revenues again at work,[42] critics point that so far the Colombian people may in fact subsidise the large-scale mining industry, given the low rate of royalties, the prevalence of tax holidays and part of the high security costs bore by the Colombian state.[43] Such tensions may result in the repression of social protests and targeted killing of community and political leaders resisting mineral exploitation.[44] As discussed below, opinions diverge about the role that 'post-war' FARC may play in this regard. Whereas FARC would be expected to consolidate or instrumentalise civil society movements opposing large-scale mining, the former guerrilla movement may use its local clout and social control to help facilitate arrangements between communities and companies.[45]

Pax mafiosa

Until a few years ago, large mining ventures resulted almost systematically into conflicts. The arrival of companies was generally resisted by artisanal and small-scale miners, who were frequently threatened, blackmailed, displaced or even assassinated by illegal armed groups seeking to directly mine or collect protection money.[46] These confrontational relations have evolved in recent years, reflecting a change of strategy among illegal armed actors now seeking to avoid open confrontations that could bring the intervention of public authorities. Some illegal armed groups have in this respect implemented two 'mafia peace' strategies. Instead of violently expulsing or extorting small artisanal miners, illegal armed groups have enrolled them through recruiting less 'outsiders' to work in the mines, as well as created and instrumentalised local miners associations to produce 'cleaner' gold.[47] Instead of directly extort mining companies through threats of violence, illegal groups have also arranged a *qui pro quo* whereby companies do not complain to the government about illegal mining taking place within or close to their concession in exchange for a relative peace; an arrangement that can even see companies laundering gold from nearby illegal mining operations for mutual profits. Such arrangements enabling illegal mining to thrive generally require the collusion of government officials, at least at a local level.[48] In some places, this collusion would be so widespread that local residents reportedly call Public Forces the 'Green Eagles' – in reference to the notorious Black Eagles (*Aguilas Negras*) criminal organisation.[49] Local mayors and landowners in gold producing municipalities with poor service delivery and bureaucratic management are also reported to tolerate illegal mining in return for bribes and 'budgetary support', thereby providing a fertile ground for illegal armed groups and criminal organisations.[50] Some mayors have also partly financed their political campaigns through donations from mining companies, while some local officials are also reported to have interests in illegal mining ventures.[51] The viability of these arrangements require profitable economic activities and a precarious but stable social environment without much direct violence.

In short, such *pax mafiosa* enables criminal organisations to maintain illegal practices lucrative for many, while being rarely violent.[52] This suggests that legalisation and formalisation efforts will not rid the sector of collusion with and pressure from illegal or criminal armed groups. In other words, 'being legal' will not solve all problems, since mining could continue being permeated by illegal armed groups and criminal organisations. In turn, the apparent 'normality' of these mining areas could leave government authorities to let such mafiosi enclaves to be 'auto-regulated', whereby criminal powers could actually continue exploiting or benefiting from gold, without much state intervention, as seen in the case of the emerald mining areas in the last 20 years.[53] The problem therefore is not only about establishing a state presence in areas where none or very little existed, but also about gaining the confidence of populations from these areas in the Colombian state. As mafiosi enclaves will likely develop, due diligence efforts in the gold mining sector might be undermined by the persistence of other criminal armed groups and mafian processes.

Post-agreement guerrilla: entrepreneurship, social order, and mining conflicts

With the demobilisation of FARC combatants (about 6000 troops and 5–7000 militias) during the first semester of 2017, future FARC's involvement with the gold mining sector remains uncertain. Demobilised FARC groups may be able to maintain some control over mining activities for a couple of months after demobilisation, in part through their front men and relays within communities.[54] As observed in other post-war situations, some demobilised FARC members may work as miners and some FARC officers have informally expressed an interest in running mining companies and securing investments. Yet, there is no survey indicating how many ex-combatants intend to work in the sector, and the FARC General Secretariat has not publicly stated an interest in running mines.[55] On the government side, neither the *Agencia Colombiana para la Reintegración* (ACR) nor the Ministry of Mines and Energy have issued statements or prepared plans for mining related livelihoods and business ventures for the FARC; a situation which reflects the more general delays experienced in demobilisation processes, but also in part because of the predominantly 'illegal' or at least 'informal' character of gold mining in most FARC-held areas (with ACR not being able to support reintegration into informal sectors), the lack of prioritisation of this issue by the Ministry of Mines and Energy, and possibly because of a government perception associating mining with various risks for the peace process – which would have led the government to try to set up quartering and demobilisation camps far from identified mining sites.[56] Involvement with the gold sector by demobilised FARC is thus, so far, most likely to take the form of informal and individualised initiatives.

In contrast to demobilised FARC units, dissident FARC groups could maintain if not increase their control (direct or indirect) over mining activities. FARC dissidents do not appear to have yet fully engaged in criminal mining, but if drug prices remain low, they might be tempted to do so. Out of the five FARC commanders, who officially announced their dissidence in December 2016, the most important is Gentil Duarte ('Euclides Mora') an Estado Mayor member sent to bring Front 1 in Guaviare (and part of the Oriental Block) back into the fold after it rejected the peace agreement; Another one, Géner Garcia Molina ('John 40'), had been reported as deeply involved in drug trafficking and to some extent in mining through his role in Front 43 in the department of Meta.[57] Both departments of Meta and Guaviare have some gold mining activities. Perhaps more relevant in terms of current gold mining activities were embryos and limited signals of dissidence in Nariño, Chocó, Cauca and Caqueta,[58] although, geographically speaking, FARC dissidence does not always coincide with gold mining regions.

More generally, there seems to be a concern, amongst both government officials (including security forces) and some gold mining communities still under FARC control, that demobilisation and disarmament will drastically reduce FARC's influence as a 'rule enforcer' and 'protection/extortion' actor in mining areas. Many expect a continued vacuum in terms of state presence, and thus a very likely take over by other illegal armed groups and criminal organisations, either conducing to a rise in violence, assassinations and extortion, or to a new modus vivendi, where direct and indirect extortion would remain the norm but violence would be less visible.[59] UNODC noted with respect to the narcotics sector that the peace process had already resulted in a rearrangement of criminal groups, and a growth in narcotics production.[60] In turn, this increase in drug revenue could further increase laundering through the gold supply chain.

The peace agreement brings FARC into mainstream politics, but the extent and character of its political engagement towards the mining sector remains debated, including within the movement itself. Given its rural roots and defence of peasant interests, FARC is expected to publicly oppose large-scale mining (*gran mineria*) as well as the vested interests of local traditional political elites in mining ventures. In 2013, FARC leader Timoleon Jimenez did situate FARC as a protector of small-scale mining, arguing that,

> [t]he national government and the large transnational companies are driven by the desire to take control of the entire mining business. Artisanal and informal miners must articulate themselves in some way to their productive projects, just as small rural owners must associate, lease or sell their land to agrofuel investors, [and as a result] the FARC, who represent and defend them, must be extinguished and condemned to hell by any means.[61]

So far, this articulation has taken several forms, including: (i) selective inclusion of informal mining operations under formalisation schemes, at time under threat of repression and following a messy and (backlash) co-existence/collusion with ex paramilitaries; (ii) extinguishment of customary mining rights, replaced by concessionary titles; (iii) a dual process including a arduous formalisation processes associated with a progressive hardening of repression. Such processes have indeed left most informal miners with few options other than continue operating as clandestinely as possible, gaining the tacit support of local-level authorities through corruption and co-optation, and joining the ranks of 'approved' miner sub-contracted by large mining companies.

On the other hand, the FARC could also prove to be pragmatic in its attitude towards mining companies, and act as a 'deal broker' between communities, informal miners, and large mining companies. FARC is expected to try to keep a certain control of social order, especially among remote communities where the movement has been replacing the Colombian state for many years. Some mining company representatives have already expressed a hope to see FARC play a regulating role in terms of social conflicts and help bring greater cohesiveness within communities, notably to reduce the influence of community members with a strong anti-mining stance.[62] The attitude of community-level mining organisations vis à vis the FARC will vary greatly according to past relations between the community and the guerrilla, but also the degree of emancipation sought out by these organisations. By early 2017, the FARC seems to face the opposition of some long-established ethnic mining communities suspecting the ex-guerrilla leaders of trying to set up and develop their own social organisations in order to gain or regain social and political support in those regions.[63]

Finally, the negotiations and peace process with the ELN are more likely to have a greater impact on the gold sector than that those with the FARC. The mining issue is for the ELN what the agrarian or rural issue was for the FARC; that is, an ideologically and historically motivated issue.[64] Beyond this historical foundation and motivational aspect, the ELN has also had closer ties and organisational involvement with gold mining communities, and it derived a much larger proportion of its revenues from extractives sectors (mostly oil and gold) than FARC. The ELN at times mixed a dual agenda of resource nationalism and extortion practices, when for example it sequestrated a Canadian executive from a junior mining company in 2013 and obtained that the company abandoned its mining concessions.[65]

Conclusion

Gold mining is not new in Colombia, yet the scale of exploitation and its criminal characterisation by the government are unprecedented. Protracted armed conflicts, a war on drugs and a decade of sustained high gold prices have encouraged illegal armed actors to diversify their portfolio of activities into the gold mining sector, either by pressing or co-opting traditional artisanal miners, or getting directly involved in the illegal exploitation of resources. The peace agreement with the FARC will help address some of the criminal dimensions of Colombia's gold sector, but many are likely to continue in the 'post-war' period.

First, the peace agreement signed with the FARC does not apply to other illegal armed groups. Furthermore, not all FARC units and members have decided to lay down their arms, and some combatants may withdraw from the DDR process, to integrate or engage into opportunistic partnerships or competition with the ELN or other illegal armed groups for control of drug trafficking routes and mining areas.[66] Second, FARC's demobilisation and the 'post-war' transition will have limited effects on the criminalities involved in the gold sector, and could even contribute to the breakdown of social ordering in some mining communities, violent struggle for control over former FARC mining territories, and aggravated criminal practices within legalised mining activities. Third, informal mining operations are unlikely to be replaced by large projects run by 'legitimate' companies, a goal often pursued by governments and donor agencies in search of greater control over the mining sector.[67] The peace agreement should entice further investments into the mining sector, but FARC was far from being the only impediment to greater investment into Colombia's gold sector, and many deposits are too small and economically marginal to be viable for large formal operations.[68]

Overall, we thus suggest that the peace agreement with the FARC – and possibly with the ELN – is unlikely to automatically or necessarily translate into an end to illegal mining or relations between illegal and/or criminal armed actors and extractive sectors in Colombia. Other actors, who are not officially part of the armed conflict, have great interests in gold mining, and although it is necessary and useful, the formalisation and legalisation of artisanal and small-scale miners will not guarantee in itself the end of the interferences and criminal dynamics in the Colombian gold sector. We emphasise in this respect that many post-conflict situations experienced a rush on resources in the wake of peace agreements and demobilisation, especially when prices are high and coalitions of demobilised armed actors, government officials and business entrepreneurs evade or instrument legalisation efforts.[69] Although concerned with the massive environmental damages and some of the fiscal losses associated with illegal mining, we note the risk posed by a large-scale militarised response against ASM activities in terms of potential loss of access to mining areas for local communities, support among communities for armed actors and criminal organisations protecting illegal activities, and social conflicts against large-scale industrial mining ventures on the part of impoverished populations marginalised by decades of conflict and growing inequalities. As such, the challenge is not only to have gold mining free of armed conflict in Colombia, but rather to have mining free of the influences and impacts of a criminalised gold sector. Given the challenges of consolidating Colombian state presence and acceptance in many mining areas, the counterproductive regulatory approach and slow pace in incentivising and assisting gold miners to formalise, and the domestic as well as international difficulties in implementing stricter and more comprehensive due diligence measures throughout the mineral supply chain, we suggest that gold mining illegalities and criminalisation will likely persist, if not increase, in the post-war period.

Disclosure statement

Frédéric Massé worked on for the OECD on due diligence within the gold sector in Colombia.

Notes

1. Collier et al., "Post-conflict Risks"; Lujala and Rustad, "High-value Natural Resources".
2. See note 1 above.
3. Vélez-Torres, "Governmental Extractivism".
4. Bloomfield, *Dirty Gold*; and Young, "Responsible Sourcing".
5. Güiza, *La Minería de hecho*; Giraldo et al., *Informalidad e ilegalidad*; Giraldo, *El Gobierno del Oro*, 63–4; Idrobo et al., "Illegal Gold"; Massé and Camargo, *Actores Armados Ilegales*; Rettberg and Ortiz-Riomalo, "Golden Opportunity"; and Romero, "Mineŕia iĺícita".
6. Presidencia de la Republica, accessed March 11, 2017, https://wsp.presidencia.gov.co/Prensa/2014/Enero/Paginas/20140117_04-La-mineria-criminal-objetivo-de-alto-valor-advirtio-el-Presidente-Santos.aspx.
7. West, *Colonial Placer*.

8. *Censo Minero Departamental, 2010–2011*.
9. Mining FDI increased from US$500 million in 2002 to a peak of US$3 billion in 2013, declining to US$533 million by 2015 (Rettberg and Ortiz-Riomalo, "Golden Opportunity"; and MinMinas, *Política Minera*).
10. Massé and Camargo, *Actores Armados Ilegales*.
11. See note 8 above.
12. ABColombia, "Alimentando el conflicto".
13. See note 3 above.
14. Goñi Pacchioni et al., *Mineria Informal*.
15. Tubb, "Muddy Decisions".
16. See note 5 above.
17. Massé and Munevar, "Due Diligence".
18. Giraldo and Muñoz, *Informalidad e ilegalidad*; and McDermott, "Ivan Rios".
19. See note 17 above.
20. Giraldo and Muñoz, *Informalidad e ilegalidad*; and McDermott, "Ivan Ríos".
21. Interview with Ministry of Mines officials.
22. Venezuelan gold would also be illegally imported into Colombia to be passed as Colombian gold and re-exported legally to benefit from lower royalty in Colombia (4% for vein/lode deposits and 6% for alluvial deposits, compared to a 13% flat rate in Venezuela). Rudas and Espitia, *Participación del Estado*.
23. *El Tiempo*, "con oro"; and Massé, "Minería y post conflicto".
24. GAFISUD, *Tipologías regionales*; OECD, *Due Diligence in Colombia*.
25. Interview with tax and customs (DIAN) officials.
26. OECD, *Due Diligence in Colombia*.
27. Massé and Munevar, "Due Diligence".
28. Accessed March 11, 2017, https://www.portafolio.co/economia/mineria-ilegal-tendra-penas-altas-en-colombia-502313.
29. Interviews with police officials, December 2016.
30. See note 8 above.
31. Echavaria, "What is Legal?"; and Ministerio de Minas y Energía, "Política Nacional".
32. Lydersen and Cardona-Maguigad, *Survival, Profit*.
33. But see, Keen, *Economic Functions*.
34. Berdal and Suhrke, *The Peace in between*; Nussio and Howe, "When Protection Collapses".
35. Massé, "¿Hacia una pax mafiosa".
36. Acuerdo Final, 24 November 2016, 79; accessed May 23, 2017, https://www.altocomisionadoparalapaz.gov.co/procesos-y-conversaciones/Documentos%20compartidos/24-11-2016NuevoAcuerdoFinal.pdf.
37. ARM staff, pers.com., 12 December 2016.
38. Interview with senior police officer, Bogota, December 2016.
39. Fundación Paz y Reconciliación, *En qué están los territorios*; and Fundación Ideas para la Paz, *Siete regiones sin las FARC*.
40. Fundación Paz y Reconciliación, *En qué están los territorios*; and Fundación Ideas para la Paz, *Siete regiones sin las FARC*.
41. Accessed September 27, 2016, https://www.wradio.com.co/noticias/actualidad/mindefensa-considera-que-la-explotacion-minera-es-necesaria-para-el-posconflicto/20160927/nota/3258099.aspx.
42. Accessed March 11, 2017, https://www.elnuevodia.com.co/nuevodia/actualidad/politica/282313-si-la-mineria-ilegal-se-legalizara-los-ingresos-para-el-pais-se-duplicari#sthash.B4OLHOPG.dpuf.
43. Garay, *Minería en Colombia*; and Rochlin, *Profits, Security*.
44. Justice for Colombia, *Silenced*.
45. Interviews with company officials and civil society representatives with access to FARC members, December 2016.
46. Massé and Camargo, *Actores Armados Ilegales*.
47. Massé, *Mineria y post conflicto*; and Tubb, "Muddy Decisions".

48. Interviews with local miners; Giraldo, "El Gobierno del Oro"; Giraldo and Muñoz, *Informalidad e ilegalidad*.
49. Interview with authors, December 2016. Colombian security forces, however, are not directly involved in illegal mining activities, contrary to many other conflict-affected mining regions around the world such as Angola or the DRC.
50. Giraldo, *El Gobierno del Oro*.
51. Interview with local authorities; Silva et al., *La Confianza*.
52. Massé, "¿Hacia una *pax mafiosa*".
53. Brazeal, "Nostalgia".
54. Interview with Ariel Avila Martinez, December 2016.
55. Interview with government official involved in peace negotiations with the FARC, December 2016.
56. Interviews with the authors, Bogotá, December 2016.
57. Hernandez-Mora, "No es solo"; Felder, "Why Colombia"; and FARC-EP, "FARC-EP Separa".
58. Accessed March 11, 2017, https://www.cronicaviva.com.pe/varios-frentes-de-las-farc-anuncian-que-no-firmaran-acuerdo-de-paz/.
59. See also Nussio and Howe, "When Protection".
60. Interviews with counter-narcotics officials, Bogota, December 2016.
61. The statement was grounded in the assertion that only 14% of gold production came from the legal sector while 11 million hectares had been allocated to industrial mining companies. See Timoleón Jiménez, "El cuento de la minería ilegal".
62. Interview with industry representative, December 2016.
63. Interview with leaders of Afro Colombian mining organisations, May 2017.
64. See for example, Medina Gallego, *FARC-EP y ELN*.
65. Drost, "Canadian Mining Executive Freed".
66. There could still be about 5400–6700 members of illegal armed groups after Peace Agreement with the FARC, including 900–1200 FARC troops (15% of its current strength refusing demobilization, and 5% rearming after demobilization), 1000–1500 ELN troops, and 3500–4000 Bacrim members and former paramilitaries released from prison. Interviews with conflicts analysts and intelligence officers, December 2016, Bogota.
67. Bray, "Attracting Reputable Companies".
68. Le Billon and Sommerville, "Landing Capital". For Colombia-specific concerns within the mining industry, see Rodriguez and Buteau, "Colombia, a Country of Challenges".
69. Lujala and Rustad, "High-value Resources"; and Le Billon, this volume.

Bibliography

ABColombia. *Alimentando el conflicto en Colombia: El impacto de la minería de oro en Chocó* [Fuelling Conflict in Colombia: The Impact of Gold Mining in Chocó]. Tierra Digna and CINEP, October 30, 2017.

Aguilera, M. *Guerrilla y Población Civil, Trayectoría de las FARC 1949–2013* [Guerrilla and Civilian Population, Trajectory of the FARC 1949–2013]. Bogotá: Informe del Centro Nacional de Memoria Histórica, 2014.

Bannon, I., and P. Collier, eds. *Natural Resources and Violent Conflict: Options and Actions*. Washington, DC: World Bank, 2003.

Berdal, M., and A. Suhrke. *The Peace in Between: Post-war Violence and Peacebuilding*. London: Routledge, 2013.

Bloomfield, M. J. *Dirty Gold: How Activism Transformed the Jewelry Industry*. Cambridge, MA: MIT Press, 2017.

Bray, J. "Attracting Reputable Companies to Risky Environments: Petroleum and Mining Companies." In *Natural Resources and Conflict: What We Can Do*, edited by Ian Bannon and Paul Collier, 287–352. Washington, DC: World Bank, 2003.

Brazeal, B. "Nostalgia for War and the Paradox of Peace in the Colombian Emerald Trade." *The Extractive Industries and Society* 3, no. 2 (2016): 340–349.

Censo Minero Departamental, 2010–2011 [Departmental Mining Census, 2010–2011]. Bogota: Ministerio de Minas y Energia, 2012.

Collier, P., A. Hoeffler, and M. Söderbom. "Post-conflict Risks." *Journal of Peace Research* 45, no. 4 (2008): 461–478.

Drost, N. "Canadian Mining Executive Freed by Colombian Rebels." *Globe and Mail*, August 27, 2013.

Echavaria, C. *What is Legal? Formalising Artisanal and Small-scale Mining in Colombia*. London/Bogota: IIED/ARM, 2014.

Echavaria, C. "The Challenges of Artisanal Mining and the Symbolism of the Nobel Peace Prize," November 30, 2016. Accessed March 11, 2017. https://www.responsiblemines.org/es/blogs/entry/the-challenges-of-artisanal-mining-and-the-symbolism-of-the-nobel-peace-prize

El Tiempo. "con oro lavan dinero y se roban regalías, revela ex jefe 'para', Salvatore Mancuso" [Former Paramilitary Chief 'Salvatore Mancuso' Reveals that Money is Laundered and Royalties Stolen], July 31, 2010. Accessed March 11, 2017. https://www.eltiempo.com/archivo/documento/CMS-7835388

FARC-EP. "FARC-EP separa a 5 mandos de sus filas." [FARC-Ep Separate Itself from 5 of its Commanders.] Estado Mayor Central de las Fuerzas Armadas Revolucionarias de Colombia, December 13, 2016.

Felder, F. "Why Colombia's Mining Sector hasn't Lived up to its Promise." *Mining Markets*, August 6, 2014. Accessed December 8, 2016. https://www.miningmarkets.ca/features/why-colombias-mining-sector-hasnt-lived-up-to-its-promise/

Fundación Ideas para la Paz. *Siete regiones sin las FARC, ¿siete problemas más?* [Seven Regions Without FARC, Seven More Problematic Regions?] Bogotá, March 13, 2017.

Fundación Paz y Reconciliación. *En qué están los territorios que dejan las FARC* [Which are the Territories That FARC is leaving?]. Bogotá, January 31, 2017.

GAFISUD. "Tipologías regionales de GAFISUD Actividades y Profesiones No-Financieras Designadas (APNFD)." [Regional Typologies of GAFISUD Designated Non-Financial Activities and Professions (APNFD).] Financial Action Task Force on Money Laundering in South America, 2010.

Garay, L. J. *Minería en Colombia, Institucionalidad y Territorio: Paradojas y Conflictos* [Mining in Colombia, Insitutionalism and Territory: Paradoxes and Conflicts]. Bogotá: Contraloría General de la República, 2013.

Goñi Pacchioni, E. A., A. Sabogal Moreno, and R. Asmat. *Minería Informal Aurífera en Colombia: Principales Resultados del Levantamiento de la Línea Debase* [Informal Gold Mining in Colombia: Main Results on the Lifting of the Base Line]. Fedesarrolo and IDB, 2014.

Guáqueta, A. "Dimensiones políticas y económicas del conflicto armado en Colombia: Anotaciones teóricas y empíricas." [Political and Economic Dimensions of the Armed Conflict in Colombia: Theoretical and Empirical Annotations]. *Colombia Internacional* 55 (2003): 19–36.

Güiza, L. *La Minería de Hecho en Colombia* [De facto mining in Colombia]. Bogotá: Imprenta Nacional, 2010.

Güiza, L., and J. D. Aristizabal. "Mercury and Gold Mining in Colombia: A Failed State." *Universitas Scientiarum* 18, no. 1 (2013): 33–49.

Giraldo, J. *El Gobierno del Oro en el Bajo Cauca, una lectura Weberiana sobre la explotación aurífera aluvial no legal, Economía Criminal y Poder Político* [The Governance of Gold in the Lower Cauca, a Weberian Reading of Illegal Gold Exploitation, Criminal Economy and Political Power]. Medellín: Universidad EAFIT, 2013.

Giraldo, J., and J. C. Muñoz. *Informalidad e Ilegalidad en la Explotación del Oro y la Madera en Antioquia* [Informality and Illegality in the Exploitation of Gold and Timber in Antioquia]. Medellín: Universidad EAFIT – Proantioquia, 2012.

Hernandez-Mora, S. "No es solo oro lo que brilla en Guainía." [Gold is not the only Thing to Shine in Guainia.] *El Tiempo*, December 14, 2015. https://www.eltiempo.com/colombia/otras-ciudades/mineria-ilegal-en-guainia/16458155

Idrobo, N., D. Mejia, and A. M. Tribin. "Illegal Gold Mining and Violence in Colombia." *Peace Economics, Peace Science and Public Policy* 20, no. 1 (2014): 83–111.

Justice for Colombia. *Silenced. The Murder of Political Activists in Colombia*. Bogota, 2016. Accessed March 11, 2017. https://www.justiceforcolombia.org/news/article/2133/534-political-activists-murdered-in-five-years-in-colombia

Keen, D. *The Economic Functions of Violence in Civil Wars*. London: Routledge, 2005.

Le Billon, P. *Wars of Plunder. Conflicts, Profits and the Politics of Resources*. Oxford: Oxford University Press, 2013.

Le Billon, P., and M. Sommerville. "Landing Capital and Assembling 'investable land'in the Extractive and Agricultural Sectors." *Geoforum* 82 (2017): 212–224.

Lujala, P., and S. A. Rustad, eds. *High-value Natural Resources and Post-conflict Peacebuilding*. London: Routledge, 2012.

Lydersen, K., and A. Cardona-Maguigad. *Survival, Profit, and War: The Many Faces of Gold Mining in Colombia*. NACLA. Accessed December 6, 2016. https://nacla.org/news/2015/11/09/survival-profit-and-war-many-faces-gold-mining-colombia

Massé, F. "¿Hacia una pax mafiosa en Colombia?" [Towards a Mafian Peace in Colombia?] *Foreign Affairs Latinoamérica* 15, no. 1 (2015): 60–69.

Massé, F. *"Minería y post conflicto: ¿es posible una minería de oro libre de conflicto en Colombia ?" in Minería y Desarrollo (Vol 4), Minería y Comunidades: impactos, conflicitos y participación ciudadana* [Mining and Post-conflict: Is Gold Mining Free of Conflict Possible in Colombia?]. Bogotá: Universidad Externado de Colombia, 2016.

Massé, F., and J. Camargo. *Actores Armados Ilegales y Sector Extractivo en Colombia* [Illegal Armed Actors and Extractive Sector in Colombia]. Madrid: Centro Internacional de Toledo para la Paz, 2012.

Massé, F., and J. Munevar. *Due Diligence in Colombia's Gold Supply Chain*. Paris: OECD, 2016.

Medina Gallego, C. *FARC-EP y ELN: Una historia política comparada (1958–2006)* [FARC-EP and ELN: A Comparative Political History (1958–2006)]. Trabajo de grado presentado para optar por el título de Doctor en Historia, Bogota, 2010.

McDermott, J. "Ivan Rios Bloc: the FARC's Most Vulnerable Fighting Division." *InsightCrime*, May 20, 2013.

Ministerio de Minas y Energía, "Política Nacional" para la Formalización de la Minería en Colombia." [National Policy for the Formalization of Mining in Colombia.] Ministerio de Minas y Energía, Julio. Accessed March 11, 2017. https://www.minminas.gov.co/documents/10180/581708/DocumentoPoliticaVersionFinal.pdf/9fd087db-7849-4728-92ff-6e426acccf9c

MinMinas. *Política Minera de Colombia. Bases para la Mineria del Futuro* [Mining Policy in Colombia. Bases for Future Mining]. Bogota, April 2016.

Nussio, E., and K. Howe. "When Protection Collapses: Post-demobilization Trajectories of Violence." *Terrorism and Political Violence* 28, no. 5 (2016): 848–867.

OECD. *Due Diligence Guidance for Responsible Supply Chains of Minerals from Conflict-affected and High-Risk Areas*. 2nd ed. Paris: OECD, 2013.

Presidencia de la Republica. *La mineria criminal es un objetivo de alto valor, advirtio el Presidente Santos* [President Santos Warns that Criminal Mining is a High-value Objective]. *Sistema Informativo del Gobierno*. Bogota: Presidencia de la Republica, 2014. Accessed December 6, 2016. https://wsp.presidencia.gov.co/Prensa/2014/Enero/Paginas/20140117_04-La-mineria-criminal-objetivo-de-alto-valor-advirtio-el-Presidente-Santos.aspx

Rettberg, A., and J. F. Ortiz-Riomalo. "Golden Opportunity, or a New Twist on the Resource-conflict Relationship: Links between the Drug Trade and Illegal Gold Mining in Colombia." *World Development* 84 (2016): 82–96.

Rochlin, J., ed. *Profits, Security, and Human Rights in Developing Countries: Global Lessons from Canada's Extractive Sector in Colombia*. London: Routledge, 2015.

Rodriguez, H., and J.-P. Buteau. "Colombia, a Country of Challenges and Opportunities." *Canadian Mining Journal*, December 1, 2015. Accessed March 11, 2017. https://www.canadianminingjournal.com/features/colombia-a-country-of-challenges-and-opportunities/

Romero, M. "Minería Ilícita: Incidencia en la Convivencia y Seguridad Ciudadana en Diez Departamentos de Colombia." [Illicit Mining: Impact on Citizen Coexistence and Security in Ten Departments of Colombia.] *Revista Criminalidad* 58, no. 1 (2016): 47–65.

Rudas, G., and L. Espitia. "Participación del Estado y la sociedad en la renta minera." [Participation of the State and Society in Mining Rents.] Chap. 4 in *Minería en Colombia, Fundamentos para superar el modelo extractivista*. Bogotá: Contraloría General de la República, 2013.

Silva, S., A. Eslava, A. Preciado, O. Zapata, L. Correa, and J. Giraldo. "La Confianza En Las Zonas Mineras De Antioquia, Bolívar Y Córdoba." [Trust in Mining Areas of Antioquia, Bolívar and Córdoba.] *Revista de Economia Institucional* 17, no. 33 (2015): 231–251.

Timoleón Jiménez. "El cuento de la minería ilegal." [The Story of Illegal Mining.] FARC-EP, April 26, 2013. Accessed December 7, 2016. https://www.farc-ep.co/unilateral/el-cuento-de-la-mineria-ilegal.html

Tubb, D. "Muddy Decisions: Gold in the Chocó, Colombia." *The Extractive Industries and Society* 2, no. 4 (2015): 722–733.

Vélez-Torres, I. "Governmental Extractivism in Colombia: Legislation, Securitization and the Local Settings of Mining Control." *Political Geography* 38 (2014): 68–78.

West, R. *Colonial Placer Mining in Colombia*. Baton Rouge: Louisiana State University Press, 1952.

Willis, A. "Colombia's 'blood gold' Turns up in Everything from Smartphones to Cars." *Bloomberg*, November 16, 2016. Accessed December 8, 2016. https://www.bloomberg.com/news/articles/2016-11-16/-blood-gold-in-u-s-cars-and-phones-funds-marxist-rebel-armies

Young, S. B. "Responsible Sourcing of Metals: Certification Approaches for Conflict Minerals and Conflict-free Metals." *The International Journal of Life Cycle Assessment* (2015): 1–19. doi:10.1007/s11367-015-0932-5.

Ex-combatants and violence in Colombia: are yesterday's villains today's principal threat?

Enzo Nussio

ABSTRACT

Ex-combatants are generally portrayed as a security threat. I present evidence that puts the ex-combatant threat perception in perspective for the case of Colombia. In-depth interviews and surveys show that ex-combatants are not destined for a life of violence, as they become less interested in risky activities over time. Also, even though former mid-ranked commanders have led criminal follower organisations of demobilised paramilitary groups, rank-and-file ex-combatants have been replaced with a new generation of recruits. According to crime statistics, participation of ex-combatants in violence is too small to unsettle overall criminal dynamics. Still, ex-combatants continue to receive a lot of attention in post-demobilisation settings, perhaps inhibiting more targeted attention for other populations with high damage potential and broader structural policies.

Introduction

In many post-conflict countries around the world, ex-combatants from non-state armed groups[1] – the human resources of war – are seen as the main danger for security. This view makes sense since most of them have skills related to violence and may apply them again after demobilisation. Further, several examples support it: some ex-combatants reorganised armed groups in Sierra Leone and the Republic of Congo,[2] others joined existing armed groups in their own country,[3] some became involved in organised crime,[4] petty crime[5] and vigilantism,[6] and still others were responsible for domestic violence.[7] Thus, it seems granted to generalise that ex-combatants are among the principal threats to post-conflict security.[8]

In Colombia, however, commonly held discourses find little support in existing evidence about ex-combatant behaviour. Colombian citizens hold very negative views of ex-combatants in general, like ex-combatants know nothing else than killing, or violence emerging after demobilisation is perpetrated by ex-combatants. In order to analyse whether such perceptions are justified, or whether yesterday's villains are today's principal threat, I make use of evidence from different sources collected over the past years. If ex-combatants were destined for a life of violence, they would have to be involved in crime and violence throughout their life course. However, evidence about Colombian reintegration processes is in line with the predictions of developmental psychologists: by growing older, ex-combatants become less attracted to violence.[9] A second common discourse about their involvement in post-demobilisation violence implies that most members of remobilised organisations are ex-combatants. However, evidence is in line with the organisational process of personnel turnover: even though dissident groups of demobilised militias and insurgencies might continue to exploit the rents of existing war economies, the share of ex-combatants in their ranks fades quickly. Similar dynamics may also apply to other cases of ex-combatant reintegration beyond Colombia.

My analysis is based on official and non-official documents about the reintegration process of former guerrilla and paramilitary fighters in Colombia, interviews with ex-combatants and key informants, and a survey with ex-combatants conducted by the Fundación Ideas para la Paz.[10] The recently started reincorporation process of the FARC-EP guerrilla is not discussed in this article, as it was written before FARC soldiers concentrated in transitory camps. However, the current process shows that the ex-combatant topic continues to absorb a lot of the Colombian public's attention.

As a collateral effect of an overestimated and generalised perception of ex-combatants as threat, more serious problems of post-demobilisation countries may become invisible. Other populations like marginalised youth might be more vulnerable to the opportunities provided by illegal organisations than ex-combatants, but rarely receive systematic and timely attention. Also, while most ex-combatants may be harmless, a certain subpopulation of ex-combatants, usually former mid-level and high-level commanders, has high damage potential. However, reintegration programming does little to keep those ex-combatants out of troubles and targets mostly former rank-and-file members.

Moreover, broader structural policies focusing on economic recovery,[11] community development and participation,[12] institution building,[13] and the management of war economies[14] might receive less attention, when politicians and citizens use ex-combatants as a scapegoat for post-conflict problems. Population-based approaches, like focusing on ex-combatants, might be problematic due to their discriminating nature,[15] but they will continue to exist, thus we should at least have a clear understanding of the reasons for focusing on a specific population.

In the remainder of this article, I first briefly review the academic and policy literature about disarmament, demobilisation, and reintegration (DDR) and its assumptions with regard to the 'ex-combatant threat'. Second, I describe recent DDR efforts in Colombia and their perception in the wider population. Third, I present the number of ex-combatant participation in crime and violence. Fourth, I assess the two commonly held discourses in the wider population ('they know nothing else than killing', and 'they are the main responsible for post-demobilisation violence'). Fifth, I stress the importance of not forgetting other and more specific post-demobilisation populations (marginalised youth and mid-ranking ex-combatants). Finally, I conclude by pointing to future research avenues and to the generalisability of the present findings.

Literature on ex-combatants as threat to security

In most post-conflict societies, the general population looks at ex-combatants with fear and distrust.[16] Early practitioners' case studies and more recent guidelines see disarmament, demobilisation, and reintegration (DDR) as a tool to overcome the threat that ex-combatants pose to security.[17] Certain academic studies seem to support this generalised suspicion of ex-combatants as a persistent security threat[18], and various scholars have tried to identify the reasons that have led ex-combatants to take up arms again or to dedicate themselves to other illegal activities.[19] Living in the vicinity of criminal organisations, having a risk-seeking personality, and not having stable family bonds are some of the predictors of recidivism.[20] Remobilisation of demobilised armed groups further depends on their ties with local communities.[21] Further, based on a cross-country time series data set, a study found that the use of child soldiers is a key risk factor for recurring war.[22]

Emerging research has questioned the underlying ex-combatant threat perception. Fogarty and Killingray studied former servicemen of colonial empires after the end of the First World War and found that 'fears [of brutalisation] were largely misplaced'.[23] Research about Northern Ireland even shows that ex-combatants are sometimes involved in community reconstruction processes inhibiting violence[24] and have in some cases been leaders of conflict transformation.[25] In Uganda, Blattman found that ex-combatants are more likely than their peers to participate in political processes.[26] Munive highlights that ex-combatants in South Sudan are able to employ themselves without the help of a reintegration programme, thus displaying more economic independence than often assumed.[27] Additionally, feared networks of ex-combatants frequently serve positive purposes, acting as informal networks that can assist with employment or simply be used to socialise.[28] In fact, Themnér found that better-organised networks are less of a threat to post-conflict Liberia and are less easily remobilised.[29]

Ultimately, ex-combatant reintegration is a hotly debated topic not only among the general public of post-conflict societies, but also among the practitioners' community and the scholars interested in this field. While practitioners often justify the introduction of DDR policies using discourse that equates ex-combatants with security threat, a more nuanced picture emerges from the review of existing scholarly literature.

Ex-combatants and their perception in Colombia

At least since the civil war, La Violencia which ended in the 1950s, combatants of non-state armed factions have disarmed and reintegrated into Colombian society. Other examples include the demobilisation of various guerrilla groups in the early 1990s, including the 19th of April Movement (M-19), the Popular Liberation Army (EPL), and other smaller insurgencies and paramilitary units.[30] In this article, I focus on more recent demobilisation processes.

Since the beginning of the Uribe government in 2002, the promotion of individual demobilisation (or desertion) of guerrilla members has become a key counterinsurgency strategy. At the same time, the paramilitary groups that largely formed in the 1980s and 1990s,[31] responsible for most human rights violations in the recent conflict history,[32] entered a negotiation process with the government and demobilised 31.671 members between 2003 and 2006. The Peace and Justice Law covered the demobilised members of the paramilitary groups which were a loose federation under the banner of the United Self-Defense Forces (AUC). Paramilitary leaders responsible for crimes against humanity received a prison sentence of up to eight years in exchange for telling the truth about their crimes and repairing their victims.

Since 2006, the High Counsellor for Reintegration (ACR – today Colombian Reintegration Agency) has been in charge of the reintegration process of the demobilised population.[33] A personalised reintegration route including psychosocial attention, education, and vocational training was designed to help ex-combatants encounter a sustainable lifestyle. The participation in this programme has been voluntary but a financial incentive coupled with attendance of reintegration activities has attracted ex-combatant interest. According to the ACR, a total of 57,907 members of non-state armed groups demobilised between 2003 and April 2016.[34] During the existence of the programme, 49,012 entered the reintegration programme, of which 13,354 finished their process, and 16,728 were still in the process in 2016. Others were either absent or left the process due to different reasons – including more than 3600 who died. Among the reintegration process participants, 74% have employment, although most of them work in the informal sector.

Internationally, the Colombian reintegration programme is seen as one of the most successful and professionally managed worldwide.[35] However, Colombia represents an untypical case since reintegration of AUC ex-combatants and individual deserters has been going on during war and has thus involved a counterinsurgent component (similar to the Philippines, Iraq, and Afghanistan). Also, Colombia is one of the richest of DDR countries and has had the capability to take on almost full institutional responsibility, while most other DDR programmes are largely externally funded.

Several studies have looked at the effect of the collective AUC demobilisation on violence in Colombia as a whole[36] as well as in certain regions.[37] Depending on the scale of analysis, these studies come to different conclusions. Early national-level gains in different violence indicators such as homicide are contrasted with hugely varying regional dynamics. Over a longer period of time, there seems to be no relationship between the diminishing homicides since 2003 and the demobilisation process, since both demobilisation and non-demobilisation areas experience the same underlying trend (see Figure 1).

While the overall effect of the DDR process on violence is difficult to identify, the AUC demobilisation gave rise to a transformation of violence, and, more specifically, it gave rise to a transformation of violent actors in Colombia. Reports about small dissident factions, reorganising demobilised people, and newly emerging armed groups started soon after the demobilisation process ended.[38] While these groups have received their income mostly from

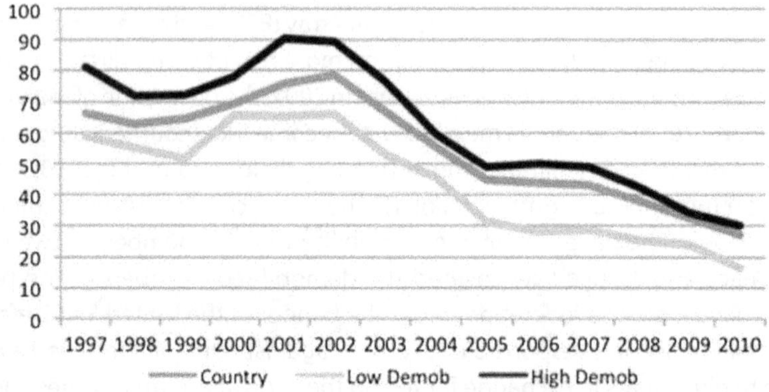

Figure 1. Homicide rates in Colombia, 1997–2010. Source: Nussio and Howe, 'When Protection Collapses: Post-Demobilization Trajectories of Violence', 5.

drug-trafficking, extortion, and illegal mining, their relationship to demobilised paramilitaries is debated.[39]

Some observers call them 'neoparamilitaries',[40] others 'new illegal armed groups'.[41] Human Rights Watch[42] calls them 'inheritors of the paramilitaries', emphasising the continuity of political violence. According to Governmental Decree 2374 of 2010, they should be called criminal bands devoid of any political agenda (in its Spanish acronym: BACRIM). Later, the Ministry of Defense released a new guideline (Directive 15 of 2016) to call them Organised Armed Groups (*Grupos Armados Oranizados*). Independent of the debate about their name (I use the terms BACRIM and neoparamilitary groups interchangeably), it is clear that these organisations are one of the main threats to security in Colombia, at least according to the former director of the National Police.[43] Until April 2016, there were more than 330.000 people registered as victims of violence perpetrated by the BACRIM, most of them were forcibly displaced.[44]

The existence of these follower organisations partially explains the negative stereotypes attached to ex-combatants in Colombia. In a survey with members of receiving communities, 41% stated that they fear ex-combatants.[45] According to the same survey, 82% said that they would not trust an ex-combatant. Similar prejudices are reflected in a national survey.[46] Only 24% of survey participants would approve of their children befriending a FARC ex-combatant. Also, respondents see ex-combatants most often as dangerous (33.6%) and violent (16.4%). Calm (15.1%) or friendly (13.9%) are less commonly selected adjectives to describe them.

Even in Bogotá, a large city with a relatively low proportion of ex-combatants per capita and a low incidence of ex-combatants in crime,[47] the Fundación Seguridad y Democracia found that 84% of survey participants thought that the presence of ex-combatants would increase insecurity.[48] In an experiment, Cárdenas et al. showed that ex-combatants receive lower transfers than other populations when study participants could choose where to allocate resources.[49]

Ex-combatants themselves frequently complain about stigmatisation in their communities and often try to hide their identity, to obtain employment and for security reasons.[50] In my own interviews around the country with diverse actors of the NGO world, local authorities, unaffiliated citizens, and even among some demobilised combatants themselves,[51] ex-combatants were largely portrayed as one of the principal threats to security in Colombia, despite the efforts of the ACR to show positive reintegration cases. In particular, Colombians are often convinced that ex-combatants know nothing else than killing. Ex-combatants are aware of these generalisations, as one of my interviewees said: 'People don't like demobilised persons, nobody wants to get together with them. Why? "Because that guy wants to kill me." It makes people step back'.[52] Another interviewee expressed how people in his community look with suspicion upon groups of ex-combatants: 'They [residents in the neighborhood] see you hanging around at the corner, and they're saying, "they're looking who they're going to rob or what are they planning?" They keep an eye on you'.[53]

The contribution of ex-combatants to violence

What is the actual contribution of ex-combatants to crime and violence in Colombia? The public debate has often focused on the number of ex-combatants who committed a crime. The term *reincidencia* which can be translated with recidivism is broadly used.[54] A recidivism rate for ex-combatants in Colombia is usually calculated for the whole period since 2003 (when the demobilisation of paramilitaries began). While in 2010, the CNRR calculated a recidivism rate of 15%,[55] more recent and sophisticated estimates by the Fundación Ideas para la Paz reported 24%.[56] The ACR itself reports a lower recidivism rate (8.3% between 2003 and April 2015), since they only count ex-combatants who have already been sentenced by a court as proven recidivists and only refer to those who joined the reintegration process. All estimates likely underreport actual recidivism rates since some crimes go unnoticed. According to the ACR, the highest numbers of crimes committed by ex-combatants were registered between 2005 and 2007, during and shortly after the demobilisation of paramilitary groups. The most common crimes committed by ex-combatants from the AUC were illegal gun possession, drug trade and possession, organised crime, and homicide.

While it is unclear which recidivism rate indicates reintegration failure, the contribution of ex-combatants to overall levels of crime is marginal, at least considering preliminary evidence. Antioquia, one of the regions with the largest ex-combatant community, includes approximately 6500 ex-combatants. The contribution of these ex-combatants to crime in Antioquia amounts to 0.13% – based on the proportion of arrests between 2011 and 2013,[57] while the amount drops to 0.10% of the total Antioquia population. Similar numbers exist for the city of Villavicencio for the period between 2005 and 2010.[58] There, ex-combatants have contributed 4.3% to the total arrests for organised crime, 4% for extortion, 3.8% for homicide, 0.6% for illegal gun possession and 0.1% for theft. Considering that the ex-combatants in this town amount to 0.2% of the total population, they are heavily overrepresented in the arrest rates, especially for serious crimes like homicide and extortion. However, their overall contribution remains below 5% for any of the mentioned crimes that occurred directly after demobilisation.

Seeing ex-combatants as a threat in Colombia is often related to the so-called BACRIM. Citizens largely identify BACRIM members with ex-combatants. Most of these organisations were founded and organised by former mid-ranking and high-ranking ex-combatants,[59] which I discuss further below. But most of their members are not ex-combatants. In 2009, the Colombian Police reported that only 12% of the members of BACRIM were ex-combatants, based on arrest numbers.[60] Later, they reported that among the 12.100 arrests of BACRIM members, 1765 or 14.6% were ex-combatants from the AUC.[61] Based on BACRIM members killed in confrontation, the rate is lower: of 1187 killed members of the BACRIM between 2006 and 2009, 71 or 6% were ex-combatants.[62]

Between 2003 and 2012, 3003 ex-combatants have been killed after their demobilisation (according to information provided by the National Police). The years shortly after the paramilitary demobilisation (2007–2009) registered the highest numbers of killed ex-combatants: more than 500 each year. The overwhelming majority (91%) were killed with a firearm, which indicates that many of these homicides were either commissioned or otherwise related to organised crime. According to the Police, 21% of those killed were arrested at least once before they were killed. There are reports that some ex-combatants were killed because they resisted joining follower organisations.[63] While some of these numbers are shocking (about 5% of ex-combatants were killed after demobilising), their overall contribution to violence in Colombia is small. As a percentage of the total homicides in Colombia between 2003 and 2012, ex-combatant homicides amount to 1.8% (in the peak year 2008 it reached 3.9%). Hence, violence against ex-combatants (who may or may not be involved in organised crime) does not significantly drive countrywide indicators of homicide.[64] Rather, ex-combatant homicides have made a marginal contribution to continuously high, though diminishing, levels of violence.

To sum up, although many ex-combatants have been involved in violence (either as perpetrators or victims), their overall contribution to violence is rather small. During the first few years after the paramilitary demobilisation, their participation in violent acts was largest. Also, they tend to commit serious crimes (like extortion, homicide, and participation in organised crime). But over time the ex-combatants' involvement in violence decreases. The relatively low contribution to overall levels of violence has several explanations, but the most important one is that there are simply not enough ex-combatants to change rates of violent crime. As a result of the collective demobilisation of the AUC and the individual demobilisations of guerrilla members, more than 57,000 members of non-state armed groups have demobilised between 2003 and 2016. They amount to about 1 per mille of the total Colombian population. Even though roughly 40% of this population is concentrated in only nine cities, according to the ACR, no municipality has more than 1% of ex-combatants among its population. Small numbers of criminals can generate large insecurity using spectacular violence and drawing on their capacity to create and lead violent organisations (see section about mid-level commanders below), but there are not enough ex-combatants to unsettle general crime tendencies in Colombia.

Also, a significant share of ex-combatants has contributed positively to their communities and to fellow ex-combatants. Mostly on a local level, they have participated in reconciliation events,[65] organised sports activities[66], and created a large number of business organisations for demobilised people in order to facilitate their economic reintegration.[67]

'They know nothing else than killing'

Are ex-combatants destined for a life of violence? General discourse has it that ex-combatants are not able to overcome their preference for a violent lifestyle after they demobilise. This is one of the arguments that justify generalised threat perception. However, it stands in contrast to a well-established finding in developmental psychology.[68] People become less interested in risky behaviour, including the participation in violent acts, with increasing age after adolescence.[69] In fact, a quantitative study about recidivism in Colombia shows that with increasing age ex-combatants tend to commit less crimes, this is especially true for ex-combatants who have children.[70] In-depth interviews with ex-combatants confirm this finding. While younger ex-combatants without family obligations were generally more inclined towards some criminal activity after demobilising, older respondents and ex-combatants who were parents were more interested in a calm family life.[71]

This may be related to what Jonsson calls the 'rebel's life-cycle', which is based on a shifting risk perception, a weakening appetite for adventure, and a growing wish for a stable family life over the life course.[72] In 2008, the respondents of an ex-combatant survey conducted by *Fundación Ideas para la Paz* were on average 29.9 years old (FARC: 28.7, AUC 31.0), while the same cohort of people joined at an average age of 21.2 (FARC: 18.5, AUC: 23.2). The typical ex-combatant in 2008, when the impact of ex-combatants on the security situation in Colombia was at its highest point, was almost 9 years older than when he or she joined, thus leaving the age group that is most inclined to risk-seeking and related criminal activities.

There is a large amount of evidence indicating that BACRIM recruits tend to be in their late adolescence. 'In different regions of the country, an increasing number of youngsters between 16 and 25 years of age have been arrested for participation in illegal activities related to these [BACRIM] organisations'.[73] The age of joiners of BACRIM today is comparable to the age profile of those who joined paramilitary and guerrilla groups back then. An interviewed representative of the Early Alert System of the Ombudsman's Office in Córdoba describes the profile of BACRIM recruits: 'Young guys with little education or job training, guys who live in marginal neighborhoods, who don't have regular employment, nor a regular income, who, at the moment when they are offered something by the recruiters, accept'.[74] BACRIM recruiters specifically target youngsters with this profile for their activities.[75] Many of the 85 to 88% of arrested BACRIM members who are not ex-combatants (see estimates by the Police mentioned above) belong to this new generation of violent people.

To sum up, a persistent preference for a violent lifestyle is uncommon among ex-combatants. Most have not become 'brutalized' by war and are not forever lost in a world of violence. The majority of them, as humans in general, develop a preference for less risk-prone activities and a calm family life. Ex-combatants are thus less of a threat to post-conflict societies than what observers assume, because – with some notable exceptions – they grow tired of violence.

'Ex-combatants are responsible for organised violence after demobilisation'

Are ex-combatants the main workforce for illegal organisations emerging after demobilisation? While the continuities and ruptures between the AUC and their follower groups, often called BACRIM, are debated,[76] many observers in Colombia view the BACRIM as a continuation of earlier paramilitary groups.[77] This view is based on the belief that they use similar methods, focus on similar income sources from war economies and rely on the same people (eg ex-combatants) as the AUC. However, this member continuity goes against a common process seen in all large organisations: personnel turnover. Even if the BACRIM were a simple continuation of the earlier AUC under a new label, it would be unlikely that they would continuously count on the same members.

As noted above, by 2009, 12% of the members of BACRIM were ex-combatants, and for the period between 2006 and 2012, 14.6% of arrested members of the BACRIM were ex-combatants. Therefore, during this time period, at least 85% of BACRIM members were either new recruits or non-demobilised members of the AUC. Considering the turnover rates in other organisations, these numbers are not surprising. Depending on the industry sector, private companies have a personnel turnover of about 20–50% per year[78], and each year one of five accountants – a profession not particularly known for job-hopping – changes his or her.[79] Members of illegal organisations might remain in their group for a longer period of time if the group constrains exit with costly punishment.[80] However, turnover in illegal organisations is also accelerated by arrests and deaths.

Assuming that the BACRIM are a continuation of the AUC, they still had 85% new members in 2009 (three years after the conclusion of the AUC demobilisation), which indicates that they suffered a large turnover in their organisation. This interpretation is consistent with evidence indicating that many demobilised and dissident members of the AUC were involved in the creation of post-demobilisation groups shortly after the AUC demobilisation[81] and new members have replaced most of them over the course of the BACRIM's existence.

Personnel turnover has a different dynamic for higher-ranking members due to the structure of career opportunities in illegal organisations. In street gangs, for example, very few have the opportunity to personally enrich themselves, while most members remain at the bottom of the pyramid.[82] This situation might lead to dissatisfaction and ultimately desistance or disaffiliation from the group for most of its rank-and-file members.[83] However, leaders might have special incentives to stay longer. This is why former paramilitary leaders and mid-ranking ex-combatants who climbed the job ladder held on to the few lucrative positions within the organisation for a longer period of time (see next section).

In summary, if the BACRIM are similar to other illegal and legal organisations, they undergo a personnel turnover that is associated with a diminishing proportion of ex-combatants among their ranks over time. This is consistent with the fact that most BACRIM members are new recruits few years after the AUC demobilisation. Higher-ranking members might stick around for longer due to their better job prospects.

Who we should not forget

A generalised perception of ex-combatants as major threat to security does not correspond to the evidence about their actual participation in violence in Colombia. This widely held perception might distract attention and resources from more important populations and structural policies. Two key populations that need more and better attention, especially in Colombia but potentially also in other cases, are marginalised youth and former mid-level fighters.

While it is not my intention to stigmatise an even larger social group than ex-combatants, marginalised youth are particularly vulnerable to participation in crime and violence in Colombia, but have received scant attention from authorities. Prevention of child and youth recruitment has been identified as an emergency issue in repeated reports of the Ombudsman's Early Alert System, as for example in Meta and Córdoba.[84] However, despite the elaboration of an important public policy document about recruitment prevention,[85] the overall attention to youth has remained largely ineffective and scattered among different government institutions.[86]

Other cases, most importantly El Salvador and Guatemala, reveal the importance of youth for post-conflict violence and stability. Gangs have been key organisations and marginalised youth the main human resources for post-war violence in these countries.[87] Similar criminal organisations are already present in several Colombian cities, like Medellín[88] or Cali,[89] and may gain more visibility in future. The fact that most BACRIM recruits belong to a new generation of violent people underlines the importance of focusing more attention and support to the human resources of post-conflict violence, who are mostly found among young males in marginalised neighbourhoods.[90]

Former mid-level and high-level combatants are not necessarily more likely to recidivate in criminal activities than other ex-combatants, but when they recidivate, they have a higher damage potential. Former mid-level fighters are potential career criminals. They moved up the ladder of their organisation's hierarchy and have accumulated 'criminal capital'.[91] Some of them might want to benefit from their know-how and their time invested in crime. They are the nodes in the criminal networks who hold the organisational memory about the extraction of criminal rents from existing war economies, ie knowledge about the smuggling routes, contacts to suppliers and customers, and strategies to cope with competitors and authorities.

It is not surprising that in the early period after the paramilitary demobilisation, all follower organisations were led by former members of the AUC.[92] Infamous drug lords like alias 'Cuchillo', 'Don Mario', and 'Otoniel' have dominated the headlines about crime in Colombia throughout the past years[93] and contributed to a generalised stigma of ex-combatants as a whole. Mid-level commanders have also been found to be important actors in other post-conflict cases like the Republic of Congo and Sierra Leone.[94]

However, while DDR policies are mostly designed for rank-and-file ex-combatants, policymakers are uninspired when it comes to mid-ranking and high-ranking commanders. More focused attention to this specific subgroup of ex-combatants would be beneficial for future demobilisation processes. Non-tangible incentives related to their leadership skills, involvement in the design of DDR programmes, political participation, personal protection schemes, and enrolment in higher education programmes might increase the willingness of some of them to put an end to their criminal career. Some of these policies already exist in Colombia,[95] but even the former High Counsellor for Reintegration accepted that the incentives offered by the reintegration programme had been insufficient for this population.[96]

Conclusions

Based on the available evidence, this article intended to put the widely perceived security threat that emanates from ex-combatants in Colombia into perspective. Many ex-combatants have committed crimes after demobilisation, mostly in the early period after their demobilisation, and others have been killed, often as a result of involvement with some criminal activity. Also, some of the ex-combatants fulfil important roles in the criminal underworld, thanks to their skills. A few 'experts' of violence may thus have a large damage potential. This is especially the case for mid-ranking and high-ranking ex-combatants, who effectively created new criminal organisations that inherited some of the war businesses from the previously existing paramilitary groups.

However, a general view of ex-combatants as acute security threat does not correspond to the underlying reality presented in this paper. Discounting the crimes committed by ex-combatants, the general dynamics of crime and violence in Colombia would have been largely unchanged since the overall contribution of ex-combatants is small. Also, ex-combatants are neither brutalised forever (due to the increased dislike of risky activities), nor are they entirely responsible for organised post-demobilisation violence (as they get replaced by a new generation of recruits). In fact, some ex-combatants have positively contributed to the reintegration of former comrades or have aided NGOs engaged in a variety of peaceful activities.[97]

The findings from the Colombian case are not directly generalisable, even though the central ideas, especially with regard to ageing and personnel turnover, may apply similarly to other cases. Observers of other cases might show similarly generalising views about ex-combatants. Perception biases push public opinion into this direction. First, ex-combatants are an easily identifiable group, and it makes sense to think of them as violent people due to their experience with armed conflict. Second, most leaders of criminal organisations in Colombia, and in other countries, have effectively been mid-ranking and high-ranking ex-combatants with pronounced criminal leadership skills and know-how about the exploitation of war economies. In Colombia, one might wrongly infer that their followers are ex-combatants too. More responsible communication about reintegration processes, especially among journalists, could help to mitigate some of these biases. However, demobilised people will continue to provide an ideal hook to stories about transition phases as they personally represent the challenges associated with peacebuilding.

With the exception of key organisers of violence, ex-combatants are largely exchangeable. Due to the low explanatory power of a human resources theory for post-demobilisation violence, we have to turn to more structural- and organisational-level explanations.[98] War economies and the governance of natural resources are important pieces in this puzzle. The Colombian case is a perfect example. While the people in charge and filling the ranks of criminal organisations have changed quickly, the war economies have seen few changes after the paramilitary demobilisation and have even expanded beyond drug-trafficking to new resources like illegal gold mining.[99] If underlying structures and war economies are not targeted, somebody (but not necessarily ex-combatants) will continue to exploit existing criminal rents.

Population-based approaches for typical post-conflict social groups, like ex-combatants, will continue to exist, and there are reasons that justify reintegration programming.[100] However, vulnerable populations like marginalised youth should not be sidelined due to continued obsession of policymakers with ex-combatants in the context of DDR policies. Furthermore, reintegration programming should not only target rank-and-file ex-combatants, but also give specific incentives to mid-ranking and high-ranking ex-combatants to participate in programming. A realistic evaluation of the danger that emanates from ex-combatants will help to reorganise population-based policies in order to spend public resources more effectively.

In line with my argument, the current collective DDR process with the FARC guerrilla will not be the biggest challenge for a successful post-conflict period in Colombia. Some guerrilla fighters have become dissidents already, and others are likely to remobilise into crime later. But the number of recidivists will likely be smaller when compared to the number of recidivists among paramilitaries, due to the larger cohesion among FARC rebels and a larger responsibility of the armed group in the design and execution of reintegration activities. This is similar to the demobilisation of guerrilla groups in the 1990s who were also more involved in the reintegration policy and were generally less associated with post-demobilisation violence.[101] Also, the sustainability of the current peace process depends to a much larger extent on wider changes in society, including among other things the capacity of the government to integrate the country, lead a nationwide reconciliation process, finally provide remote areas with decent public services, and tackle pervasive organised crime that continues to benefit from war economies.

Disclosure statement

No potential conflict of interest was reported by the author.

Acknowledgements

I thank all the participants of the Workshop on Post-conflict Crime for their valuable feedback on earlier versions of this essay, especially the workshop conveners Angelika Rettberg and Sabine Kurtenbach, and Bridget Steele. Earlier versions of this paper were also presented at Universidad de los Andes in 2015 and Universidad del Rosario 2016.

Notes

1. In this article, I focus on ex-combatants from non-state armed groups who demobilise as a result of a negotiation process or individual desertion.
2. Themnér, *Violence in Post-Conflict Societies*.
3. Zyck, 'Former Combatant Reintegration and Fragmentation'.
4. Moratti and Sabic-El-Rayess, *Transitional Justice and DDR*.
5. Subedi, 'Ex-Combatants, Security and Post-Conflict Violence'.
6. Maringira, 'Militarised Minds'.
7. Londoño and Ramírez, *Estudio Sobre El Impacto de La Reinserción*.
8. While security threats are constructed, in this article, I am less interested in the process of threat construction as in the underlying reality of ex-combatant involvement in violent activities.
9. Other factors that explain recidivism of ex-combatants but are not directly related to this perception that ex-combatants would continuously favour a violent lifestyle are analysed by Kaplan and Nussio, 'Explaining Recidivism'.
10. Documents include newspaper articles, reports from the Colombian Reintegration Agency, the Police, and other organisations overseeing the DDR process in Colombia, and academic studies. Interview material was mainly collected for my doctoral dissertation – 68 interviews mostly with former paramilitary members, described at length in Nussio, *La Vida Después de La Desmovilización*. Also, I interviewed a large number of key observers from the Police, the Military, the Attorney General's Office and other governmental bodies, NGOs, church representatives, officials of international organisations like the Organisation of American States and the United Nations, and community leaders in Bogotá, Medellín, Tierralta, Montería, Santa Marta, Ciénaga, Villavicencio, Cúcuta, and Florencia. This interview material provides key background for my analysis. The ex-combatant survey with 1485 participants was conducted by the Fundación Ideas para la Paz in 2008. It is used to illustrate general characteristics of ex-combatants in Colombia. This survey is described at length in Kaplan and Nussio, 'Community Counts'.
11. Collier et al., *Breaking the Conflict Trap*.
12. King and Samii, 'Fast-Track Institution Building in Conflict-Affected Countries?'; and Kaplan and Nussio, 'Community Counts'.
13. Le Billon, 'The Political Ecology of War'.
14. Kurtenbach and Rettberg, 'War Economies and Postwar Crime'.
15. Söderström, 'The Political Consequences of Reintegration'.
16. McFee, 'The Double Bind of "playing Double"'; McMullin, 'Integration or Separation?'; Subedi, 'Ex-Combatants, Security and Post-Conflict Violence'. Exceptions might include cases where ex-combatants are seen as liberators or heroes, as for example the members of the Kosovo Liberation Army or the Free Aceh Movement.
17. Colletta, Kostner, and Wiederhofer, *Case Studies in War-to-Peace Transition*; United Nations, *Integrated Disarmament, Demobilisation*.
18. Maringira, 'Militarised Minds'; Muggah, *Security and Post-Conflict Reconstruction*.
19. FIP, 'Retorno a La Legalidad O Reincidencia'; Hill, Taylor, and Temin, 'Would You Fight Again?'; and Kaplan and Nussio, 'Explaining Recidivism'.
20. Kaplan and Nussio, 'Explaining Recidivism'.
21. Daly, *Organized Violence after Civil War*.
22. For example, Haer and Böhmelt, 'Child Soldiers as Time Bombs?'.
23. Fogarty and Killingray, 'Demobilization in British and French Africa', 106.

24. Clubb, 'From Terrorists to Peacekeepers'.
25. McEvoy and Shirlow, 'Re-Imagining DDR'.
26. Blattman, 'From Violence to Voting'; see also Söderström, 'Second Time around'; and Ugarriza, 'La Dimensión Política Del Postconflicto'.
27. Munive, 'Invisible Labour'.
28. Utas, Themnér, and Lindberg, 'Commanders for Good and Bad. Alternative Post-War'; Zyck, 'Former Combatant Reintegration and Fragmentation'.
29. Themnér, 'Former Military Networks and the Micro-Politics'.
30. CNMH, *Desmovilización Y Reintegración Paramilitar*. Even though limited recidivism accompanied these processes as well, they were judged as largely successful in terms of security Palou and Méndez, 'Balance de Los Procesos de DDR'.
31. Romero, *Paramilitares Y Autodefensas, 1982–2003*.
32. CNMH, *¡Basta Ya!*.
33. The recent Colombian DDR process has been widely analysed, eg CNMH, *Desmovilización Y Reintegración Paramilitar*; Restrepo and Bagley, *La Desmovilización de Los Paramilitares*; Villarraga, 'Experiencias Históricas Recientes de Reintegración'; Nussio, 'Learning from Shortcomings'; and Palou and Méndez, 'Balance de Los Procesos de DDR'.
34. Updated numbers can be found on the ACR web page (accessed 15 February 2017), http://www.reintegracion.gov.co/es/la-reintegracion/Paginas/cifras.aspx.
35. See, for example, Rohrlich, 'How Do You Turn 57,000 Former Militants'.
36. CNMH, *Grupos Armados Posdesmovilización*; Daly, *Organized Violence after Civil War*; Gutiérrez Sanín and González Peña, 'Colombia's Paramilitary DDR and Its Limits'; Howe, 'Violent Momentum'; and Restrepo and Muggah, 'Colombia's Quiet Demobilization'.
37. Krakowski, 'Colombian Paramilitaries Since Demobilization'; Massé et al., 'La Evolución de Las Estructuras Armadas Post-Desmovilización'; Munévar and Nussio, 'Desmovilizados'; and Nussio and Howe, 'When Protection Collapses'.
38. CNRR, *Disidentes, Rearmados Y Emergentes*.
39. Echandía, 'Narcotráfico'; Massé et al., 'La Evolución de Las Estructuras Armadas Post-Desmovilización'.
40. Granada, Restrepo, and Tobón, 'Neoparamilitarismo En Colombia'.
41. International Crisis Group, 'Dismantling Colombia's New Illegal Armed Groups: Lessons from a Surrender'.
42. Human Rights Watch, *Herederos de Los Paramilitares*.
43. Semana, 'Las Bandas Criminales Son La Principal Amenaza Para El País'.
44. El Tiempo, 'Ya van 332.149 Víctimas de Las Bandas'.
45. CNC, *Informe Final Evaluación de Impacto*.
46. García-Sánchez, Montalvo, and Seligson, *Cultura Política de La Democracia*.
47. Massé et al., 'Presencia de Desmovilizados'.
48. Seguridad y Democracia, *Criminalidad Y Victimización*.
49. Cárdenas, Casas-Casas, and Méndez, 'The Hidden Face of Justice'.
50. Nussio, *La Vida Después de La Desmovilización*; Nussio, 'How Ex-Combatants Talk about Personal Security'.
51. Nussio, *La Vida Después de La Desmovilización*.
52. Interview in Bogotá, January 2009.
53. Interview in Barrancabermeja, March 2009.
54. Kaplan and Nussio, 'Explaining Recidivism'. *Reincidencia* or recidivism is understood as engagement in some illegal activity after demobilisation.
55. CNRR, *La Reintegración*.
56. FIP, 'Retorno a La Legalidad O Reincidencia'. Included in these estimates are ex-combatants who were killed in operations against organised crime.
57. Calculations based on Ocampo, 'Criminalidad, Grupos Armados Y Reinserción'.
58. Massé et al., 'Presencia de Desmovilizados'.
59. CNMH, *Grupos Armados Posdesmovilización*.
60. Semana, '12 Por Ciento de Las Bacrim Son Desmovilizados'.

61. Prieto, *Las Bacrim Y El Crimen Organizado*; see also Munévar and Nussio, 'Desmovilizados'.
62. Observatorio de Procesos de DDR, 'DDR Y Acciones Violentas (2008–2009)', 36.
63. Munévar and Nussio, 'Desmovilizados'.
64. However, in certain regions, homicides of ex-combatants reached enormous levels. In Córdoba in 2008, ex-combatant homicides amounted to 38% of all homicides in this department, in Nussio and Howe, 'When Protection Collapses'.
65. Ugarriza and Nussio, 'The Effect of Perspective-Giving'.
66. Nussio, *La Vida Después de La Desmovilización*.
67. Observatorio de DDR, *Las Formas Organizativas*.
68. Boyer, 'The Development of Risk-Taking'.
69. Gottfredson and Hirschi, *A General Theory of Crime*.
70. Kaplan and Nussio, 'Explaining Recidivism'.
71. Examples taken from Nussio, *La Vida Después de La Desmovilización*. 'I didn't have anybody to think about, I didn't have any obligations, I didn't have children. And now, I have a daughter, she gives me a lot of motivation not to go back there' (Barrancabermeja). 'The only thing that hinders me from going back is my family. I try to keep my family out of any problem. They know where my family lives. In the end, it's the family that pays the price' (Bogotá).
72. Jonsson, 'Comrades in Arms'; Nussio, 'The Role of Sensation Seeking in Violent Armed Group Participation'.
73. Prieto, *Las Bacrim Y El Crimen Organizado*, 3.
74. Interview in Montería, December 2010.
75. Nussio and Howe, 'When Protection Collapses', 11.
76. CNRR, *Disidentes, Rearmados Y Emergentes*, 135; Massé et al., 'La Evolución de Las Estructuras Armadas Post-Desmovilización'.
77. Human Rights Watch, *Herederos de Los Paramilitares*.
78. Khatri, Fern, and Budhwar, 'Explaining Employee Turnover'.
79. Arnold and Feldman, 'A Multivariate Analysis of the Determinants of Job Turnover'.
80. Altier, Thoroughgood, and Horgan, 'Turning Away from Terrorism'; Nussio and Oppenheim, 'Anti-Social Capital in Former Members'.
81. CNMH, *Desmovilización Y Reintegración Paramilitar*; Munévar and Nussio, 'Desmovilizados'.
82. Levitt and Venkatesh, 'An Economic Analysis of a Drug-Selling'.
83. Altier, Thoroughgood, and Horgan, 'Turning Away from Terrorism'.
84. Sistema de Alertas Tempranas, *Informe de Riesgo No. 006-10*; Sistema de Alertas Tempranas, *Informe de Riesgo No. 015-13*.
85. Conpes 3673, *Política de Prevención Del Reclutamiento*.
86. Rubio Serrano, 'Los Niños: El Futuro de La Guerra… Y de La Paz'.
87. Kurtenbach, 'The "Happy Outcomes"'.
88. Baird, 'Swimming against the Tide'.
89. El Tiempo, '"No Nos Enfrentamos a Unas Pandillitas": Alcalde de Cali'.
90. Rodgers and Jensen, 'The Problem with Templates'.
91. McCarthy and Hagan, 'Getting into Street Crime'.
92. CNMH, *Desmovilización Y Reintegración Paramilitar*; CNRR, *Disidentes, Rearmados Y Emergentes*.
93. After arrests and killings of former AUC members who initially organised the BACRIM, a new generation of criminal leaders is starting to emerge, see El Tiempo, 'Con "Pijarvey" Muere Segunda Generación'.
94. Themnér, *Violence in Post-Conflict Societies*.
95. Arias, Prieto, and Herrera, 'Mandos Medios de Las FARC Y Su Proceso de Desmovilización'.
96. Semana, 'Desmovilización de Guerrilleros Y Paramilitares'.
97. Observatorio de DDR, *Las Formas Organizativas*.
98. Collier, Hoeffler, and Söderbom, 'Post-Conflict Risks'; Kurtenbach, 'The "Happy Outcomes"'; Nussio and Howe, 'When Protection Collapses'.
99. Rettberg and Ortiz-Riomalo, 'Golden Opportunity, or a New Twist'.
100. United Nations, *Integrated Disarmament, Demobilisation*.
101. Palou and Méndez, 'Balance de Los Procesos de DDR'.

Bibliography

Altier, Mary Beth, Christian N. Thoroughgood, and John G. Horgan. "Turning Away from Terrorism. Lessons from Psychology, Sociology, and Criminology." *Journal of Peace Research* 51, no. 5 (2014): 647–661.

Arias, Gerson, Carlos Prieto, and Natalia Herrera. "Mandos Medios de Las FARC Y Su Proceso de Desmovilización En El Conflicto Colombiano: ¿Una Apuesta Para La Paz O Para La Guerra?" Informes FIP No. 10. Bogotá: Fundación Ideas para la Paz, 2010.

Arnold, Hugh J., and Daniel C. Feldman. "A Multivariate Analysis of the Determinants of Job Turnover." *Journal of Applied Psychology* 67, no. 3 (1982): 350–360.

Baird, Adam. "Swimming against the Tide: Youth Policy and Contexts of Chronic Violence in Medellín." In *Jugend Und Politik*, edited by Peter Filzmaier, Peter Plaikner, Christina Hainzl, and Karl A Duffek, 77–91. Wien: Facultas, 2015.

Blattman, Christopher. "From Violence to Voting: War and Political Participation in Uganda." *American Political Science Review* 103, no. 2 (2009): 231–247.

Boyer, Ty W. "The Development of Risk-taking: A Multi-perspective Review." *Developmental Review* 26, no. 3 (2006): 291–345.

Cárdenas, Juan Camilo, Andrés Casas-Casas, and Nathalie Méndez Méndez. "The Hidden Face of Justice: Fairness, Discrimination and Distribution in Transitional Justice Processes." *Peace Economics, Peace Science and Public Policy* 20, no. 1 (2014): 33–60.

Clubb, Gordon. "'From Terrorists to Peacekeepers': The IRA's Disengagement and the Role of Community Networks." *Studies in Conflict & Terrorism* 37, no. 10 (2014): 842–861.

CNC. *Informe Final Evaluación de Impacto, Seguimiento Y Sistematización de La Estrategia de Reintegración Comunitaria*. Bogotá: Centro Nacional de Consultoría, 2011.

CNMH. *¡Basta Ya! Colombia: Memoria de Guerra Y Dignidad*. Bogotá: Centro Nacional de Memoria Histórica, 2013.

CNMH. *Desmovilización Y Reintegración Paramilitar. Panorama Posacuerdos Con Las AUC*. Bogotá: CNMH, 2015.

CNMH. *Grupos Armados Posdesmovilización (2006-2015). Trayectorias, Rupturas Y Continuidades*. Bogotá: Centro Nacional de Memoria Histórica, 2017.

CNRR. *Disidentes, Rearmados Y Emergentes: ¿Bandas Criminales O Tercera Generación Paramilitar?* Bogotá: CNRR, 2007.

CNRR. *La Reintegración: Logros En Medio de Rearmes Y Dificultades No Resueltas. II Informe de La Comisión Nacional de Reparación Y Reconociliación*. Bogotá: CNRR, 2010.

Colletta, Nat J., Markus Kostner, and Ingo Wiederhofer. *Case Studies in War-to-Peace Transition: The Demobilization and Reintegration of Ex-Combatants in Ethiopia, Namibia, and Uganda*. Washington, DC: World Bank, 1996.

Collier, Paul, V. L. Elliott, Havard Hegre, Anke Hoeffler, Marta Reynal-Querol, and Nicholas Sambanis. *Breaking the Conflict Trap: Civil War and Development Policy*. Washington, DC: World Bank, 2003.

Collier, Paul, Anke Hoeffler, and Måns Söderbom. "Post-Conflict Risks." *Journal of Peace Research* 45, no. 4 (2008): 461–478.

Conpes 3673. *Política de Prevención Del Reclutamiento*. Bogotá: DNP, 2010.

Daly, Sarah Zukerman. *Organized Violence after Civil War: The Geography of Recruitment in Latin America*. New York: Cambridge University Press, 2016.

Echandía, Camilo. "Narcotráfico: Génesis de Los Paramilitares Y Herencia de Bandas Criminales." Informes FIP No. 19. Bogotá: Fundación Ideas para la Paz, 2013.

El Tiempo. "Con 'Pijarvey' Muere Segunda Generación de Jefes de Bandas Criminales." September 28, 2015. http://www.eltiempo.com/archivo/documento/CMS-16389853.

El Tiempo. "'No Nos Enfrentamos a Unas Pandillitas': Alcalde de Cali." February 15, 2014. http://www.eltiempo.com/archivo/documento/CMS-13508296.

El Tiempo. "Ya van 332.149 Víctimas de Las Bandas Criminales En El País." April 28, 2016. http://www.eltiempo.com/archivo/documento/CMS-16575453.

FIP. "Retorno a La Legalidad O Reincidencia." Informes FIP. Bogotá: Fundación Ideas para la Paz, 2014.

Fogarty, Richard S., and David Killingray. "Demobilization in British and French Africa at the End of the First World War." *Journal of Contemporary History* 50, no. 1 (2015): 100–123.

García-Sánchez, Miguel, Jorge Montalvo, and Mitchell A. Seligson. *Cultura Política de La Democracia En Colombia, 2015*. Bogotá: LAPOP, 2015.

Gottfredson, Michael, and Travis Hirschi. *A General Theory of Crime*. Stanford, CA: Stanford University Press, 1990.

Granada, Soledad, Jorge Restrepo, and Alonso Tobón. "Neoparamilitarismo En Colombia." In *Guerra Y Violencias En Colombia. Herramientas E Interpretaciones*, edited by Jorge Restrepo and David Aponte, 467–500. Bogotá: Pontificia Universidad Javeriana, 2009.

Gutiérrez Sanín, Francisco, and Andrea González Peña. "Colombia's Paramilitary DDR and Its Limits." In *Post-Conflict Disarmament Demobilization and Reintegration: Bringing State-Building Back In*, edited by Antonio Giustozzi, 113–132. Burlington, VT: Ashgate, 2013.

Haer, Roos, and Tobias Böhmelt. "Child Soldiers as Time Bombs? Adolescents' Participation in Rebel Groups and the Recurrence of Armed Conflict." *European Journal of International Relations* 22, no. 2 (2016): 408–436.

Hill, Richard, Gwendolyn Taylor, and Jonathan Temin. "Would You Fight Again? Understanding Liberian Ex-Combatant Reintegration." Special Report No. 211. Washington, DC: USIP, 2008.

Howe, Kimberly. "Violent Momentum: Paramilitary Demobilization, Grey Zones and the Search for Wealth in Contemporary Colombia." Doctoral thesis, Tufts University, 2012.

Human Rights Watch. *Herederos de Los Paramilitares. La Nueva Cara de La Violencia En Colombia*. Bogotá: Human Rights Watch, 2010.

International Crisis Group. "Dismantling Colombia's New Illegal Armed Groups: Lessons from a Surrender." Latin America Report No. 41. Bogotá: International Crisis Group, 2012.

Jonsson, Michael. "Comrades in Arms. Motivational Change and Divergence Inside FARC-EP 2002-2010." PhD diss., University of Uppsala, 2014.

Kaplan, Oliver, and Enzo Nussio. "Community Counts: The Social Reintegration of Ex-Combatants in Colombia." *Conflict Management and Peace Science* (2015).

Kaplan, Oliver, and Enzo Nussio. "Explaining Recidivism of Ex-Combatants in Colombia." *Journal of Conflict Resolution* (2016).

Khatri, Naresh, Chong Tze Fern, and Pawan Budhwar. "Explaining Employee Turnover in an Asian Context." *Human Resource Management Journal* 11, no. 1 (2001): 54–74.

King, Elisabeth, and Cyrus Samii. "Fast-Track Institution Building in Conflict-Affected Countries? Insights from Recent Field Experiments." *World Development* 64 (2014): 740–754.

Krakowski, Krzysztof. "Colombian Paramilitaries Since Demobilization: Between State Crackdown and Increased Violence." *Latin American Politics and Society* 57, no. 4 (2015): 28–50.

Kurtenbach, Sabine. "The 'Happy Outcomes' May Not Come at All – Postwar Violence in Central America." *Civil Wars* 15, no. sup1 (2013): 105–122.

Kurtenbach, Sabine, and Angelika Rettberg. "War Economies and Postwar Crime. An Exploratory Framework for Discussion." *Third World Thematics* (Forthcoming).

Le Billon, Philippe. "The Political Ecology of War: Natural Resources and Armed Conflicts." *Political Geography* 20, no. 5 (2001): 561–584.

Levitt, Steven D., and Sudhir Alladi Venkatesh. "An Economic Analysis of a Drug-Selling Gang's Finances." *Quarterly Journal of Economics* 115, no. 3 (2000): 755–789.

Londoño, Luz María, and Patricia Ramírez. *Estudio Sobre El Impacto de La Reinserción Paramilitar En La Vida de Las Mujeres de Comunidades Receptoras de Medellín, Bajo Cauca Y Urabá*. Medellín: Universidad de Antioquia and Unifem, 2007.

Maringira, Godfrey. "Militarised Minds: The Lives of Ex-combatants in South Africa." *Sociology* 49, no. 1 (2015): 72–87.

Massé, Frédéric, Juan Munévar, Eduardo Álvarez Vanegas, and William Renán. "La Evolución de Las Estructuras Armadas Post-Desmovilización: Pasado, Presente Y Futuro." Tercer Informe Del Observatorio de DDR Y Ley de Justicia Y Paz. Madrid: CITpax, 2010.

Massé, Frédéric, Victor Negrete, Enzo Nussio, and Juan E. Ugarriza. "Presencia de Desmovilizados E Inseguridad En Las Ciudades. Casos de Estudio: Villavicencio, Montería Y Bogotá." Cuarto Informe Del Observatorio de DDR Y Ley de Justicia Y Paz. Madrid: CITpax, 2011.

McCarthy, Bill, and John Hagan. "Getting into Street Crime: The Structure and Process of Criminal Embeddedness." *Social Science Research* 24, no. 1 (1995): 63–95.

McEvoy, Kieran, and Peter Shirlow. "Re-Imagining DDR: Ex-Combatants, Leadership and Moral Agency in Conflict Transformation." *Theoretical Criminology* 13, no. 1 (2009): 31–59.

McFee, Erin. "The Double Bind of 'playing Double': Passing and Identity Among Ex-combatants in Colombia." *Peace and Conflict: Journal of Peace Psychology* 22, no. 1 (2016): 52–59.

McMullin, Jaremey R. "Integration or Separation? The Stigmatisation of Ex-combatants After War." *Review of International Studies* 39, no. 2 (2013): 385–414.

Moratti, Massimo, and Amra Sabic-El-Rayess. *Transitional Justice and DDR: The Case of Bosnia and Herzegovina*. New York: International Center for Transitional Justice, 2009.

Muggah, Robert, ed. *Security and Post-Conflict Reconstruction. Dealing with Fighters in the Aftermath of War*. Abingdon: Routledge, 2009.

Munévar, Juan, and Enzo Nussio. "Desmovilizados: Víctimas Y Causas de Inseguridad. Estudio de Caso Sobre El Municipio de Tierralta En El Departamento de Córdoba." Segundo Informe Del Observatorio de DDR Y Ley de Justicia Y Paz. Bogotá: CITpax, 2009.

Munive, Jairo. "Invisible Labour: The Political Economy of Reintegration in South Sudan." *Journal of Intervention and Statebuilding* 8, no. 4 (2014): 1–23.

Nussio, Enzo. "How Ex-combatants Talk about Personal Security. Narratives of Former Paramilitaries in Colombia." *Conflict, Security & Development* 11, no. 5 (2011): 579–606.

Nussio, Enzo. *La Vida Después de La Desmovilización. Percepciones, Emociones Y Estrategias de Exparamilitares En Colombia*. Bogotá: Universidad de los Andes, 2012.

Nussio, Enzo. "Learning from Shortcomings: The Demobilisation of Paramilitaries in Colombia." *Journal of Peacebuilding and Development* 6, no. 2 (2011): 88–92.

Nussio, Enzo. "The Role of Sensation Seeking in Violent Armed Group Participation." *Terrorism & Political Violence* (2017). doi:10.1080/09546553.2017.1342633.

Nussio, Enzo, and Kimberly Howe. "When Protection Collapses: Post-Demobilization Trajectories of Violence." *Terrorism and Political Violence* 28, no. 5 (2016): 848–867.

Nussio, Enzo, and Ben Oppenheim. "Anti-Social Capital in Former Members of Non-State Armed Groups: A Case Study of Colombia." *Studies in Conflict & Terrorism* 37, no. 12 (2014): 999–1023.

Observatorio de DDR. *Las Formas Organizativas Y Asociativas de Desmovilizados (FOAD) En Colombia*. Bogotá: ODDR, 2009.

Observatorio de Procesos de DDR. *DDR Y Acciones Violentas (2008–2009)*. Bogotá: Universidad Nacional de Colombia, 2010.

Ocampo, Melina. "Criminalidad, Grupos Armados Y Reinserción: Perfiles Y Motivaciones." *Ciencias Sociales Y Educación* 3, no. 5 (2014): 17–57.

Palou, Juan Carlos, and María Lucía Méndez. "Balance de Los Procesos de Desmovilización Desarme Y Reintegración En Colombia: 1990-2009." In *Construcción de Paz En Colombia*, edited by Angelika Rettberg, 349–381. Bogotá: Universidad de los Andes, 2012.

Prieto, Carlos Andrés. *Las Bacrim Y El Crimen Organizado En Colombia*. Bogotá: Friedrich Ebert Stiftung Colombia, 2013.

Restrepo, Elvira María, and Bruce Bagley, eds. *La Desmovilización de Los Paramilitares En Colombia*. Bogotá: Universidad de los Andes, 2011.

Restrepo, Jorge, and Robert Muggah. "Colombia's Quiet Demobilization. A Security Dividend?" In *Security and Post-Conflict Reconstruction. Dealing with Fighters in the Aftermath of War*, edited by Robert Muggah, 30–46. Abingdon: Routledge, 2009.

Rettberg, Angelika, and Juan Felipe Ortiz-Riomalo. "Golden Opportunity, or a New Twist on the Resource-Conflict Relationship: Links Between the Drug Trade and Illegal Gold Mining in Colombia." *World Development* 84 (2016): 82–96.

Rodgers, Dennis, and Steffen Jensen. "The Problem with Templates: Learning from Organic Gang-Related Violence Reduction." *Stability: International Journal of Security and Development* 4, no. 1 (2015): 1–16.

Rohrlich, Justin. "How Do You Turn 57,000 Former Militants Into Model Citizens?" *Vice News*, December 16, 2014.

Romero, Mauricio. *Paramilitares Y Autodefensas, 1982–2003*. Bogotá: Planeta, 2003.

Rubio Serrano, Rocío. "Los Niños: El Futuro de La Guerra… Y de La Paz." *Razón Pública*, February 18, 2013.

Seguridad y Democracia. *Criminalidad Y Victimización En Las 6 Principales Ciudades de Colombia*. Bogotá: Fundación Seguridad y Democracia, 2008.

Semana. "12 Por Ciento de Las Bacrim Son Desmovilizados: Policía Nacional." August 1, 2009. http://www.semana.com/nacion/justicia/articulo/12-ciento-bacrim-desmovilizados-policia-nacional/111725-3.

Semana. "Desmovilización de Guerrilleros Y Paramilitares. El Ensayo Y Error de La Reintegración." *Semana.com*, July 24, 2008. http://www.semana.com/on-line/articulo/el-ensayo-error-reintegracion/94109-3.

Semana. "'Las Bandas Criminales Son La Principal Amenaza Para El País': General Naranjo." January 25, 2011. http://www.semana.com/nacion/articulo/las-bandas-criminales-principal-amenaza-para-pais-general-naranjo/234587-3.

Sistema de Alertas Tempranas. *Informe de Riesgo No. 006-10*. Defensoría del Pueblo, June 2010.

Sistema de Alertas Tempranas. *Informe de Riesgo No. 015-13*. Defensoría del Pueblo, 2013.

Söderström, Johanna. "Second Time Around: Ex-combatants at the Polls in Liberia." *The Journal of Modern African Studies* 51, no. 03 (2013): 409–433.

Söderström, Johanna. "The Political Consequences of Reintegration Programmes in Current Peace-building: a Framework for Analysis." *Conflict, Security & Development* 13, no. 1 (2013): 87–116.

Subedi, Dambaru B. "Ex-combatants, Security and Post-conflict Violence: Unpacking the Experience from Nepal." *Millennial Asia* 5, no. 1 (2014): 41–65.

Themnér, Anders. "Former Military Networks and the Micro-Politics of Violence and Statebuilding in Liberia." *Comparative Politics* 47, no. 3 (2015): 334–353.

Themnér, Anders. *Violence in Post-Conflict Societies: Remarginalization, Remobilizers and Relationships*. London: Routledge, 2011.

Ugarriza, Juan E. "La Dimensión Política Del Postconflicto: Discusiones Conceptuales Y Avances Empíricos." *Colombia Internacional* 77 (2013): 141–176.

Ugarriza, Juan E., and Enzo Nussio. "The Effect of Perspective-Giving on Postconflict Reconciliation. An Experimental Approach." *Political Psychology* 38, no. 1 (2017): 3–19.

United Nations. *Integrated Disarmament, Demobilisation and Reintegration Standards*. New York: UNDDR, 2006.

Utas, Mats, Anders Themnér, and Emy Lindberg. "Commanders for Good and Bad. Alternative Post-War Reconstruction and Ex-Commanders in Liberia." Policy Note 6. Uppsala: Nordic Africa Institute, 2014.

Villarraga, Álvaro. "Experiencias Históricas Recientes de Reintegración de Excombatientes En Colombia." *Colombia Internacional* 77 (2013): 107–140.

Zyck, Steven A. "Former Combatant Reintegration and Fragmentation in Contemporary Afghanistan – Analysis." *Conflict, Security & Development* 9, no. 1 (2009): 111–131.

Index

Note Page numbers in **bold** refer to tables
Page numbers in *italics* to figures

For Product Safety Concerns and Information please contact our EU representative GPSR@taylorandfrancis.com
Taylor & Francis Verlag GmbH, Kaufingerstraße 24, 80331 München, Germany

www.ingramcontent.com/pod-product-compliance
Lightning Source LLC
LaVergne TN
LVHW080656011026
849160LV00014B/1443
* 9 7 8 1 0 3 2 0 8 9 5 7 7 *